Bloom's Major Literary Characters

King Arthur

Nick Adams

George F. Babbitt

Elizabeth Bennet

Leopold Bloom

Holden Caulfield

Sir John Falstaff

Huck Finn

Frankenstein

Jay Gatsby

Hamlet

Willy Loman

Macbeth

Hester Prynne

Raskolnikov and Svidrigailov

Satan

Bloom's Major Literary Characters

Macbeth

Edited and with an introduction by
Harold Bloom
Sterling Professor of the Humanities
Yale University

CHELSEA HOUSE
P U B L I S H E R S
A Haights Cross Communications Company

P h i l a d e l p h i a

Library of Congress Cataloging-in-Publication Data applied for.

Macbeth / edited and with an introduction by Harold Bloom.
    p. cm. — (Bloom's major literary characters)
  Includes bibliographical references and index.
  ISBN 0-7910-8176-1 (alk. paper)   0-7910-8385-3 (pb)
  1. Shakespeare, William, 1564-1616. Macbeth. 2. Macbeth, King of Scotland, 11th
cent.—In literature. 3. Scotland—In literature. 4. Regicides in literature. I. Bloom,
Harold. II. Major literary characters.
  PR2823.M2294 2004
  822.3'3—dc22
                                        2004023878

Contributing editor: Grace Kim

Cover design by Keith Trego

Cover: © Getty Images

Layout by EJB Publishing Services

All links and web addresses were checked and verified to be correct at the time of
publication. Because of the dynamic nature of the web, some addresses and links may
have changed since publication and may no longer be valid.

Every effort has been made to trace the owners of copyrighted material and secure
copyright permission. Articles appearing in this volume generally appear much as they did
in their original publication with little to no editorial changes. Those interested in
locating the original source will find bibliographic information on the first page of each
article as well as in the bibliography and acknowledgments sections of this volume.

Contents

Pg 27
? Pg 73

HAROLD BLOOM

The Analysis of Character

"Character," according to our dictionaries, still has as a primary meaning a graphic symbol, such as a letter of the alphabet. This meaning reflects the word's apparent origin in the ancient Greek character, a sharp stylus. *Charactēr* also meant the mark of the stylus' incisions. Recent fashions in literary criticism have reduced "character" in literature to a matter of marks upon a page. But our word "character" also has a very different meaning, matching that of the ancient Greek *ēthos*, "habitual way of life." Shall we say then that literary character is an imitation of human character, or is it just a grouping of marks? The issue is between a critic like Dr. Samuel Johnson, for whom words were as much like people as like things, and a critic like the late Roland Barthes, who told us that "the fact can only exist linguistically, as a term of discourse." Who is closer to our experience of reading literature, Johnson or Barthes? What difference does it make, if we side with one critic rather than the other?

Barthes is famous, like Foucault and other recent French theorists, for having added to Nietzsche's proclamation of the death of God a subsidiary demise, that of the literary author. If there are no authors, then there are no fictional personages, presumably because literature does not refer to a world outside language. Words indeed necessarily refer to other words in the first place, but the impact of words ultimately is drawn from a universe of fact. Stories, poems, and plays are recognizable as such because they are human utterances within traditions of utterances, and traditions, by achieving authority, become a kind of fact, or at least the sense of a fact. Our sense that literary characters, within the context of a fictive cosmos, indeed are fictional personages is also a kind of fact. The meaning and value of every character in a successful work of literary representation depend upon our ideas of persons in the factual reality of our lives.

Literary character is always an invention, and inventions generally are indebted to prior inventions. Shakespeare is the inventor of literary character as we know it; he reformed the universal human expectations for the verbal imitation of personality, and the reformation appears now to be permanent and uncannily inevitable. Remarkable as the Bible and Homer are at representing personages, their characters are relatively unchanging. They age within their stories, but their habitual modes of being do not develop. Jacob and Achilles unfold before us, but without metamorphoses. Lear and Macbeth, Hamlet and Othello severely modify themselves not only by their actions, but by their utterances, and most of all through *overhearing themselves*, whether they speak to themselves or to others. Pondering what they themselves have said, they will to change, and actually do change, sometimes extravagantly yet always persuasively. Or else they suffer change, without willing it, but in reaction not so much to their language as to their relation to that language.

I do not think it useful to say that Shakespeare successfully imitated elements in our characters. Rather, it could be argued that he compelled aspects of character to appear that previously were concealed, or not available to representation. This is not to say that Shakespeare is God, but to remind us that language is not God either. The mimesis of character in Shakespeare's dramas now seems to us normative, and indeed became the accepted mode almost immediately, as Ben Jonson shrewdly and somewhat grudgingly implied. And yet, Shakespearean representation has surprisingly little in common with the imitation of reality in Jonson or in Christopher Marlowe. The origins of Shakespeare's originality in the portrayal of men and women are to be found in the *Canterbury Tales* of Geoffrey Chaucer, insofar as they can be located anywhere before Shakespeare himself, Chaucer's savage and superb Pardoner overhears his own tale-telling, as well as his mocking rehearsal of his own spiel, and through this overhearing he is emboldened to forget himself, and enthusiastically urges all his fellow-pilgrims to come forward to be fleeced by him. His self-awareness, and apocalyptically rancid sense of spiritual fall, are preludes to the even grander abysses of the perverted will in Iago and in Edmund. What might be called the character trait of a negative charisma may be Chaucer's invention, but came to its perfection in Shakespearean mimesis.

The analysis of character is as much Shakespeare's invention as the representation of character is, since Iago and Edmund are adepts at analyzing both themselves and their victims. Hamlet, whose overwhelming charisma has many negative components, is certainly the most comprehensive of all literary characters, and so necessarily prophesies the labyrinthine complexities of the will in Iago and Edmund. Charisma, according to Max Weber, its first codifier, is primarily a natural endowment, and implies a primordial and idiosyncratic power over nature, and so finally over death. Hamlet's uncanniness is at its most suggestive in the scene of his long dying, where the audience, through the mediation of Horatio, itself is compelled to meditate upon suicide, if only because outliving the prince of Denmark scarcely seems an option.

Shakespearean representation has usurped not only our sense of literary character, but our sense of ourselves as characters, with Hamlet playing the part of the largest of these usurpations. Insofar as we have an idea of human disinterestedness, we tend to derive it from the Hamlet of Act V, whose quietism has about it a ghostly authority. Oscar Wilde, in his profound and profoundly witty dialogue, "The Decay of Lying," expressed a permanent insight when he insisted that art shaped every era, far more than any age formed art. Life imitates art, we imitate Shakespeare, because without Shakespeare we would perish for lack of images. Wilde's grandest audacity demystifies Shakespearean mimesis with a Shakespearean vivaciousness: "This unfortunate aphorism about art holding the mirror up to Nature is deliberately said by Hamlet in order to convince the bystanders of his absolute insanity in all art-matters." Of *Hamlet*'s influence upon the ages Wilde remarked that: "The world has grown sad because a puppet was once melancholy." "Puppet" is Wilde's own deconstruction, a brilliant reminder that Shakespeare's artistry of illusion has so mastered reality as to have changed reality, evidently forever.

The analysis of character, as a critical pursuit, seems to me as much a Shakespearean invention as literary character was, since much of what we know about how to analyze character necessarily follows Shakespearean procedures. His hero-villains, from Richard III through Iago, Edmund, and Macbeth, are shrewd and endless questers into their own self-motivations. If we could bear to see Hamlet, in his unwearied negations, as another hero-villain, then we would judge him the supreme analyst of the darker recalcitrances in the selfhood. Freud followed the pre-Socratic Empedocles, in arguing that character is fate, a frightening doctrine that maintains the fear that there are no accidents, that overdetermination rules us all of our lives. Hamlet assumes the same, yet adds to this argument the terrible passivity he manifests in Act V. Throughout Shakespeare's tragedies, the most interesting personages seem doom-eager, reminding us again that a Shakespearean reading of Freud would be more illuminating than a Freudian exegesis of

Shakespeare. We learn more when we discover Hamlet in the Freudian Death Drive, than when we read *Beyond the Pleasure Principle* into *Hamlet*.

In Shakespearean comedy, character achieves its true literary apotheosis, which is the representation of the inner freedom that can be created by great wit alone. Rosalind and Falstaff, perhaps alone among Shakespeare's personages, match Hamlet in wit, though hardly in the metaphysics of consciousness. Whether in the comic or the modern mode, Shakespeare has set the standard of measurement in the balance between character and passion.

In Shakespeare the self is more dramatized than theatricalized, which is why a Shakespearean reading of Freud works out so well. Character-formation after the passing of the Oedipal stage takes the place of fetishistic fragmentings of the self. Critics who now call literary character into question, and who proclaim also the death of the author, invariably also regard all notions, literary and human, of a stable character as being mere reductions of deeper pre-Oedipal desires. It becomes clear that the fortunes of literary character rise and fall with the prestige of normative conceptions of the ego. Shakespeare's Iago, who wars against being, may be the first deconstructionist of the self, with his proclamation of "I am not what I am." This constitutes the necessary prologue to any view that would regard a fixed ego as a virtual abnormality. But deconstructions of the self are no more modern than Modernism is. Like literary modernism, the decentered ego came out of the Hellenistic culture of ancient Alexandria. The Gnostic heretics believed that the psyche, like the body, was a fallen entity, mechanically fashioned by the Demiurge or false creator. They held however that each of us possessed also a spark or pneuma, which was a fragment of the original Abyss or true, alien God. The soul or psyche within every one of us was thus at war with the self or pneuma, and only that sparklike self could be saved.

Shakespeare, following after Chaucer in this respect, was the first and remains still the greatest master of representing character both as a stable soul and a wavering self. There is a substance that endures in Shakespeare's figures, and there is also a quicksilver rendition of the unsettling sparks. Racine and Tolstoy, Balzac and Dickens, follow in Shakespeare's wake by giving us some sense of pre-Oedipal sparks or drives, and considerably more sense of post-Oedipal character and personality, stabilizations or sublimations of the fetish-seeking drives. Critics like Leo Bersani and René Girard argue eloquently against our taking this mimesis as the only proper work of literature. I would suggest that strong fictions of the self, from the Bible through Samuel Beckett, necessarily participate in both modes, the sublimation of desire, and the persistence of a primordial desire. The mystery of Hamlet or of Lear is intimately invested in the tangled mixture of the two modes of representation.

Psychic mobility is proposed by Bersani as the ideal to which deconstructions of the literary self may yet guide us. The ideal has its pathos, but the realities of literary representation seem to me very different, perhaps destructively so. When a novelist like D. H. Lawrence sought to reduce his characters to Eros and the Death Drive, he still had to persuade us of his authority at mimesis by lavishing upon the figures of *The Rainbow* and *Women in Love* all of the vivid stigmata of normative personality. Birkin and Ursula may represent antithetical and uncanny drives, but they develop and change as characters pondering their own pronouncements and reactions to self and others. The cost of a non-Shakespearean representation is enormous. Pynchon, in *The Crying of Lot 49* and *Gravity's Rainbow*, evades the burden of the normative by resorting to something like Christopher Marlowe's art of caricature in *The Jew of Malta*. Marlowe's Barabas is a marvelous rhetorician, yet he is a cartoon alongside the troublingly equivocal Shylock. Pynchon's personages are deliberate cartoons also, as flat as comic strips. Marlowe's achievement, and Pynchon's, are beyond dispute, yet they are like the prelude and the postlude to Shakespearean reality. They do not wish to engage with our hunger for the empirical world and so they enter the problematic cosmos of literary fantasy.

No writer, not even Shakespeare or Proust, alters the available stock that we agree to call reality, but Shakespeare, more than any other, does show us how much of reality we could encounter if only we retained adequate desire. The strong literary representation of character is already an analysis of character, and is part of the healing work of a literary culture, which implicitly seeks to cure violence through a normative mimesis of ego, *as if it were stable*, whether in actuality it is or is not. I do not believe that this is a social quest taken on by literary culture, but rather that we confront here the aesthetic essence of what makes a culture *literary*, rather than metaphysical or ethical or religious. A culture becomes literary when its conceptual modes have failed it, which means when religion, philosophy, and science have begun to lose their authority. If they cannot heal violence, then literature attempts to do so, which may be only a turning inside out of the critical arguments of Girard and Bersani.

I conclude by offering a particular instance or special case as a paradigm for the healing enterprise that is at once the representation and the analysis of literary character. Let us call it the aesthetics of being outraged, or rather of successfully representing the state of being outraged. W. C. Fields was one modern master of such representation, and Nathanael West was another, as was Faulkner before him. Here also the greatest master remains Shakespeare, whose Macbeth, himself a bloody outrage, yet retains our imaginative sympathy precisely because he grows increasingly outraged as he experiences the equivocation of the fiend that lies like truth. The double-natured promises and the prophecies of the weird sisters finally induce in Macbeth an apocalyptic version of the stage actor's anxiety at missing cues, the horror of a phantasmagoric stage fright of missing one's time, of always reacting too late. Macbeth, a veritable monster of solipsistic inwardness but no intellectual, counters his dilemma by fresh murders, that prolong him in time yet provoke him only to a perpetually freshened sense of being outraged, as all his expectations become still worse confounded. We are moved by Macbeth, however estrangedly, because his terrible inwardness is a paradigm for our own solipsism, but also because none of us can resist a strong and successful representation of the human in a state of being outraged.

The ultimate outrage is the necessity of dying, an outrage concealed in a multitude of masks, including the tyrannical ambitions of Macbeth. I suspect that our outrage at being outraged is the most difficult of all our affects for us to represent to ourselves, which is why we are so inclined to imaginative sympathy for a character who strongly conveys that affect to us. The Shrike of West's *Miss Lonelyhearts* or Faulkner's Joe Christmas of *Light in August* are crucial modern instances, but such figures can be located in many other works, since the ability to represent this extreme emotion is one of the tests that strong writers are driven to set for themselves.

However a reader seeks to reduce literary character to a question of marks on a page, she will come at last to the impasse constituted by the thought of death, her death, and before that to all the stations of being outraged that memorialize her own drive towards death. In reading, she quests for evidences that are strong representations, whether of her desire or her despair. Such questings constitute the necessary basis for the analysis of literary character, an enterprise that always will survive every vagary of critical fashion.

Editor's Note

My Introduction centers upon the dangerous prevalence of the imagination in *Macbeth*.

George Wilson Knight usefully compares Brutus and Macbeth as tragic protagonists, finding them poetically alike though very different ethically, while Bernard McElroy finds Macbeth to be a tragic hero *because* of his criminality and his initial compunctions.

Irony and disjunction in *Macbeth* are analyzed by Howard Felperin, after which Robert Watson uncovers a pattern in which regenerative nature takes revenge upon Macbeth.

Kay Stockholder interestingly hints at sexual impotence in Macbeth's curious passivity towards Lady Macbeth, while Christopher Pye also meditates upon Macbeth's sexual anxieties, but in relation to images of theatrical spectacle.

Deconstructing the contraries of "absence" and "presence" in the usurper Macbeth is the project of H.W. Fawkner, after which Rebecca Bushnell sets forth a dialectic between gender and politics in the tragedy.

Robert Lanier Reid concludes this volume by chronicling the loss of everything that is childlike and woman-nurtured in Macbeth.

HAROLD BLOOM

Introduction

Macbeth is the culminating figure in the sequence of what might be called Shakespeare's Grand Negations: Richard III, Iago, Edmund, Macbeth. He differs from his precursors in lacking their dark intellectuality, and their manipulative power over other selves. But he surpasses them in imagination, in its High Romantic sense, even though that is hardly a faculty in which they are deficient. His imagination is so strong that it exceeds even Hamlet's, so strong indeed that we can see that it is imagination, rather than ambition or the Witches, that victimizes and destroys Macbeth. The bloodiest tyrant and villain in Shakespeare, Macbeth nevertheless engages our imaginations precisely because he is so large a representation of the dangerous prevalence of the imagination. The tragedy *Macbeth* constitutes an implicit self-critique of the Shakespearean imagination, and therefore also of a crucial element in your own imagination, whoever you are.

Not even Hamlet dominates his play as Macbeth does; he speaks about one third of the text as we have it. Compared to him, the other figures in the drama take on a common grayness, except for Lady Macbeth, and she largely vanishes after the middle of Act III. No Shakespearean protagonist, again not even Hamlet, is revealed to us so inwardly as Macbeth. Shakespeare quite deliberately places us under a very paradoxical stress: we intimately accompany Macbeth in his interior journey, and yet we attempt to refuse all identity with Macbeth; an impossible refusal, since his imagination becomes our own. We are contaminated by Macbeth's fantasies; perhaps someday our

critical instruments will be keen enough so that we will comprehend just how
much Sigmund Freud's theories owe to precisely Macbethian contamination.
I myself am inclined to place *The Tragedy of Macbeth* foremost among
Shakespeare's works, above even *Hamlet* and *Lear*, because of the unique
power of contamination manifested by its protagonist's fantasy-making
faculty. Everything that Macbeth says, particularly to himself, is notoriously
memorable, yet I would assign a crucial function to a passage in Act I that
defines the exact nature of Macbeth's imagination:

> Present fears
> Are less than horrible imaginings.
> My thought, whose murder yet is but fantastical,
> Shakes so my single state of man that function
> Is smothered in surmise, and nothing is
> But what is not.

What does Macbeth mean by "single" here? Perhaps "alone" or
"unaided," perhaps "total," but either way the word indicates vulnerability to
phantasmagoria. To smother function or thought's ordinary operation by
surmise, which is anticipation but not action, is to be dominated by what
might be called the proleptic imagination, which is Macbeth's great burden
and his tragedy. Though the murder of Duncan is still a pure prolepsis,
Macbeth has but to imagine an act or event and instantly he is on the other
side of it, brooding retrospectively. The negations of Iago and Edmund were
willed nihilisms, but Macbeth's imagination does the work of his will, so that
"nothing is / But what is not." Macbeth represents an enormous
enhancement of that element in us that allows us to see Shakespeare acted,
whether in the theatre, or the mind's eye of the reader, without protesting or
denying the illusion. It is not that Macbeth has faith in the imagination, but
that he is enslaved to his version of fantasy. Brooding on Macduff's absence
from court, Macbeth sums up his proleptic mode in one powerful couplet:

> Strange things I have in head that will to hand,
> Which must be acted ere they may be scanned.

He seems to know already that he seeks to murder every member of
Macduff's family, yet he will not truly have the knowledge until the massacre
is accomplished, as though the image in his head is wholly independent of his
will. This is the burden of his great soliloquy at the start of Act I, Scene vii,
with its Hamlet-like onset:

If it were done when 'tis done, then 'twere well
It were done quickly. If th'assassination
Could trammel up the consequence, and catch,
With his surcease, success; that but this blow
Might be the be-all and the end-all—here,
But here, upon this bank and shoal of time,
We'd jump the life to come.

"Bank and shoal of time" is a brilliant trope, whether or not it is Shakespeare's, since "shoal" there is a scholarly emendation, and perhaps Shakespeare wrote "school," which would make "bank" into a schoolbench. Scholars tell us also that "jump" here means "hazard," but I think Macbeth means both: to leap and to risk, and I suspect that Shakespeare actually wrote "shoal." The metaphor is superbly characteristic of precisely how Macbeth's imagination works, by leaping over present time and over a future act also, so as to land upon the other bank of time, looking back to the bank where he stood before action. The soliloquy ends with the same figuration, but now broken off by the entry of Lady Macbeth. Vaulting and overleaping, Macbeth's ambition, which is another name for the proleptic aspect of his imagination, falls upon the other side of his intent, which is to say, the other bank both of his aim and his meaning:

                    I have no spur
To prick the sides of my intent, but only
Vaulting ambition, which o'erleaps itself
And falls on th'other—

The intent is a horse all will, but Macbeth's imagination again falls on the other side of the will, and dominates the perpetually rapt protagonist, who is condemned always to be in a kind of trance or phantasmagoria that governs him, yet also is augmented by every action that he undertakes. Though Shakespeare doubtless gave full credence to his Witches, weird or wayward demiurges of the Gnostic cosmos of *Macbeth*, they may also be projections of Macbeth's own rapt state of prolepsis, his inability to control the temporal elements of his imagination. The Witches embody the temporal gap between what is imagined and what is done, so that they take the place of Macbeth's Will. We could not envision Iago or Edmund being sought out by the Witches, because Iago and Edmund will their own grand negations, or indeed will to become grand negations of every value. Macbeth imagines his negations, and becomes the grandest negation of them all.

Why then do we sympathize with Macbeth's inwardness, in spite of our own wills? He shares Hamlet's dark side, but is totally without Hamlet's intellect. It is almost as though Shakespeare deliberately cut away Hamlet's cognitive gifts while preserving Hamlet's sensibility in the immensely powerful if purely involuntary imagination of Macbeth. Hamlet interests us for reasons very different from why we interest ourselves; Macbeth precisely is interesting to us exactly as we are interesting, in our own judgment. We know Macbeth's inwardness as we know our own, but Hamlet's vast theatre of mind remains an abyss to us. Both Macbeth and Lady Macbeth are well aware that in murdering Duncan they are slaying the good father. We share their Oedipal intensity (which becomes her madness) if not their guilt. The primal act of imagination, as Freud had learned from Shakespeare, is the ambitious act of desiring the father's death. The first part of Macbeth's appeal to us is his rapt state of being or Oedipal ambition, but the second part, even more appealing, is his power of representing an increasing state of being outraged, outraged by time, by mortality, and by the equivocation of the fiend that lies like truth.

William Hazlitt shrewdly observed of Macbeth that: "His energy springs from the anxiety and agitation of his mind." I would add that, as the drama advances, the principal agitation is the energy of being outraged by the baffling of expectations. Increasingly obsessed with time, Macbeth fears becoming an actor who always misses his cue, and constantly learns that the cues he was given are wrong. The energy that stems from an adroit representation of a state of being outraged is one that imbues us with a remarkable degree of sympathy. I recall watching a television film of Alec Guinness playing the last days of Hitler, portrayed accurately as progressing to a greater intensity of being outraged from start to end. One had to keep recalling that this was a representation of Hitler in order to fight off an involuntary sympathy. Our common fate is an outrage: each of us must die. Shakespeare, implicating us in Macbeth's fate, profoundly associates the proleptic imagination with the sense of being outraged, nowhere more than in Macbeth's extraordinary refusal to mourn the death of his afflicted wife. All of Western literature does not afford us an utterance so superbly outraged as this, or one that so abruptly jumps over every possible life to come:

> She should have died hereafter;
> There would have been a time for such a word.
> Tomorrow, and tomorrow, and tomorrow
> Creeps in this petty pace from day to day,
> To the last syllable of recorded time;
> And all our yesterdays have lighted fools
> The way to dusty death. Out, out, brief candle!

Life's but a walking shadow, a poor player
That struts and frets his hour upon the stage
And then is heard no more. It is a tale
Told by an idiot, full of sound and fury
Signifying nothing.

Dr. Samuel Johnson was so disturbed by this speech that initially he wished to emend "such a word" to "such a world." Upon reflection, he accepted "word," but interpreted it as meaning "intelligence," in the sense that we say we send "word" when we give intelligence. Macbeth, outraged yet refusing to mourn, perhaps begins with the distancing observation that his wife would have died sooner or later anyway, but then centers ironically upon the meaninglessness now, for him, of such a word as "hereafter," since he *knows* that quite literally there will be no tomorrow for him. In the grim music of the word "tomorrow" he hears his own horror of time, his proleptic imagining of all of remaining life, and not just for himself alone. Recorded time, history, will end with the last syllable of the word "tomorrow," but that will refer to a tomorrow that will not come. If all our yesterdays have existed to light "fools" (presumably meaning "victims") the way to a death that is only ourselves (Adam being created from the dust of red clay), then the brief candle of Lady Macbeth's life just as well has gone out. By the light of that candle, Shakespeare grants Macbeth an outraged but astonishing vision of life as an actor in a Shakespearean play, rather like *The Tragedy of Macbeth*. The best in this kind are but shadows, but life is not one of the best, being a bad actor, strutting and fretting away his performance, and lacking reverberation in the memories of the audience after they have left the theatre. Varying the figurative identification, Macbeth moves life's status from bad actor to bad drama or tale, composed by a professional jester or court fool, an idiot indulged in his idiocy. The story is either meaningless or a total negation, signifying nothing because there is nothing to signify. Theatrical metaphors are more fully appropriate for Shakespeare himself than for the tyrant Macbeth, we might think at first, but then we remember that Macbeth's peculiar imagination necessarily has made him into a poetic dramatist. Iago and Edmund, nihilistic dramatists, manipulated others, while Macbeth has manipulated himself, leaping over the present and the actions not yet taken into the scenes that followed the actions, as though they already had occurred.

Critics of Macbeth always have noted the terrible awe he provokes in us. Sublime in himself, the usurper also partakes in the dreadful sublimity of the apocalyptic cosmos of his drama. When Duncan is slain, lamentings are heard in the air, great winds blow, owls clamor through the night, and behave like hawks, killing falcons as if they were mice. And Duncan's horses break loose, warring against men, and then devour one another. It is as though the daemonic underworld of the Weird Sisters and Hecate had broken upwards into Duncan's realm, which in some sense they had done by helping to spur on the rapt Macbeth. Shakespeare's protagonist pays a fearful price for his sublimity, and yet as audience and readers we do not wish Macbeth to be otherwise than the grand negation he becomes. I think this is because Macbeth is not only a criticism of our imaginations, which are as guilty and Oedipal as his own, but also because Macbeth is Shakespeare's critique of his own tragic imagination, an imagination beyond guilt.

G. WILSON KNIGHT

Brutus and Macbeth

From the crystal lucidity, even flow, and brilliant imagery of the style of *Julius Caesar* stand out two main personal themes: the Brutus-theme and the Cassius-theme. The one predominates at the start, the other at the finish. The two men are finely contrasted. But I shall not concern myself in this essay primarily with that contrast. Nor shall I consider the play as a whole in its romantic and spiritual significance. The *Julius Caesar* universe is one of high-spirited adventure and nobility, of heroic optimism, erotic emotion. It is differentiated sharply from the plays succeeding it. It is essentially a play of keen spiritual faith and vision, curiously preceding the sequence of the hate-theme which starts with *Hamlet*. These important elements I do not analyse here.[1] Rather I outline the imaginative nature of the Brutus-theme alone; and, in considering the figure of Brutus, I shall indicate how his soul-experience resembles that of Macbeth. The process is interesting, since it forces us to cut below the surface crust of plot and 'character', and to expose those riches of poetic imagination too often deep-buried in our purely unconscious enjoyment of Shakespeare's art. Moreover, it will serve as a valuable introduction to the complexities of the *Macbeth* vision itself.

Brutus is confronted with a task from which his nature revolts. He, like Macbeth, embarks on a line of action destructive rather than creative; directed against the symbol of established authority; at root, perhaps, selfish. For, though he may tell himself that his ideals force him to a work of secrecy,

From *The Wheel of Fire*. ©1998 Routledge.

conspiracy, and destruction, he is not at peace. He suffers a state of spiritual or mental division. Two impulses diverge: one urges him to conspiracy and murder, the other reminds him of Caesar's goodness and the normal methods of upright men. He is thus divided—torn between a certain sense of duty and his instinct for peaceful and civilized behaviour. Now his state is very similar to that of Macbeth. Though their motives at first sight appear to be very different, yet in each the resulting disharmony is almost identical in imaginative impact. We should not let our sight of a poetic reality be blurred by consideration of 'causes'. With Macbeth it is almost impossible to fit clear terms of conceptual thought to the motives tangled in his mind or soul. Therein lies the fine truth of the *Macbeth* conception: a deep, poetic, psychology or metaphysic of the birth of evil. He himself is hopelessly at a loss, and has little idea as to why he is going to murder Duncan. He tries to fit names to his reasons—'ambition', for instance—but this is only a name. The poet's mind is here at grips with the problem of spiritual evil—the inner state of disintegration, disharmony and fear, from which is born an act of crime and destruction. And the state of evil endured by Macbeth is less powerfully, but similarly, experienced by Brutus. Its signs are loneliness, a sense of unreality, a sickly vision of nightmare forms. It contemplates murder and anarchy to symbolize outwardly its own inner anarchy, and so, by forcibly creating itself in things around it, to restore contact with its environment for its severed and lonely individuality. Now one simple statement can be made of both Macbeth and Brutus: they both suffer a state of division, due to conflicting impulses for and against murder. Their inner disharmony is given an almost identical reflection in words—not only in terms of logical statement, but in terms, too, of the more important verbal colour and association, imagery, rhythm—in short, of poetry:

Consider Brutus' speech:

> Since Cassius first did whet me against Caesar
> I have not slept.
> Between the acting of a dreadful thing
> And the first motion, all the interim is
> Like a phantasma or a hideous dream
> The genius and the mortal instruments
> Are then in council; and the state of man.
> Like to a little kingdom, suffers then
> The nature of an insurrection.   (II. i. 62)

Compare Macbeth's:

This supernatural soliciting
Cannot be good, cannot be ill: if ill,
Why hath it given me earnest of success
Commencing with a truth? I am Thane of Cawdor.
If good, why do I yield to that suggestion
Whose horrid image doth unfix my hair,
And make my seated heart knock at my ribs
Against the use of nature? Present fears
Are less than horrible imaginings:
My thought, whose murder yet is but fantastical,
Shakes so my single state of man that function
Is smother'd in surmise, and nothing is
But what is not.   (I. iii. 130)

The second speech is more vivid, powerful, and tense: but in quality they are alike. One is only a more packed and pregnant verbal expression of the state of being expressed by the other. Each gives us a sickly sense of nightmare unreality. The ordinary forms of reality, to the self-contemplating mind in the grip of evil, have become 'nothing': and a ghastly negation, a black abyss of nothing, has usurped the significance of reality. Thus the mind endures 'horrible imaginings' which are 'like a phantasma or a hideous dream'. Both speeches use the metaphor, 'the state of man'. This 'state' is shaken from its normal balance of faculties, so that it endures anarchy and disorder. This anarchy of the soul reflects the outer anarchy which it is fated to impose by its act of murder, directed against the symbol of ordered community, the King, or Caesar: the soul mirrors as in a glass the disharmony and disruption to be brought about by its act of nihilism. All three realities are intertwined: the chaos in the 'state of man'; the act of murder; the resulting chaos in the state of the community.

The instigation in both plays comes partly from within, partly from without. Though Cassius' words 'whet' Brutus against Caesar we know that he has already suffered the beginnings of inward division. He is already, as he tells Cassius, 'with himself at war' (I. ii. 46). In the same way, though Macbeth is urged on by his wife, he has already been in contact with the Weird Sisters. Both Brutus and Macbeth find their own vague mental suggestions brought to rapid growth by outside influences. Both, too, promise to consider the matter further:

Brutus.   ... for this present
    I would not, so with love I might entreat you,
    Be any further moved. What you have said

> I will consider. What you have to say
> I will with patience hear ...   (I. ii. 164)

and,

> *Macbeth.* We will speak further.   (I. v. 72)

In *Macbeth* the tragic tension is always more powerful than in *Julius Caesar*; gained, too, within a minimum of space either by the most perfect and powerful simplicity, or by the complexity of highly-charged, compressed, and pregnant metaphoric thought. The effects in the Brutus-theme are so much more prolix, and therefore less powerful, especially in the matter of blood-imagery, which I notice later.

Both Brutus and Macbeth meditate in solitude concerning the proposed act (I quote only their first words):

> *Brutus.* It must be by his death: and for my part
> I know no personal cause to spurn at him,
> But for the general ...   (II. i. 10)

and,

> *Macbeth.* If it were done, when 'tis done, then 'twere well
> It were done quickly. If the assassination
> Could trammel up the consequence and catch
> With his surcease success ...   (I. vii. 1)

Though the intellectual meanings of these soliloquies are different, their poetic qualities are similar. Each reflects unrest, indecision; in a style of broken and disjointed, meditative, flashes of thought. They give one the impression that the personality of the thinker is momentarily relaxed; letting arguments and reasons pass rapidly and automatically across the screen of his own mind for the hundredth time: they are merely chaotic shapes and shadows of the active intellect, which the contemplating mind watches projected away from its centre, trying to understand. They are not vitally immediate and concentrated thought-adventures, like Hamlet's 'To be or not to be ...'. They reflect a mind trying to get its own motives clear. Brutus' is throughout rhythmically uneven and jerky; so is Macbeth's in the first half. Each of them is characterized by a quite unexpected and, it would seem, untrue method of presenting irrelevant arguments: they are both getting their reasons and motives hopelessly wrong. So Brutus tells himself that Caesar must be assassinated to avoid the dangers contingent on his nature possibly changing after he becomes king. Yet, he says, he has never known

him let passion master reason. There is a hopeless confusion: Brutus'
strongest method of justifying his act is to assert that the Roman ideal of a
commonwealth must not be shattered by the accession of a king, good or
bad. Yet, in his confused desire to justify himself, he does not do this, but falls
back on a quite indefensible sophistry. He does not understand himself.
Who, at a really testing moment, does? Similarly Macbeth, whose conscience
revolts from the crime, persuades himself that he is a most cold-blooded
villain, and only fears actual and personal punishment. How untrue this is
may be apparent from the latter half of his soliloquy where he begins to speak
with a passionate sincerity: then he miserably images to himself the
excellences of Duncan, as Brutus contemplates those of Caesar, and sees that
his virtues are as angels trumpet-tongued to plead against the crime. He
concludes by crying:

> I have no spur
> To prick the sides of my intent, save only
> Vaulting ambition, which o'erleaps itself
> And falls on the other.   (I. vii. 25)

He is perfectly aware of the futility of such 'ambition': yet he can find no
better name. So, too, Brutus sighs:

> I know no personal cause to spurn at him,
> But for the general ...   (II. i. 11)

And neither is, it seems, quite convinced: though Brutus is much nearer
peace of mind and clarity of motive than Macbeth. But both are in the same
kind of confusion. And it may be noticed that Brutus' speech in point of
complexity and condensation of thought and phrase stands out remarkably
from a play of a lucidity and crystal transparence of diction unparalleled in
Shakespeare: it has a typical *Macbeth* ring.

Soon after both these soliloquies the impulse to assassinate definitely
wins. Both are appealed to on grounds of personal pride: Brutus by the paper
which Lucius brings him, Macbeth by his wife. They assent at moments of
dramatic intensity again remarkably similar in their sudden, finality:

> *Brutus.* 'Speak, strike, redress!' Am I entreated
>   To speak and strike? O Rome, I make thee promise,
>   If the redress will follow, thou receivest
>   Thy full petition at the hand of Brutus!   (II. i. 55)

Macbeth likewise reaches decision with a similar finality:

> *Macbeth.*   I am settled and bend up
>   Each corporal agent to this terrible feat.
>   Away, and mock the time with fairest show.
>   False face must hide what the false heart doth know.   (I. vii. 79)

Why does Macbeth thus decide on a course repellant to his instinct and unsound to his own reasoning? One of the finest interpretative remarks ever made on Macbeth is A. C. Bradley's to the effect that Macbeth sets about the murder 'as an appalling duty'. This is profoundly true. Like Brutus he has to be appealed to on grounds of pride: like Brutus, he undertakes a terrible and appalling duty. So Macbeth counsels his wife to 'mock the time with fairest show'. This is a typical *Macbeth* thought and occurs in slightly different forms elsewhere (I. iv. 52; I. v. 65; I. v. 72). At first sight it seems far from a Brutus. But we have the same counsel given by Brutus:

>   O conspiracy,
>   Shamest thou to show thy dangerous brow by night,
>   When evils are most free? O, then by day,
>   Where wilt thou find a cavern dark enough
>   To mask thy monstrous visage? Seek none, conspiracy;
>   Hide it in smiles and affability ...   (II. i. 77)

Again, he advises cunning as follows:

>   And let out hearts as subtle masters do,
>   Stir up their servants to an act of rage,
>   And after seem to chide 'em. This shall make
>   Our purpose necessary and not envious ...   (II. i. 175)

And finally,

>   Good gentlemen, look fresh and merrily;
>   Let not our looks put on our purposes ...   (II. i, 224)

The prolix and diffuse expression in *Julius Caesar* corresponds, as elsewhere, to a more packed and condensed explosive poetry in *Macbeth*. This recurrent thought in both plays emphasizes the essential isolation of the hero from surrounding human reality: the act to be is an act of darkness whose very conception bears the Ishmael stamp of outlawry and tends to make the perpetrator a pariah from the ways of men. Both Brutus and Macbeth endure this spiritual loneliness: it is at the root of their suffering. Loneliness, deception, and loss of that daily nurse of anguish, sleep.

Sleeplessness and nightmare vision are twined with this loneliness, this severance of individual consciousness—consciousness feverishly awake and aware of its deception and isolation due to—or urging towards—the proposed deed of blood. There is insistence on sleep in both plays. Macbeth's crime is a hideous murder of sleep: Caesar is waked from sleep by Calpurnia's cries in nightmare— 'Help, ho! they murder Caesar!' (II. ii. 3). Calpurnia has a dream of Caesar's statue spouting blood (II. ii. 76). Cinna the poet dreamt that he feasted with Caesar and is next mobbed and, we suppose, slain. He reminds us of Banquo:

> I dreamt to-night that I did feast with Caesar,
> And things unluckily charge my fantasy;
> I have no will to wander forth of doors,
> Yet something leads me forth. (III. iii. 1)

Compare Banquo's:

> A heavy summons lies like lead upon me,
> And yet I would not sleep: merciful powers,
> Restrain in me the cursed thoughts that nature
> Gives way to in repose! (II. i. 6)

There is a nightmare fear powerful throughout both plays. Sleep-imagery is recurrent in the Brutus-theme and in *Macbeth* to an extent paralleled in no other of Shakespeare's tragedies. Brutus has not slept since Cassius first instigated him against Caesar (II. i. 61). He calls:

> Boy! Lucius! Fast sleep? It is no matter;
> Enjoy the honey-heavy dew of slumber.
> Thou hast no figures nor no fantasies,
> Which busy care draws in the brains of men;
> Therefore thou sleep'st so sound. (II. i. 229)

Again:

> I would it were my fault to sleep so soundly. (II. i. 4)

And Portia, too, refers to Brutus' sleeplessness (II. i. 252). At the close of the tent-scene in Act IV, it is sleep and the drowsy tune of Lucius' instrument that touches for a while these latter hours with the faery wand of a gentleness and beauty that are remorselessly shattered by the Ghost of Caesar—the 'evil spirit' of Brutus; the evil that has gripped him, symbolized itself in murder, and left him condemned, like Macbeth, to 'sleep no more'. So, too, the most terrible element in the punishment of Macbeth and Lady Macbeth is a loss of sleep:

> *Macbeth*. Methought I heard a voice cry, 'Sleep no more!
>   Macbeth does murder sleep'—the innocent sleep,
>   Sleep that knits up the ravell'd sleeve of care,
>   The death of each day's life, sore labour's bath,
>   Balm of hurt minds, great nature's second course,
>   Chief nourisher in life's feast—
> *L. Macbeth*.   What do you mean?
> *Macbeth*. Still it cried 'Sleep no more!' to all the house.
>   'Glamis hath murder'd sleep, and therefore Cawdor
>   Shall sleep no more; Macbeth shall sleep no more.'
>
> (II. ii. 36)

Again, later:

> But let the frame of things disjoint, both the worlds suffer,
> Ere we will eat our meal in fear and sleep
> In the affliction of these terrible dreams
> That shake us nightly: better be with the dead,
> Whom we, to gain our peace, have sent to peace,
> Than on the torture of the mind to lie
> In restless ecstasy. Duncan is in his grave;
> After life's fitful fever he sleeps well;
> Treason has done his worst; nor steel, nor poison,
> Malice domestic, foreign levy, nothing,
> Can touch him further.   (III. ii. 16)

There is the dread sleep-walking of Lady Macbeth: Macbeth asks the doctor for some 'sweet oblivious antidote' (V. iii. 43) to give rest to her agonized consciousness. One of the worst terrors of the Macbeth and Brutus experience is imaged as a loss of the sweet curative of sleep.

In so far as we regard Brutus as the hero of *Julius Caesar*, it will be evident that the falling action continues to present similarities to *Macbeth*. The act of blood looses chaos and destruction on earth. So Antony prophesies:

Domestic fury and fierce civil strife
Shall cumber all the parts of Italy;
Blood and destruction shall be so in use
And dreadful objects so familiar
That mothers shall but smile when they behold
Their infants quarter'd with the hands of war;
All pity chok'd with custom of fell deeds ...   (III. i. 263)

Similar is the description by Ross of the horrors alive in Scotland:

Alas, poor country!
Almost afraid to know itself. It cannot
Be call'd our mother, but our grave; where nothing,
But who knows nothing, is once seen to smile;
Where sighs and groans and shrieks that rend the air
Are made, not mark'd; where violent sorrow seems
A modern ecstasy: the dead man's knell
Is there scarce ask'd for who; and good men's lives
Expire before the flowers in their caps,
Dying or ere they sicken.   (IV. iii. 164)

These exaggerated speeches—tending away from realism to pure poetic, symbolism, like the storms and strange behaviour of beasts that accompany the central actions—emphasize the essentially chaotic and destructive nature of the first murders. Also after the murder each hero experiences a purely subjective vision of a ghost. This suggests the continuance of the divided state of evil: though Brutus may continually refer to his high motives, the Ghost of Caesar introduces himself as 'Thy evil spirit, Brutus'.[2] The inward division tends to prevent any continued success. Both Brutus and Macbeth fail in their schemes not so much because of outward events and forces, but through the working of that part of their natures which originally forbade murder. Macbeth's additional and unnecessary crimes are in reality due to his agonized conscience. Had he from the first been a hardened and callous murderer, had he undertaken the act without any conflict of mind or soul, there was nothing to prevent his establishing himself safely on the throne. Conscience, which had urged him not to murder Duncan, now forces him to murder many others. With Brutus, much the same cause produces the same final result by different means: his conscience, or instinct, or whatever it was which urged him not to assassinate Caesar, tells him not to risk further unnecessary bloodshed, and even to allow Antony's oration—all in the nature of a peace-offering to his own uneasy conscience. The result in both cases determines the downfall of the hero.

At the end Brutus and Macbeth are attacked each by two main enemies: the symbols of (i) their original deed of destruction, and (ii) their own trammelling and hindering conscience. Which has profound significance, since had either remained absolutely true to one side of his nature there would, probably, have been no failure. They are thus tracked down by this dual representation of their originally divided selves: it is apparent throughout that the same division is at the root of both their original state of evil and their eventual failure. So here the conquering forces are to be led against Brutus by the young Octavius, nephew of Caesar, and Antony, whom Brutus' conscience has indirectly placed in power; and against Macbeth by the young Malcolm, son of Duncan, and Macduff, whom Macbeth's tortured conscience has roused against him. And before the end, each is left more lonely than ever by the death of his nearest partner. Brutus finds Cassius dead soon after having heard of his wife's suicide. Macbeth, too, loses his wife. Each receives such news callously: for, after all, what has this new element of loneliness to add to that spiritual isolation that has been so long a torment? The death of each is unspectacular:

> *Brutus.* So fare you well at once; for Brutus' tongue
> Hath almost ended his life's history:
> Night hangs upon mine eyes; my bones would rest
> That have but laboured to attain this hour.   (V. v. 39)

Macbeth meets Macduff and is killed. With each hero the sleepless agony of spiritual division finds rest and unity in the vaster sleep of death.

The similarities I have noticed between the Brutus-theme and *Macbeth* are essentially imaginative similarities: only in so far as we are submerged in the poetic quality of the plays will this similarity be powerfully and significantly in evidence. Therefore it is not strange that on the plane of pure poetic symbolism and attendant atmosphere there should be more, and striking, parallels. The most obvious forms of symbolism in these two plays are (i) storm-symbolism, (ii) blood-imagery, and (iii) animal-symbolism. The Brutus and Macbeth themes alone in Shakespeare are accompanied by these three forms of poetic atmosphere and suggestion in full force. They stand for contest, destruction, and disorder in the outer world and in the reader's mind, mirroring the contest, destruction, and disorder both in the soul of the hero and in that element of the poet's intuitive experience to which the plays concerned give vivid and concrete dramatic form.

The storm-imagery in the early scenes of *Julius Caesar* is insistent and lurid:

Casca. Are you not moved when all the sway of earth
    Shakes like a thing unfirm? O, Cicero,
    I have seen tempests, when the scolding winds
    Have rived the knotty oaks, and I have seen
    The ambitious ocean swell and rage and foam,
    To be exalted with the threatening clouds
    But never till to-night, never till now,
    Did I go through a tempest dropping fire.
    Either there is a civil strife in heaven,
    Or else the world, too saucy with the gods,
    Incenses them to send destruction.   (I. iii. 3)

More storm references occur throughout the scene. So, too, Lennox speaks to Macbeth on the night of the murder:

    The night has been unruly: where we lay,
    Our chimneys were blown down; and, as they say,
    Lamentings heard i' the air—strange screams of death;
    And, prophesying with accents terrible
    Of dire combustion and confus'd events
    New-hatch'd to the woeful time, the obscure bird
    Clamour'd the live-long night: some say the earth
    Was feverous, and did shake.   (II. iii. 60).

The storm-imagery in *Macbeth*, as, too, the whole imaginative atmosphere is less fiery and bright and scintillating: more black, smoky, foul. There is nothing so vividly pictorial as the 'fierce fiery warriors' fighting in the heavens above Rome (II. ii. 19). But the same order of imagery occurs, reflecting the same kind of theme. Macbeth answers to Lennox merely:

    'Twas a rough night.

The storm itself has little meaning for him: it is merely a pale reflex—for our benefit—of the tempest conflicting in his soul. Nor is Brutus affected by it— it serves as a convenient method of illumination:

    The exhalations whizzing in the air
    Give so much light that I may read by them.   (II. i. 44)

The phantasms that make terrible the skies of Rome, and drizzle blood upon the Capitol, are nothing to the phantasma and hideous dream in his own mind. He is, in fact, ignorant of them: they are for us, not for him. But their effect on the minor characters, and thence on the reader, is great. It is, however, noteworthy that Lady Macbeth and Cassius will not be shown to us as struck with any kind of awe: since, enduring no inward conflict and chaos of soul, it is inevitable that they should be presented as untouched by the symbol of conflict. Lady Macbeth is coldly realistic at the time of the murder:

> I heard the owl scream and the crickets cry.   (II. ii. 17)

Cassius even revels in the storm. To him it symbolizes not the act of destruction, but rather the present state of things which he whole-heartedly intends to alter:

> *Casca.*   Cassius, what night is this!
> *Cassius.* A very pleasing night to honest men.
> *Casca.* Who ever knew the heavens menace so?
> *Cassius.* Those that have known the earth so full of faults.
> For my part, I have walked about the streets,
> Submitting me unto the perilous night,
> And, thus unbraced, Casca, as you see,
> Have bared my bosom to the thunder-stone;
> And when the cross-blue lightning seem'd to open
> The breast of heaven, I did present myself
> Even in the aim and very flash of it.   (I. iii. 42)

Cassius, in conspiring against Caesar, is being true, to his own nature. Suffering no consciousness of evil in himself, being, that is, in harmony with himself, he can say that the night is pleasing 'to honest men'. The storm has no terrors for Cassius, since to him the murder of Caesar is creative, not destructive—the act is one to restore, not disturb, the order of Rome. Now, though the storm effects in *Macbeth* are, as are most other effects, less prolix than in *Julius Caesar*, they are in their impact even more powerful. They are less coloured and less varied, but more grim and thick with a choking atmosphere of evil. Foul weather, thunder, and lightning, accompany the Weird Sisters from the start. But, though imaginatively the whole of the Brutus-theme is on a more brilliant, optimistic, almost cheerfully heroic plane than the action of *Macbeth*, one is only a more concentrated and explosive development of the other: though one flower be bright and the other dark, the roots are of the same species—destruction, spiritual division, disharmony and anarchy within and without.

The blood-imagery of *Julius Caesar* is flagrant and excessive. Images

of blood and human wounds abound. Such lines as the following are
typical:

> O mighty Caesar! dost thou lie so low?
> Are all thy conquests, glories, triumphs, spoils,
> Shrunk to this little measure? Fare thee well.
> I know not, gentlemen, what you intend,
> Who else must be let blood, who else is rank:
> If I myself, there is no hour so fit
> As Caesar's death's hour, nor no instrument
> Of half that worth as those your swords, made rich
> With the most noble blood of all this world.
> I do beseech you, if you bear me hard,
> Now whilst your purpled hands do reek and smoke,
> Fulfil your pleasure.   (III. i. 148)

There is Brutus' elaborate and rather horrible description of the proposed
'carving' of Caesar (II. i. 173); there are the 'fierce fiery warriors' who
'drizzled blood upon the Capitol' (II. ii. 19); there is Caesar's dream of the
statue

> Which like a fountain with a hundred spouts
> Did run pure blood.   (II. ii. 77)

'Blood' or 'bloody' occurs seventeen times in III. i. alone. Brutus advises the
conspirators to stoop and bathe their swords and arms in Caesar's blood.
Blood is again emphasized in Antony's oration—blood and Caesar's wounds.
The pages of this play are drenched in it. And yet the whole of the blood-
imagery here does not hold a quarter of the terror and the misery of the
blood-speeches in *Macbeth*; of Lady Macbeth's

> Yet who would have thought the old man to have had so much
> blood in him?   (V. i. 42)

or Angus'

> Now does he feel
> His secret murders sticking on his hands   (V. ii. 16)

—terrible bloodless metaphor! or of Macbeth's

> What hands are these? Ha! they pluck out mine eyes.
> Will all great Neptune's ocean wash this blood
> Clean from my hand? No, this my hand will rather
> The multitudinous seas incarnadine,
> Making the green one red.   (II. ii. 60)

In comparison with such lines those in *Julius Caesar* show more of a blood-zest than a blood-horror: just as the storm in *Julius Caesar* is lurid, fiery, bizarre, and picturesque—a kind of tragic fireworks; whereas the atmosphere of *Macbeth* is gloomy, black, and fearful. But in both plays the essentially murderous and destructive nature of the action is emphasized by recurrent blood-imagery.

And, finally, there is the animal-symbolism. Many of the creatures mentioned are either unnatural in form or unnatural in behaviour. They are creatures suggestive of a disjointed and disorganized state, creatures of unnatural disorder, reflecting the unnatural and disorderly acts of Brutus and Macbeth: for it is, in the present era, now that 'human statute' has 'purged the general weal' (*Macbeth*, III. iv. 76), as natural to man to aim at harmony and order both without and within the individual 'state of man' as it is to birds and beasts to follow the instinctive laws of their kind. Hence the murder of Caesar is heralded by varied unnatural phenomena. Not only do 'birds and beasts' break from all habits of their 'quality and kind' (I. iii. 64); all laws of nature are interrupted:

> *Casca*. A common slave—you know him well by sight—
>   Held up his left hand, which did flame and burn
>   Like twenty torches join'd, and yet his hand,
>   Not sensible of fire, remain'd unscorch'd.
>   Besides—I ha' not since put up my sword—
>   Against the Capitol I met a lion,
>   Who glared upon me and went surly by,
>   Without annoying me.   (I. iii. 15)

He tells how

> Men all in fire walk up and down the streets.
> And yesterday the bird of night did sit
> Even at noon-day upon the market place,
> Hooting and shrieking.   (I. iii. 25)

A lioness 'hath whelped in the streets' (II. ii. 17). Graves have opened, and the dead walk forth shrieking (II. ii. 18, 24). All things seem to have changed

> from their ordinance
> Their natures and preformed faculties
> To monstrous quality.   (I. iii. 66)

There is no heart within the sacrificial offering (II. ii 40). We are confronted with things apparently beyond the workings of causality. In *Julius Caesar* all order is inverted: 'old men fool and children calculate' (I. iii. 65). And all this shadows vaguely the terrors and dangers of an act against the symbol of order and authority: an act of destruction directed against the state, a rough tearing of the woven fabric of society and order and peace. Now the action of *Macbeth* is accompanied by similar extraordinary manifestations. Not only have we the familiars of the Weird Sisters and their references to animals of unnatural form as 'the rat without a tail'[3] and the numerous evil forms of life mentioned in the cauldron incantation scene, but, as in *Julius Caesar*, weird phenomena in the animal and stellar worlds strike fear and wonder into the minds of men. In both plays, the comparison of these outward forms to the central act of disorder is clearly pointed. Cassius tells us:

> And the complexion of the element
> In favour's like the work we have in hand,
> Most bloody, fiery, and most terrible.   (I. iii. 128)

Calpurnia knows that 'when beggars die there are no comets seen' (II. ii. 30). In *Macbeth* we are told clearly, in a short scene of choric commentary, that these strange events reflect the essential unnaturalness of murder—that is, the essential disorderliness of destruction: and this reflects—or is reflected in—the unnatural disharmony in Macbeth's soul. Ross and an Old Man talk:

> *Old Man.* Three score and ten I can remember well:
>   Within the volume of which time I have seen
>   Hours dreadful and things strange; but this sore night
>   Hath trifled former knowings.
> *Ross.*   Ah, good father,
>   Thou seest, the heavens, as troubled with man's act,
>   Threaten his bloody stage; by the clock, 'tis day,
>   And yet dark night strangles the travelling lamp;
>   Is't night's predominance, or the day's shame,
>   That darkness does the face of earth entomb,

When living light should kiss it?
Old Man.   'Tis unnatural,
　Even like the deed that's done. On Tuesday last,
　A falcon, towering in her pride of place,
　Was by a mousing owl hawk'd at and kill'd.
Ross. And Duncan's horses—a thing most strange and certain—
　Beauteous and swift, the minions of their race,
　Turn'd wild in nature, broke their stalls, flung out,
　Contending 'gainst obedience, as they would make
　War with mankind.
Old Man. 'Tis said they eat each other.
Ross. They did so, to the amazement of mine eyes
　That look'd upon't.   (II. iv. 1)

Again the insistence on disorder: the suspension and interruption of natural laws corresponding to the unlawful and so unnatural deed. Earlier in the play Lennox told us that:

　... prophesying with accents terrible
　Of dire combustion and confus'd events
　New-hatch'd to the woeful time, the obscure bird
　Clamour'd the live-long night ...   (II. iii. 62)

—like 'the bird of night' in *Julius Caesar*, 'hooting and shrieking' (I. iii. 26) in the market-place.

　Such portents are harbingers of 'confused events', of disorder. So Macbeth, who has, like Brutus; 'let slip the dogs of war' within himself, but determines not to return but 'go o'er', tells the Weird Sisters that he must be satisfied whatever confusion and disorder follow: again, an emphasis on chaos, disorder, 'confused events':

　I conjure you, by that which you profess,
　Howe'er you come to know it, answer me:
　Though you untie the winds and let them fight
　Against the churches; though the yesty waves
　Confound and swallow navigation up;
　Though bladed corn be lodg'd and trees blown down;
　Though castles topple on their warders' heads;
　Though palaces and pyramids do slope
　Their heads to their foundations; though the treasure
　Of nature's germens tumble all together,

> Even till destruction sicken; answer me
> To what I ask you.   (IV. i. 50)

These are the forces of destruction and disorder Macbeth must now loose—against himself. This speech is followed by the three 'apparitions'; and we see how the interruption of natural laws itself recoils on him—Birnam Wood is to move to Dunsinane, or appear to him to do so; and Macduff, not 'born of woman', will be the appointed angel of revenge. Brutus also finds he has released forces against himself and his party. Antony's prophecy is fulfilled:

> ... Caesar's spirit, ranging for revenge,
> With Ate by his side, come hot from Hell,
> Shall in these confines, with a monarch's voice,
> Cry 'Havoc!' and let slip the dogs of war.   (III. i. 270)

In both plays it is seen that good does not come from evil; order from disorder; harmony, from conflict. But a new good must take, the place of the old, a new order, like the old, must come back to Rome and Scotland; the new harmony will be as the old harmony that was shattered by the rash act of conflict.

The poetic symbolism and imaginative atmosphere of these two plays tend to mirror the spiritual significance. The outer conflict is a symbol of an inner conflict. The unnatural 'phenomena' of earth and sky show a disorder in things: so, too, is there disorder in the souls—or minds—of Brutus and Macbeth. An exact reference of these disorder-symbols to the mental experience of the protagonists is most important. I shall next attempt to show why the disorder-symbols of *Julius Caesar* must be related to Brutus, and not elsewhere.

The horror of Caesar's assassination is apparent most strongly to two people in the play: Brutus and Antony. Its necessity is apparent most strongly to Brutus and Cassius. Cassius and Antony are both sure of themselves, and enjoy a oneness of vision, which results in clear and concise action. To neither does the act present a twofold and agonizingly inconsistent appearance. But it is exactly this incertitude, this wavering between two aspects of reality, which is at the root of disorder.[4] It is this which torments Brutus; it is this twofold fated necessity and yet rational absurdity of Caesar's assassination which the play, as a whole, gives the reader; it is this consciousness of the wrongness and unnaturalness of destruction in a mind that is yet involved automatically and half-willingly in that very destruction which forms the poetic experience of Brutus and Macbeth; and the poetic experience of the poet which created, and that in the reader which is induced by, the attendant symbolism of storm, blood, and chaos in nature. For the poet and the reader, like Brutus, see both sides of the question, and suffer a division of sympathy. And it is only in respect of this division of sympathy in the beholder that the murders can ultimately be considered unnatural. That they are 'unnatural' in themselves and absolutely cannot ultimately be asserted they happened and were therefore natural. Absolute disorder is inconceivable. So though to Antony the murder is purely hateful, unnecessary and in a sense unnatural, and though he may prophesy external disorder, he is in no doubt as to his own course, he endures no division of sympathy, no unnatural experience, no spiritual conflict, and so, not suffering inward disorder, he promptly expresses himself by recreating 'order'. The murder of Caesar is natural to Antony in that it falls readily into his scheme of thought: he therefore knows just what to do about it. But Brutus, like the reader, is twined in the meshes of the immediately actual and impending— and so in one sense perfectly natural—fact of the murder, and yet sees all the time its essential breaking of the natural evolved laws of humanity. It is this twofold consciousness of the unnatural within the actual that creates disorder in the souls of Brutus and Macbeth. And we, in reading, are made to feel a similar symbolic disorder within the order of nature. The poetic symbolism accordingly forces us to see the central act of *Julius Caesar* more nearly through the vision of a Brutus than that of any other of the chief persons.

This is the peculiar technique of mature Shakespearian tragedy. The hero and his universe are interdependent. In *Macbeth* and *King Lear* this interdependence is obvious: in *Julius Caesar* it is only evident, perhaps, on the analogy of *Macbeth*. But, whether in *Macbeth* or *Julius Caesar*, this interpenetration of the protagonist with his environment is a supreme act of poetry. It not merely forces our vision to the focus of the hero's consciousness but is philosophically profound: for the play then contains more than an historical sequence of events. In so closely fusing protagonist with plot, the poet has created a living reality in that he shows us, not merely a series of persons and events, but a profound relation between the mind and its environment; a relation bridged by action. There is disorder in Brutus, in Macbeth: there is a disorderly act: there is disorder in the world. And yet this is not a purely logical sequence. The original spiritual disorder may equally be said either to cause, or to be caused by, the final disorder in the world: since, if the murderer were at peace with himself originally, his deed might not lead—as I have shown—to political chaos; and yet it is the fear of final disorder—that is, of crime—which originally seems to cause disorder in the hero's soul. Thus there is no rigid time-sequence of cause and effect between the hero and his environment: there is, however, a relation, and this relation is cemented and fused by the use of prophecy and poetic symbolism, merging subject with object, present with future. We are shown not merely the story of a murder; not merely the mind of a murderer; nor merely the effect of murder; but rather a single reality built of these three interacting, reciprocal, co-existent. The future disorder of Rome is mirrored in the skies before Caesar's death: the Weird Sisters foreshadow the death of Duncan, the Soothsayer that of Caesar: the future is half felt as existing within the present and the time-sequence has a secondary reality only. In this way we are shown the essence of destruction, of evil. This essence is not purely human, though it uses humanity; it is contingent on human action, and it is therefore not inhuman either. It exists purely as a reciprocity, or relation: and in so far as the poetic symbolism alone directly expresses this relation it is of more importance than either the protagonist himself or the action of the play. It alone reflects an absolute reality. It is, in fact, the pivot and core of the drama. In this way *Julius Caesar* and *Macbeth* expose the nature of an evil reality: an abnormal and dynamic relation between a unit and its environment.

I do not claim in this essay to have done more than indicate wherein the Brutus and Macbeth conceptions are poetically alike. The divergences are readily apparent. I do not deny a difference on the plane of ethics. Brutus is more conscious of integrity and harmony in his aims—if not in himself—than Macbeth. And partly for this reason, the whole of the first part of *Julius Caesar* with its fire and blood imagery and its picturesque menagerie of beasts, is always heroic and romantic and colourful against the darkness, and contrasts with the gloom and murk of *Macbeth*; its muffled thunder; and the unclean rites of the Weird Sisters. But in essence the conflicts are similar. Though the contestants in the souls of the two heroes be not exactly commensurable with each other, the conflict is of the same nature. The courses of their tragedies follow channels of the same curves. The Brutus-theme, though pitched in a different ethical key, presents the same rhythm as *Macbeth*.

NOTES

1. My comprehensive analysis of *Julius Caesar* is presented in *The Imperial Theme*.

2. That this phrase comes from Plutarch is not relevant here. Shakespeare need not have used it. Nor, in any case, does its legendary survival prove its artistic sterility: rather the reverse.

3. The fact that this was a popular superstition in no way lessens its imaginative value in *Macbeth*.

4. Cf. Bergson's contention (to which I am indebted) that the concept of disorder is the result of a mind oscillating between *two kinds of order*. In writing of 'orders' he says: 'There is not first the incoherent, then the geometrical, then the vital; there is only the geometrical and the vital and then, by a swaying of the mind between them, the idea of the incoherent' (*Creative Evolution*, translated A. Mitchell, p. 249). This appears to me to have relevance to the Brutus-theme and *Macbeth*; both of which turn on the idea of 'disorder' and that of a mind suffering division and conflict.

BERNARD McELROY

Macbeth:
The Torture of the Mind

In *Macbeth*, Shakespeare focuses his attention fully upon a problem he had dealt with peripherally in *Hamlet* and *Measure for Measure*: that of the criminal who is deeply aware of his own criminality, is repulsed by it, but is driven by internal and external pressures ever further into crime. What differentiates such villains as Claudius, Angelo, and Macbeth from Richard III, Iago, and Edmund is that the former fully admit the validity and worth of the moral laws they violate, while the latter dismiss the ethical standards of the world as so much folly and delusion. The latter three relish their superiority over their victims, while the former judge themselves from the same ethical perspectives as their victims. The descendants of the Vice believe in what they do, while the conscience-stricken criminals are in the agonizing position of being committed by their actions to one set of values while committed by their beliefs to quite another. *Macbeth* dramatizes this predicament as experienced by a man who possesses the fundamental qualities of the Shakespearean tragic hero.

For all its emphasis upon blood and violence, *Macbeth* is the most completely internal of all Shakespeare's tragedies. It presents us with a man who has a clear conception of the universe and his own proper place in it. But, when confronted with the possibility of committing a daring though criminal act, he wilfully deceives himself for a short time and embraces an

---

From *Shakespeare's Mature Tragedies*. ©1973 Princeton University Press, 2001 renewed PUP.

opposite view of the world. In the aftermath of an irrevocable act, he finds himself irrevocably committed to a world-view in which he does not believe. The key to his savagery, and, even more, to the soul-sickness that elevates him to tragedy, is that he must proceed as if the self-delusion were true, when in his mind and heart he knows that it is not. This constant lying to himself, and the discrepancy between his beliefs and the world that he has chosen for himself, produce the self-loathing and the numbing sense of loss that are the essence of his tragedy.

The *Macbeth*-world is one of the most distinctive Shakespeare ever created, having an atmosphere very much its own, upon which almost all extensive commentaries have remarked. Like the *Hamlet*-world, the world of *Macbeth* can be divided into three spheres or loci—the court over which Macbeth gains bloody sway, the world outside that court from which the forces of retribution issue, and a metaphysical sphere which intrudes physically upon the action. But the *Macbeth*-world has none of *Hamlet*'s variegation; it is all very much of a piece, and the same nightmarish qualities of violence, fear, equivocation, and diabolism permeate every corner of it. The metaphysical realm seems scarcely more than an extension of the dark recesses of the hero's mind, a projection of his own inner promptings and fears. The consistency and intensity of the *Macbeth*-world have given rise to the widespread impression that this play is the most unified product of Shakespeare's art, that it issued as if a single breath from the most profoundly disturbing recesses of his imagination.[1]

The world Macbeth sees corresponds in striking detail to the world that the play presents us. Indeed, when the Thane describes his microcosm on the eve of the murder, he presents us with a most haunting delineation of the macrocosm, the world of the play:

> Now o'er the one half-world
> Nature seems dead, and wicked dreams abuse
> The curtained sleep. Witchcraft celebrates
> Pale Hecate's offerings; and withered murder,
> Alarumed by his sentinel, the wolf,
> Whose howl's his watch, thus with his stealthy pace,
> With Tarquin's ravishing strides, towards his design
> Moves like a ghost.
>
> (II.i.49–56)

Because of this coalescence between the macrocosm and the microcosm, Macbeth's own words provide us with the most useful index to the salient qualities of the *Macbeth*-world.

Nature seems dead. In the world of *Macbeth*, the inverted and the unnatural constitute the normal state of affairs. Paradox, antithesis, and equivocation are the characteristic idiom of the play.[2] The word "strange" and its derivatives appear twenty times, far more often than in any other tragedy by Shakespeare, and more often than in any other of his plays except *The Tempest*. All the characters, young and old, good and bad, are troubled by a sense of being estranged from the "natural touch," of being surrounded by conditions which are "'gainst nature still." Disruptions in the natural order occur everywhere, from the firmament to the stables, "even like the deed that's done." Darkness at noon, predatory animals, night's black agents, murdering ministers, crying orphans, weeping widows, and innumerable other large and small touches all combine to delineate a macrocosm which, like the microcosm of the hero, has suffered the death of nature. As if to underscore the ubiquitousness of the strange, the weird, and the inverted in Macbeth's Scotland, the one presentation of the benificent face of nature occurs in a context of extreme irony. The temple-haunting martlet may seem to approve by his loved mansionry that the heavens' breath smells wooingly around Macbeth's castle, yet we know from the previous scene that it is the raven, not the martlet, which croaks the fatal entrance of Duncan under those grim battlements.

Wicked dreams abuse the curtained sleep. The *Macbeth*-world is predominantly nocturnal, and the aberrations that can occur in sleep are central to the play. Though this has been amply pointed out, what has not received sufficient attention is the nightmarish quality of the *Macbeth*-world itself. Like *The Winter's Tale*, *Cymbeline*, and *The Tempest*, *Macbeth* is in a sense a dream-play; that is, its world is informed by the same meaningful distortions which, in universal human experience, characterize the world seen in dreams—the same combination of the real and the unreal, the logical and the absurd, the probable and the fantastic, the frightening and the grotesque.[3] Like a dream, the play seems both to rush forward with inexorable speed and yet to move with the agonizing slowness of stupor. The two main characters engage in swift, violent action, yet their lives wind down to absolute stasis, the frozen horror of Lady Macbeth's nightmares and the bedrock of Macbeth's despair. The *Macbeth*-world is a projection of Macbeth's mind in exactly the way the world seen in dreams is a projection of the mind of the dreamer. Like a dream-world, the *Macbeth*-world is filled with symbols, both obvious and obscure, which portray to Macbeth's mind the essential qualities of his thoughts and acts. Like the world of nightmare, the *Macbeth*-world is oppressive, airless, and claustrophobic, a quality suggested by "curtained sleep," and made explicit by Macbeth's feeling of being "cabined, cribbed, confined." Memories are filled with rooted sorrows, the stuffed bosom is fraught with perilous stuff which weighs upon the heart, and the imagination quails before nameless terrors. Even the good characters describe their native country in terms which, like the world of nightmare, embody at once distortion and reality, exaggeration and absolute conviction:

> Where signs and groans, and shrieks that rent the air,
> Are made, not marked; where violent sorrow seems
> A modern ecstacy. The dead man's knell
> Is there scarce asked for who, and good men's lives
> Expire before the flowers in their caps,
> Dying or ere they sicken.
>
> (IV.iii.168–173)

As in the world of dreams, the boundaries between what is and what is not are thin and flexible. That the witches are real seems pretty clear, since Banquo sees them, but, like the contingent "realities" of dreams, they are as insubstantial as breath or bubbles, and they can melt into the wind, leaving their astonished interlocutors wondering, "Were such things here?" There has been no unanimity in either the theater or in criticism about whether Banquo's ghost, the air-drawn dagger, and the disembodied voices that haunt Macbeth are strictly the products of his imagination or manifestations of the supernaturalism of the *Macbeth*-world. Shakespeare seems to have left the matter purposely vague; Macbeth is tortured by both external and internal "sights," symbolic manifestations both in the macrocosm and the microcosm, and it is not always possible for him to say where one leaves off and the other begins.

'Twere best not know myself. In the *Macbeth*-world, characters are constantly turning their eyes toward the innermost recesses of nature, especially their own natures, and they are invariably appalled by what they find there. Macbeth, in his first appearance, is horrified by his own propensities, and, as the play progresses, an unstintingly negative appraisal of himself and of life in general becomes the substance of his tragedy. But he is not the only one who is repulsed by what he sees within himself. The discreet Banquo can keep his mind under control when he is awake, but is shaken by nameless "cursed thoughts" that nature gives way to in repose. Lady Macbeth, too, can cope with the waking world by embracing the worst she sees there with ferocious assent and enthusiasm. But in sleep, with her defenses—her rationalizations and ruthless will—in abeyance, she is brought to a horrified recognition of herself. Watching her, the Doctor cries, "God, God forgive us all!" (v.i.70), which could well serve as an epigraph for the play. Both the young Lennox and the Old Man are appalled by natural

aberrations and the deeds which initiate them. Ross delivers the nightmare description of Scotland quoted above. The Porter sees Macbeth's courtyard as the entrance to hell. Both Lady Macduff and her son paint a glum picture of the relation of innocence and experience, a picture that proves all too accurate in their case. Even Malcolm recites a whole catalog of fictitious vices of which he is supposedly guilty. The constant discernment of evil supports the play's overall impression that both microcosm and macrocosm are vast repositories of the unspeakable, that the serpent lurks beneath every innocent flower, readily apparent to anyone who has the nerve or misfortune to look. And the devil laughs.

Witchcraft celebrates. Whatever one may make of the reality of Banquo's ghost, the witches most certainly have a more vivid dramatic reality than Banquo living. The problem that their presence poses is central to the tragedy, for it involves the degree of freedom Macbeth exercises in committing his succession of crimes. If the witches can accurately foresee the future in the instant, then the future must be fixed. If the future is fixed, had Macbeth any real choice? If he had no choice, what becomes of the moral significance of his actions? The quest for a solution has run the gamut from the venerable Kittredge, who saw the sisters as Norns who could not only see the future but could determine it, to Stoll, for whom the problem scarcely existed, since the witches are primarily devices intended to sustain an illusion.[4] Walter Clyde Curry attempted to steer a middle course, pointing out that in the mainstream of theology in Shakespeare's England, evil was both subjective and objective, existing both in the mind of man as a result of the Fall, and also in a whole realm of devils, imps, and spirits, whose existence was in no way dependent upon the human mind.[5] The degree of their influence upon human actions, he tells us, depended largely upon how a given individual was disposed at the time of temptation. The critic suggests that Macbeth had free will to begin with, but appears to have forfeited it after the crime. "We have a passage from strict indeterminism to apparent determinism" (p. 105). The insight is valuable insofar as Macbeth, as he himself realizes, does drastically circumscribe his range of possible choices after he commits regicide. Yet, when Curry attributes to the witches "a dignity, a dark grandeur, and a terror-inspiring aspect" (p. 77), he commits the same error Kittredge had before him, placing more confidence in exhaustive research among arcane books on witchcraft than in the witches Shakespeare has given us in the play. Far from being awesome demons or implacable Norns, they are filthy old hags who possess very little grandeur of any kind; when not trifling with the destiny of kings, they seem to derive equal pleasure from killing swine, cadging chestnuts, collecting thumbs, and gathering from ditch and gibbet the loathsome ingredients of their brew.[6]

Besides, to attempt a cogent theological explanation of *Macbeth* is almost as grave an error as to seek one for *Hamlet*. For one thing, the doctrine of free will itself has always been a particularly controversial and ambiguous one in Christian theology, resting upon the essentially paradoxical formulation that God's foreknowledge of the future, even though infallible and at one with His omnipotent will, is not the cause of the future.[7] Ultimately, the whole matter was usually presented as a mystery beyond the full understanding of the finite intellect, a seeming contradiction which had to be accepted on faith. Shakespeare, for the purposes of this play, seems to have accepted it on exactly those terms. The sisters can indeed look into the seeds of time, and their predictions are always right. The play accepts a central paradox of Christian thought; though the future is foreknown, it is not fixed. Macbeth himself alternately trusts the prophecies completely and ignores them entirely; more precisely, he attempts to skirt around those prophecies he does not want to believe, as when he plans the murders of Banquo and Fleance so that the prediction about Banquo's issue will never come true.[8] Shakespeare, in contrast to Milton, does not even explore the problem of foreknowledge and free will directly; he takes it for granted and goes on to those aspects of man and evil that interested him more.

The witches are not instruments of a power that *causes* destruction and suffering; they are instruments of a power that *enjoys* destruction and suffering. They go about their work with gusto and enthusiasm, inverting values, reporting their exploits, and gleefully anticipating fresh trouble. Their principal function in the drama is to embody a supernatural order which desires suffering and evil, does what it can to promote them, and finally exults in the destruction that follows. As such, they have more to do with the tone and atmosphere of the work than with the metaphysics of the *Macbeth*-world. Shakespeare could have chosen to omit them entirely and still have written essentially the same kind of play about the same characters. What would have been lost, however, is the haunting sense that the center of the universe depicted in *Macbeth* is not heaven but hell. They serve not so much to tempt Macbeth as to tantalize him; they do not so much impel his deed as insure that it will be as bitter as possible to him. When they first encounter him, they whet his appetite for the crown, but then in the next breath predict that Banquo's issue, not his own, will be the ultimate beneficiaries of disruption in the royal line. More prudent tempters might wish to conceal this, for it could deter Macbeth from regicide. But, characteristically, Macbeth defers recognition of all that does not immediately suit his bent of mind. It is only after he has killed the king that he turns to the second prophecy, and then the prospect of Banquo's heirs enjoying his spoils becomes the source of unbearable torment to him, torment which the sisters increase by showing him Banquo's successors triumphantly crowned. So, too, they produce spirits to instill in him a false sense of confidence, and the bursting of that bubble of imagined security is Macbeth's final agony. The witches, then, are not on hand to make wounds, but to rub salt in them and relish the howls that follow. They do not cause Macbeth's fall; they do not even contribute much to it; rather, their most characteristic function is to exacerbate it, to revel in it, and profanely celebrate it: "Show his eyes, and grieve his heart! / Come like shadows, so depart!" (IV.i.110–111).

This even-handed justice. Perhaps the most extraordinary thing about the *Macbeth*-world is that it contains a strong, effective principle of retributive justice in operation throughout the play. This is not something which our experience with the worlds of Shakespeare's tragedies would lead us to expect. In *Hamlet*, to be sure, there is a heavenly inclination toward justice, but, like all things in the *Hamlet*-world, it works in obscure and devious ways. In *Othello*, there is only that justice which the characters can make for themselves—too late. In *King Lear*, tragedy occurs finally because there is no justice, no way to make ethics and experience congruent. But in *Macbeth*, the title character describes a verifiable phenomenon when he observes:

> But in these cases
> We still have judgment here, that we but teach
> Bloody instructions, which, being taught, return
> To plague th' inventor. This even-handed justice
> Commends th' ingredience of our poisoned chalice
> To our own lips.
>
> (I.vii.7–12)

Paradoxically, it is the presence rather than the absence of justice in the *Macbeth*-world that gives the tragedy its particularly grim and futile outlook. The forces of conventional good triumph completely, but their triumph is strangely hollow, almost devoid of any power to mitigate the reality of evil or reconcile humanity to its condition. Justice in the *Macbeth*-world gives the impression of being less real and significant than the problems it successfully confronts.[9] That evil exists is the essential fact in the world of the play; that, in the face of its existence, there is nothing to do but punish it is the essential futility. It is at the moment of justice's complete triumph that the most famous statement of futility echoes sepulchrally from the depths of Macbeth's world and from the *Macbeth*-world itself. It will not do to say that "tomorrow and tomorrow" are the embittered words of a man who has lost his humanity, for they carry far more weight within the context of the play than does anything spoken by the lackluster defenders of right. Justice is necessary, and we greet its reestablishment with a sigh of relief; but to say that justice is necessary is not the same as to say it is meaningful. When Macbeth commits his crime, he seems to embody a dimension of mankind left quite untouched by Macduff's and Malcolm's vengeance upon the individual man. It is almost as if Shakespeare were taking the most optimistic theological explanation of the operation of divine justice and demonstrating that it, too, contains the seeds of tragedy.

No other Shakespearean hero faces so pallid an array of antagonists. Hamlet must deal with the cunning and capable Claudius; Othello faces the super-subtle Iago; and Lear is pitted against a conspiracy of no less than four ruthless and determined predators. But whom does Macbeth face? Banquo, Malcolm, and Macduff. Bradley's futile attempt to build a character for the first shows effectively how little the progenitor of kings is fleshed out, while Wilbur Sanders has effectively refuted those who would make a heroic, saintly king figure out of Malcolm.[10] Macduff is more sympathetic and impressive than the other two, but, by the time he becomes a significant figure, his motivation rests more upon personal grief and thirst for vengeance than upon the desire to reestablish justice:

> If thou beest slain and with no stroke of mine,
> My wife and children's ghosts will haunt me still.
> I cannot strike at wretched kerns, whose arms
> Are hired to bear their staves. Either thou, Macbeth,
> Or else my sword with an unbattered edge
> I sheathe again undeeded.
>
> (v. vii.15–20)

Macduff's grief does not animate the new order which is established at the end of the play; Malcolm's cautious politics do, and they loom much smaller in our imagination than the bloody criminal whom they supplant.

By pitting Macbeth against a combination of forces whose sum total is so much less compelling than himself, Shakespeare emphasizes that in this play, the protagonist is his own most formidable adversary. As I say, *Macbeth* is the most private and internal of Shakespeare's tragedies, and the tragic suffering that occurs is the torture of the mind that goes on within the hero and heroine. But, further, the comparatively pallid nature of the hero's opponents is essential to the complementary tension of the play, a tension that accounts for the deep ambivalence of feeling which the tragedy prompts toward its title character.[11] The central question to which almost all critics have addressed themselves is, "How can anyone who does what Macbeth does command not only our interest but our awe and empathy throughout the play? How can a man who violates his humanity tell us so much about what humanity is?" There is no doubt that Macbeth is wrong, but in his mammoth wrongness he completely overshadows the pint-size rightness of Malcolm and is much closer to realizing the outer limits of human potential than the even-handed characters who remain cautiously in the center. Like many tragic protagonists from Oedipus and Orestes to Kurtz and Raskolnikov, he is a lone voyager into the forbidden, who severs his ties with the comfort and security of the community. Such mythic figures do not merely circumvent conventional moral judgment; they pass through and beyond it. Throughout the play, Macbeth is surrounded by men who accept the limitations imposed upon them by the world, and he, too, initially considers his extraordinary powers to be "children and servants" to his king. He transgresses all the bounds that others accept, and in doing so he becomes evil and must be destroyed. But at the same time, in transgressing, fully aware of the enormity of his transgression, he assumes awe-inspiring dimensions quite beyond Duncan, Malcolm, Banquo, and Macduff. Humanity as Macbeth is terrible, but humanity as Malcolm is merely insipid.

Over the years, a theatrical tradition has sprung up, encouraged by much of the critical commentary, which casts Macbeth as a gruff, burly character of no mental prowess, one who is distinguished from other roughnecks only by his hyperactive imagination.[12] Such an interpretation, I feel certain, falls far short of the intricate characterization Shakespeare created. Macbeth's imagination is fired by a mind of considerable power and discernment; his imagination is the violent instrument by which his intellect attempts to make itself heard over the all but indomitable voice of his will. No other Shakespearean hero has so firm and correct a sense of self-knowledge, nor so fully developed a concept of the universe and his place in it. Macbeth has a unique ability to foresee both the practical and the ethical outcome of his actions.[13] Lear, in contrast, starts off with a completely mistaken notion of who he is and what the world is like; he blindly pulls down tragedy upon his own head and is shocked and outraged when disaster strikes. Othello, because of his predisposition, convinces himself of a falsehood upon virtually no evidence. Hamlet, for all his mercurial brilliance, is hopelessly inept at foreseeing the logical outcome of his actions. But Macbeth suffers from none of these perceptual shortcomings. The most terrible thing about his tragedy is that he goes to it with his eyes wide open, his vision unclouded, his moral judgment still in perfect working order. He wilfully disregards his own best perceptions and intuitions, but he is never rid of them. More than any other Shakespearean hero, he has a perfectly clear concept of who he is and where he stands—and it is exactly this perception that torments and spiritually destroys him.

In the opening scenes, Macbeth's mind is already under that kind of tension which we have seen to be so characteristic of mature Shakespearean tragedy, the tension that precedes the collapse of the personal world. The opposites are basic and the opposition is total. Macbeth is the most honored peer in the realm, but his honor is based upon incongruous and irreconcilable qualities; on the one hand, he is able and willing to dare anything and fear nothing, but, on the other, he accepts limits and boundaries which cannot under any circumstances be transgressed. Gory descriptions of his individual fearless deeds alternate with praise of him as a loyal subject who curbs the lavish spirits of those who dare to rise against their king. The tension of Macbeth's position in the macrocosm is reflected by a corresponding tension in the microcosm, the tension between a deeply moral intellect and an utterly amoral will.[14]

> The service and the loyalty I owe,
> In doing pays itself. Your Highness' part
> Is to receive our duties, and our duties
> Are to your throne and state children and servants,
> Which do but what they should by doing everything
> Safe toward your love and honor.
>
> (I.iv.22–27)

These are not the oily words of a political intriguer.[15] Macbeth really believes this version of his position in life, or at least a part of him believes it. But another part is impelled with terrible force to the ruthless action of the man for whom bounds do not exist, the man who dares to do anything.[16]

In many respects, Macbeth is, right from the beginning, a poor candidate for the job of political assassin. For one thing, he is not really ambitious in the usual sense of the word. In the scenes leading up to the murder, he scarcely mentions the crown; he has none of his wife's sanguine anticipation of a golden round or nights and days of solely sovereign sway and masterdom. Unlike Tamburlane, he does not find kingship a sort of apotheosis of the human condition, and, unlike Richard of Gloucester, he is not driven by a compulsive need to command, to check, and to o'erbear such as are of better person than himself. In conventionally ambitious men, anticipation of the fruits of crime blunts the sensibilities to the crime itself. But Macbeth is just the opposite of this; he scarcely gives a thought to the spoils that will proceed from the act and keeps his attention unwaveringly upon the act itself; and his attitude toward the object of his fixation is mixed attraction and repulsion. His repulsion springs from the deeply moral side of his nature. No other character is so acutely aware of himself as living in the eye of heaven. When he looks into himself and finds there inclinations that are anything but celestial, he is frightened and revolted, and he extends his abhorrence of his own instinct to heaven nature:

> Stars, hide your fires;
> Let not light see my black and deep desires.
> The eye wink at the hand.
>
> (I.iv.50–52)

Yet on the heels of this can come a reassertion of the impulse to terrible and forbidden action: "yet let that be / Which the eye fears, when it is done, to see" (52–53). It is the very fearfulness of the deed that seems to exert the strongest attraction for him, since it calls for a degree of resolution and daring quite beyond the slaying of rebels. For Macbeth, action is self-definition; he is revolted by the act, but tantalized by the possibility of doing exactly that which is most expressly forbidden by all laws, sacred and humane. He dares to kill his king not so much to become king himself as to become the man who dared to do it.[17]

In such a frame of mind—revolted by his own inner promptings, but drawn to them nonetheless—he goes home to his wife Much of the commentary on the play has centered upon how well Lady Macbeth knows her man, perfectly or not at all. The answer, I believe, is that she has an unfailing instinct for his weaknesses and fixes them precisely, though his strengths come as a complete surprise to her. Her misunderstanding of him is the reverse of her misunderstanding of herself: she has perfect confidence in her strengths; but her weaknesses, when they declare themselves, catch her defenseless and unaware. Throughout the play, she is most self-assured in those moments when Macbeth's nerve is failing, but her own nerve fails in those scenes where he is most independent and ruthless.

Macbeth and his lady have the makings of one murderer between them. She is capable of contemplating the crime with something that borders upon exaltation, but is not, it turns out, capable of dealing the fatal stroke herself. He is quite capable of doing that, but cannot even think of the moral quality of the act without horror and aversion. He would, no doubt, be capable of resisting the temptation to strike were it not for the devastating attack she launches against the foundation of his world-view, his concept of what it means to be a man.[18] Thus, the great confrontation between them in Act I, scene vii, presents the disconcerting picture of two people inciting each other to crime, for the presence of each makes crime possible for the other.

Macbeth's soliloquy at the opening of the scene gives us our first full view of the hero's subjective world; it is a world in which action is a continuum, an ongoing process of cause and effect, act and consequence, a world in which retributive justice is not merely possible but certain. It is also a world of relatedness, a world in which duties and obligations are well defined and divinely sanctioned.[19] In such a world, vaulting ambition, far from being heroic self-assertion, is unconscionable overreaching, a violation of the sacrosanct bonds that define one's humanity. By the end of the soliloquy, Macbeth has decided to abandon all thoughts of regicide, for in such a world, to proceed would be not only appalling, but positively suicidal. When he announces his decision to his wife, the reason he gives, the "golden opinions" his valor has just won from all sorts of people, is an evasion. He cannot explain his real reasons—retribution from heaven, the sacred bonds of obligation—because she simply would not comprehend them, would, in fact, heap scorn upon them.[20] But his stated reason is a significant and characteristic evasion; the golden opinions epitomize his position as a valorous subject who is content to accept the status of subject and live as an honored member of the community.

Lady Macbeth is able to undermine his resolution so quickly not simply because she calls his virility into question, and not simply because she exerts enormous personal power over their relationship; Macbeth is quite capable of withstanding such pressures. She finally achieves her purposes by suggesting to him that his whole apprehension of reality is mistaken, that action is not an open-ended continuum, but is final and conclusive, and that the essence of humanity is not living within the limits of an assigned place, but daring to do anything. Her attack on Macbeth is the same as Goneril's attack upon Albany; because he is moral, he is a coward and a fool who deceives himself about the way the world really operates.[21] But her arguments are far more effective than Goneril's because she is not telling her husband anything new, but reiterating things he had already told himself. Like Hamlet and Othello, Macbeth has a divided mind about some of the most fundamental issues of existence; Lady Macbeth is the voice of one side of it.

However, she makes not one but two false beginnings, first taunting him with the "hope" he has of being king, and then trying to use love to blackmail him. These tactics elicit no reaction whatsoever; Macbeth usually stays out of trouble as long as he can keep his mouth shut. But then she puts her finger squarely on the central paradox of his present position:

> Wouldst thou have that
> Which thou esteem'st the ornament of life,
> And live a coward in thine own esteem,

Letting 'I dare not' wait upon 'I would,'
Like the poor cat i' th' adage?

(I.vii.41–45)

The ornament of life, his present position as first peer of the realm, is contingent upon his willingness to accept one limitation, not to dare to rise up against his king. She tantalizes him with his own self-image as a man who dares anything, for whom no limits of any kind exist. This line of argument draws an immediate reaction, not because he cannot stand her taunts of cowardice, but because she has touched upon a deep ambivalence in his own mind about what it is to be a man. He counters with a reassertion of the idea that to be a man is to live within human limits, and she responds with an assertion of the opposite:

MACBETH: I dare do all that may become a man:
Who dares do more is none.

(46–47)

LADY: When you durst do it, then you were a man;
And to be more than what you were, you would
Be so much more the man.

(49–51)

But this pro and contra is getting nowhere. Clearly, she needs something to break the deadlock, and her instinct leads her surely to the clincher: her version of the world and of man was once *his* version too. She undermines his confidence in the vision of the soliloquy, by pointing out that he does not fully believe in it himself. At one time he had been more than willing to kill the king if only the opportunity would present itself. "If we should fail?" (59). This, Macbeth's last attempt at resistance, has been widely misunderstood. As the soliloquy showed, he is not in the least worried about the practical possibility of executing the murder: if that were all there were to it, he would proceed at once. But the failure Macbeth fears is the long-range failure in a world of relatedness, where action is a continuum and justice is certain—to be cut off forever from the rest of humanity, to be hated and cursed by all men, and finally to be hounded down by inexorable retribution. It is the long-range failure he had pictured in harrowing detail, and it is, in fact, exactly what happens. Lady Macbeth, however, misunderstands him completely; she thinks he is worried about the practicability of getting away with the crime in the short run, and so she reassures him that her plan is foolproof. We come now to the most crucial moment of the tragedy, when

Macbeth changes his mind for the second time and commits himself to murdering the king. He is not really persuaded; rather, as at several other junctures in the play, he wilfully disregards his own better judgment, pushing to the back of his mind all his best perceptions and most passionately held beliefs, and substitutes in their place the shallow, faulty rationalizations for which his wife has been spokesman.[22] First of all, he unequivocally accepts the idea that the essence of manhood is unbounded action:

> Bring forth men-children only;
> For thy undaunted mettle should compose
> Nothing but males.
>
> (72–74)

There is gruesome irony in his praising her fitness to bear sons, since she has just declared that she would kill her own child without compunction were it necessary to vindicate her will. But far more important, Macbeth accepts the notion that action is final and conclusive, that accomplishment of the deed is tantamount to success, that the consequences of an action may be circumvented:

> Will it not be received,
> When we have marked with blood those sleepy two
> Of his own chamber and used their very daggers,
> That they have done't?
>
> (74–77)

Like Othello's "And yet, how nature erring from itself—," it is the point of no return, for it signals not simply a change of mind, but a movement from one world-view to another. The seeds of Macbeth's tragedy are planted here, not only because he dedicates himself to the first of many brutal crimes, but even more because he does not really *believe* in a world in which a man may dare anything, in which action is final and conclusive. He wants to believe in it, for such a world poses no impediments to action. His ruthless will scores a temporary victory over his own best perceptions.[23] But the shallowness and patent self-deception of this speech contrast sharply with the intense and passionate conviction of the soliloquy. From this point on, Macbeth is in the position of having to insist with all the vigor of his will upon the truth of something which, in his own mind, he does not really believe. His method of insistence will be action, and the result will be tragedy.

The undermining of the subjective world is different in Macbeth's case from the undermining of the world-views of the other three heroes. They all found, for one reason or another, that their most fundamental assumptions about the world and themselves were erroneous: he, on the other hand, finds himself irremediably estranged by his actions from his most fundamental beliefs, an estrangement which deepens until he finds the absolute bedrock of the final soliloquy.[24] For the remainder of the play, Macbeth sees himself as being in fundamental conflict with the world itself, with his indomitable will pitted against its moral order, its communal obligations, its immutable and inescapable ethical laws. Like all the Shakespearean tragic heroes, he sees his own actions in cosmic terms; but after the dreadful finality of "I am resolved," he is positively obsessed by the notion of being at the center of a universe which is fundamentally opposed to what he is doing. Like Hamlet, he declares total, all-out war upon the world of the play, but his attack is not against duplicity and corruption, but against humane feeling and divine justice.

In the famous dagger speech, Macbeth animates and vivifies the elements themselves, endowing them with a moral attitude toward his actions. Nature itself is atrophied by the enormity of what he is about to do; the darkest and most sinister powers have usurped the primacy of nature and, like himself, hover breathlessly on the brink of an abyss. The night seems full of sentient beings all watching what he is about to do, and the very stones of the earth are ready to cry out. It is the same vision he had seen in the first soliloquy, but now charged and animated, for the action is no longer hypothetical, but is about to become an actuality. Having thus projected his own emotional state onto the world, he turns from this harrowing vision and forces to the front of his mind the simple imperative of action; action and only action has value, action is the very substance of life itself: "Words to the heat of deeds too cold breath gives. / I go, and it is done" (II.i.61–62).

Yet in the very commission of his act, he is still haunted by the conviction that the entire universe is opposed to his breech of nature, as, in the *Macbeth*-world, it clearly is. His hysteria after the crime reflects not merely fear of real and imagined horrors; the purport of all his speeches after the murder is a sense of incalculable loss, panic-stricken realization of his estrangement from all that had formerly constituted his life, from his subjective world itself. First of all, he is cut off from the metaphysical order that is one of the givens of the *Macbeth*-world:

> But wherefore could not I pronounce 'Amen'?
> I had most need of blessing, and 'Amen'
> Stuck in my throat.
>
> (II.ii.30–32)

He is cut off from the normal, life-sustaining processes of nature:

> —the innocent sleep,
> Sleep that knits up the ravelled sleave of care,
> The death of each day's life, sore labor's bath,
> Balm of hurt minds, great nature's second course,
> Chief nourisher in life's feast.
>
> (35–39)

The self-delusion that action is final and conclusive crumbles before the realization that the consequences of his deed will last as long as his life: "Macbeth shall sleep no more" (42). He is fully aware that he can never by any means get back to the bank and shoal of time from which he has so precipitously leaped; nothing can change or mitigate the consequences of his act:

> Will all great Neptune's ocean wash this blood
> Clean from my hand? No, this my hand will rather
> The multitudinous seas incarnadine,
> Making the green one red.
>
> (59–62)

But most of all, his crime destroys his capacity to respect or even to tolerate himself. For the remainder of the play, the vantage point from which he judges himself is the world-view from which he is hopelessly estranged. His own hands are unrecognizable to him, savage, hangman's hands that would pluck out his eyes. But, in fact, they do not obliterate his vision; he must continue staring at them and at the self they epitomize. The primary purpose of his act had been to define his manhood. Ironically, it does, but the definition is one he cannot contemplate without horror and revulsion: "To know my deed, 'twere best not know myself" (72). This line sets the tone for the remainder of the tragedy. He is his deed in his own eyes, and in his own eyes his deed is appalling. Hence, he faces the characteristic problem of the Shakespearean tragic hero, how to endure what is, for him, simply unendurable. I do not read *Macbeth* as a tragedy of ambition, nor as a tragedy of fear. It is above all a tragedy of self-loathing, of self-horror that leads to spiritual paralysis, the tragedy of a man who comes to condemn all that is in him for being there. Macbeth is indeed terror-stricken in this scene, but what strikes him full of terror is not the deed itself, and still less the fear of being caught, but rather a full realization of what his action has done to him. He has cut himself off from the world he believes in and has committed himself to its antithesis, a world in which man is a predatory animal. The commitment is irrevocable, and all he can do is follow it remorselessly to its conclusion. It is as if by insisting vehemently enough on such a world-view, Macbeth believes he can validate it, can establish its reality by sheer force of will. It is the desperate need to validate the world-view to which he is committed, his determination to win a battle of wills with the macrocosm itself, that plunges him into steadily deepening cruelty in Acts III and IV. Where before he had refused to return to the chamber and look upon what he had done, he now rushes in without hesitation, feigning astonishment and grief. Where before the stirring and muttering of the sleeping grooms had all but paralyzed him, he is now capable of killing them without compunction. But despite the increasing vigor and brutality of his actions, he is never able to rid himself of his former vision of a world of relatedness and justice; rather, it becomes a kind of waking nightmare, forcing him to contemplate what he has lost and what he has become. The tension between the two world-views is clearly evident in his next soliloquy.

Macbeth had known all along that the prophecies in which he places such confidence decreed that Banquo's issue would ultimately come to the throne. Indeed, just a few minutes before the murder, he had discussed the weird sisters with Banquo, but did not for an instant allow the fact that his own posterity would benefit nothing from his crime to deter him. Characteristically, he pushed it out of his mind and wilfully ignored it until after he had committed the act toward which he was so strongly impelled. His soliloquy now is animated not so much by fear of Banquo as by intense envy of him, for Banquo is incumbent in exactly the position Macbeth himself has lost, that of a loyal peer whose daring and valor are exercised within the prescribed, acceptable limits:[25]

> 'Tis much he dares;
> And to that dauntless temper of his mind
> He hath a wisdom that doth guide his valor
> To act in safety.
>
> (III.i.51–54)

Moreover, Macbeth, as in the scene immediately following the murder, is acutely aware of his own enormous loss: he has filed his mind, put rancors in the vessel of his peace, slain a gracious king, and delivered up his soul to eternal damnation. It is a terrible self-awareness with which to live, and the knowledge that he has sacrificed everything to gain "nothing" makes it intolerable. Macbeth's solution, as at every crisis in the play, is ruthless, unrestrained action, the action of self-assertion, action based upon a world-view which makes of man a predatory hunter. Many critics have observed that, in the scene with the murderers, Macbeth uses the same line of argument that Lady Macbeth had used upon him. This is not because he has been learning tactics from his wife, but because he is now speaking from the same point of vantage as she had spoken from previously, attempting to validate the idea of manhood that underlies all his crimes. The hired assassins are to prove that their station in the file is not in the worst rank of manhood by ambushing a lone man and a boy. "Your spirits shine through you," Macbeth lauds them as soon as they agree (III.i.128).

The next scene displays even more vividly Macbeth's determination to impose, by sheer force of will, the version of reality to which he is committed upon the macrocosm itself

> But let the frame of things disjoint, both the
>   worlds suffer,
> Ere we will eat our meal in fear, and sleep
> In the affliction of these terrible dreams
> That shake us nightly.
>
>   (III.ii.16–19)

But the affliction and the fears, like his own judgment of himself, arise from that other world-view where his emotions are really engaged, a world which demands his destruction for having violated its most basic laws. "Treason has done his worst" Macbeth reflects, thinking of Duncan's peaceful sleep (24); there is a terrible self-indictment implied in the line. His image of his own mind as a rack upon which he lies being tortured is most apt and precise, for it is the torture of tension, of being torn between irreconcilable opposites. When Macbeth undertook his crime, he undertook living with its aftermath, and now the most abhorrent aspect of that aftermath is the need to be a hypocrite, to give mouth-honor to a man whom at that very moment he is causing to be treacherously struck down:[26]

> Unsafe the while, that we must lave
> Our honors in these flattering streams
> And make our faces vizards to our hearts,
> Disguising what they are.
>
>   (32–35)

Like the other Shakespearean tragic heroes, Macbeth is constitutionally incapable of tolerating false appearances, especially evil masquerading as good. What his heart is is bad enough in his eyes, but the realization that he must mask it under false magnanimity elicits from him one of the most anguished outbursts in Shakespeare: "O, full of scorpions is my mind, dear wife!" (36). Yet it seems to me that this is the only point in the scene at which the two protagonists are in emotional touch with each other. Throughout the rest of the encounter, she is trying desperately to bridge the gulf between them and he is consciously trying to widen it. Just as she had not foreseen her own failure of nerve in the aftermath of the murder, so she had not foreseen the emergence of a ruthless and completely independent will in her husband. She can no longer pour her spirits in his ear or chastize him with the valor of her tongue, and this signals a complete breakdown of their relationship, a breakdown which is at least as responsible as pangs of conscience for her own psychic disintegration. Over half her famous sleepwalking scene will be addressed to him, and will recreate exactly those moments when she was sustaining him through a crisis. But at this present juncture, all she can do is stare in astonishment and apprehension at the man he has, at her urgent insistence, become: "Come on. / Gentle my lord, sleek o'er your rugged looks" (26–27). But his struggle is with himself; it has very little to do with her: "Thou marvell'st at my words, but hold thee still; / Things bad begun make strong themselves by ill" (54–55). The last line is significant in two senses: first, it reasserts Macbeth's determination to validate by force of will the world-view to which he is committed, and, second, it implies that having embarked upon his course, he can now steel *himself* to commit further crimes. He no longer needs her to do it for him.

Of course, this does not prove to be the case, at least not all the time. In the banquet scene, Macbeth completely loses his nerve, and, just as suddenly, she finds hers again. His weakness is an absolute prerequisite for her strength. In assuming that the murder of Banquo and Fleance would set his mind at rest, Macbeth was once again wilfully deluding himself, pretending that, if he insisted vehemently enough upon something, and put that insistence into act, then the thing would be true. But even if Fleance had shared his father's fate, it would be difficult to imagine a Macbeth who was not cabined, cribbed, and confined; his prison, his torture chamber, is not the macrocosm but the microcosm, and the death of one man or of thousands is incapable of setting things to rights there. But the escape of Fleance once again makes him see that the murder of Duncan was not a final or definitive act. It will go on through a continuum of cause and effect to produce consequences completely beyond his control. When he confronts the shade of Banquo (or the evil spirit sent by the witches in Banquo's shape, or the product of his own haunted imagination—there is no way of telling which, and no need to tell), he gives voice, even in his hysteria, to the basic rift in his own subjective world. On the one hand there is the world of infinite daring, but on the other there is the world of swift and terrible justice, in which dead victims rise again to push murderers from their stools. On the one hand there is the primitive world of the olden time when blood was shed in perfect impunity without compunction, but there is also the later order, in which humane statute has purged the gentle weal. Lady Macbeth tries once again to shame him into manhood, but he will have none of it. The visible emblem of what he has done terrifies him more than any consequences he may have to face as a result of revealing his guilt.

In the aftermath of his great feast, Macbeth is more convinced than ever that he is living in a macrocosm which implacably requires his destruction:

> It will have blood, they say: blood will have blood.
> Stones have been known to move and trees to speak;
> Augures and understood relations have
> By maggot-pies and choughs and rooks brought forth
> The secret'st man of blood.
>
> (III.iv.122–126)

Yet, far from impeding him from further action, his conviction only impels him to ever more ruthless action; his insistence upon the world to which he is committed is now fired by desperation. In the face of his implacable will, all causes shall give way. His image of himself is not simply of a man with bloody, hangman's hands, but of a man inundated in blood, bathed in it from head to foot, literally into it over his head. But the total estrangement from all his previous values confers upon Macbeth, as it has upon other Shakespearean heroes, a terrible, lonely freedom. The man who has lost positively everything he cherishes is the freest of all possible men; he has nothing further to lose and nothing to worry about salvaging.

By the time he reaches the witches' abode, the naked force of his will has reached apocalyptic proportions reminiscent of the third act of *King Lear*. Macbeth thinks he has come to learn by the worst means the worst, for to know the worst is to lose a large part of fear of the worst. But the witches *want* Macbeth to struggle and hope, for they know that struggle is futile and hope groundless, and therefore torture.[27] Thus, they tell him what appears to be better news than he had expected to hear. He greets the prophecies so eagerly not primarily because they promise him apparent invulnerability, but more because they confirm him in his chosen course, urge him to become exactly the kind of man he has been trying desperately to become: "Be bloody, bold, and resolute! Laugh to scorn / The pow'r of man" (IV.i.79–80); "Be lion-mettled, proud, and take no care" (90). But if one side of Macbeth is impelled to mindless violence, another side knows that actions have consequences, and he must discover what the consequences of his initial crime will be. The parade of kings is far more than merely a salute to Shakespeare's royal patron, and productions that cut it err seriously; for the sight of Banquo's crowned progeny enjoying the fruits for which he himself has lost everything of real importance to him forces Macbeth to confront the futility of all his actions, past, present, and future. In the face of this, paradoxically, his will to act is increased to almost manic intensity:

> The flighty purpose never is o'ertook
> Unless the deed go with it. From this moment
> The very firstlings of my heart shall be
> The firstlings of my hand.
>
> (145–148)

The more aware he becomes of his estrangement from the real world, the more vehemently he must insist upon the validity of the world he has embraced—even when he does not believe in its validity himself. This conflict between vehement action and conviction of the futility of action rages through his mind for the rest of the play. In the great scenes at Dunsinane, boasting speeches of furious resolve alternate with the most soul-sick contemplations ever written.

By far the most usual interpretation of the last act is that Macbeth has completely lost his humanity, has become the monster he set out to be, and though we continue to have grudging admiration for his animal courage, we rejoice with the followers of Malcolm when the tyrant and his fiend-like queen are overthrown. Rather, it seems to me that we are so absorbed in Macbeth's private conflict that his death and the triumph of unimpressive right is almost incidental to the tragedy. Moreover, Macbeth does not lose his humanity because he *cannot* lose his humanity no matter how hard he tries; that is exactly what makes him a tragic hero.[28] His case is in one way analogous to Othello's: the Moor repeatedly resolves to cast away all love for Desdemona, but he simply cannot do it. His love remains, coexistent with his belief she has betrayed him, and the result is excruciating inner torture. Macbeth's humanity is vested in that world-view he unfolded in his first major soliloquy, and, though his most vigorous efforts throughout the play have been to rid himself of that vision, he has never even come close to doing so. It remains as a vantage point from which he must assess all that he has done, all that he has lost, all that he has become: "I am sick at heart, / When I behold—" (v.iii.19–20). The thought is left uncompleted, but clearly what Macbeth beholds all through these scenes is himself:

> I have lived long enough. My way of life
> Is fall'n into the sear, the yellow leaf,
> And that which should accompany old age,
> As honor, love, obedience, troops of friends,
> I must not look to have.
>
>   (22–26)

Honor, love, obedience, and troops of friends are the values of the limited, structured world he had abandoned; in the predatory world he embraced, they should have no importance whatsoever. "To be tender-minded / Does not become a sword," Edmund had observed. But those values are terribly important to Macbeth, and only his loss of them has made him realize how important they are. Alfred Harbage has observed that "no voice in literature has sounded with greater sadness" than Macbeth's in the above speech.[29] To have a passionately held, demonstrably valid vision of the world, and yet to be cut off from it by one's own actions, to be hated and cursed by all humanity, to have to struggle against one's own most deeply felt emotions, and to be *aware* of all this with perfect, unblinking clarity, is surely the most harrowing vision of human isolation that has ever been realized in drama. It is perhaps the degree of his self-awareness that most differentiates him from other Shakespearean malefactors: he sees his own situation unflinchingly and refuses either to soften it or to be sentimental about himself. He drains the ingredients of his poisoned chalice to the last bitter dregs. Self-awareness is one of the hallmarks of the Shakespearean tragic hero, and in Macbeth's case, it is the very essence of his tragedy. Also, like the other three, he has a desperate need to have his actions in consonance with a broader scheme of reality, including the rest of humanity and the metaphysical order. But, as Macbeth fully realizes, such consonance is impossible for him because he is so utterly cut off from the only world he believes in or values. In self-recognition and self-horror he realizes he has lost even the capacity to feel fear, and a moment later he cannot feel normal human grief at the death of his wife. Above all, he realizes he has committed himself to action and yet he believes action to be futile, full of sound and fury, but signifying nothing.

That the vision of life offered in Macbeth's final soliloquy is not Shakespeare's ultimate or only significant pronouncement upon the human condition we need only our experience with the canon, including the other tragedies, to attest. Besides, *Macbeth* does not "make a statement" any more than *Lear* did. What Shakespeare was dramatizing was a potentiality of the human condition, in this case a most grim potentiality, but as true in its context as any other embodied in his dramas. It is realized with exceptional conviction and power, and to shrug it off as the observation of a man who has lost his humanity may make the play easier to live with, but undermines its imaginative vigor and ruthless integrity. Macbeth's pronouncement is the only pronouncement on life in the *Macbeth*-world; nothing of comparable weight is there to counterbalance it, and it draws its power not only from the greatness of the verse but also from its dramatic context. And here, I think, is the center of the problem, for is not its context a world which finally is moral, surely the most thoroughly just world Shakespeare created for a tragedy? The *Macbeth*-world is a moral world founded upon a moral incongruity, for while evil seems to issue spontaneously and irrepressibly from its very core, its most basic law is that evil is evil and must be destroyed. The same incongruity is repeated in the microcosm; Macbeth is strongly impelled to evil, but he is no less strongly impelled to abhor evil. Hence, he comes to abhor himself. If the world is basically inclined to evil, as the *Macbeth*-world is, then justice becomes little more than a tragic necessity. Its pyrrhic victory is retributive but not redemptive.

The play, then, explores dialectically the complementary tension between proneness to evil and abhorrence of evil in both the macrocosm and the microcosm. Macbeth is not a tragic hero in *spite* of his criminality but *because* of his criminality. Had he been able to resist his own inclinations and the promptings of his wife, he would be of no more interest than any other successful general. Had he been able to kill without compunction, he would be simply one of our rarer monsters. But he is caught in the tension between his action and his reaction, the primary tension of the *Macbeth*-world, and in his struggle and his failure to reconcile irreconcilable conflicts, he assumes tragic dimensions.

NOTES

1. Knight gives a particularly good account of this view on p. 155. Paul A. Jorgensen's fine study, *Our Naked Frailties* (Berkeley and Los Angeles: Univ. of California Press, 1971), appeared too late to be of use to me in writing this chapter. The similarities and ultimate differences between his thinking on this play and my own will be apparent to anyone familiar with his book.

2. For detailed analysis see Margaret Burrell, "*Macbeth*: A Study In Paradox," *Shakespeare Jahrbuch*, 90 (1954), 167–190. Also George Duthie, "Antithesis in *Macbeth*," *Shakespeare Survey*, 19 (1966), 25–32.

3. "He is living in an unreal world, a fantastic mockery, a ghoulish dream: he strives to make this single nightmare to rule the outward things of his nation. He would make all Scotland a nightmare thing of dripping blood" (Knight, p. 170).

4. George Lyman Kittredge, ed., *Macbeth* (Boston: Ginn, 1939), pp. xviii–xx; Elmer Edgar Stoll, *Art and Artifice in Shakespeare* (Cambridge, Eng.: Cambridge Univ. Press, 1933), pp. 87–88.

5. *Shakespeare's Philosophical Patterns*, p. 58.

6. See Robert Reed, *The Occult on the Tudor and Stuart Stage* (Boston: Christopher, 1965), pp. 168–171.

7. See Roland M. Frye, *Shakespeare and Christian Doctrine* (Princeton: Princeton Univ. Press, 1963), pp. 147–148, 157–165.

8. Wilbur Sanders, in *The Dramatist and the Received Idea* (Cambridge, Eng.: Cambridge Univ. Press, 1968), pp. 280–281, analyzes Macbeth's complex reaction to the prophecies.

9. See Sanders, p. 275.

10. Bradley, pp. 379–387; Sanders, pp. 258–263. Nevil Coghill, who brings to the play the experience of both critic and director, also finds Malcolm a lightweight: "Listening to Shakespeare," in *Stratford Papers on Shakespeare, 1962*, ed. B.W. Jackson (Toronto: Gage, 1963), pp. 25–32. On the matter of Banquo, see Kirschbaum, *Character and Characterization*, 52–58.

11. Willard Farnham, in *Shakespeare's Tragic Frontier*, p. 10, notes the duality of feeling Macbeth prompts, and makes that duality the basis of his study (pp. 79–137). Sanders also analyzes "the essential ambivalence of our reaction to the 'criminal' Macbeth," on pp. 292ff. Sanders seems to have arrived independently and almost simultaneously at a reading of the play somewhat similar to Rabkin's idea of complementarity in *Shakespeare and the Common Understanding*. Cf. Sanders, p. 299; Rabkin, pp. 12–13.

12. See esp. Bradley, pp. 352–358; and J.Q. Adams, ed., *Macbeth* (Boston: Houghton Mifflin, 1931), p. 135.

13. Robert Pack, "*Macbeth*: The Anatomy of Loss," *Yale Review*, 45 (1956), 536–537.

14. Robert Heilman, "'Twere Best Not Know Myself: Othello, Lear, Macbeth," in *Shakespeare 400*, ed. James McManaway (New York: Holt, 1964), p. 94: "When a protagonist 'knows' that his course is morally intolerable, but strains frantically against that knowledge lest it impair his obsessive pursuit of the course, the tension between knowing and willing may itself destroy him."

15. William Rosen, in *Shakespeare and the Craft of Tragedy* (Cambridge, Mass.: Harvard Univ. Press, 1960), p. 68, notes that only in retrospect is the speech ironic.

16. George Duthie, "Shakespeare's *Macbeth*: A Study in Tragic Absurdity," in *English Studies Today*, ed. G.A. Bonnard (Bern: Franke, 1961), pp. 121–128, analyzes the division in Macbeth's mind before and after the murder.

17. A.P. Rossiter, in *Angel With Horns and Other Shakespearean Lectures*, ed. Graham Storey (London: Longmans, 1961), pp. 210–211, also rejects conventional ambition as Macbeth's motive. See also Stewart, *Character and Motive in Shakespeare*, p. 93.

18. Both Charlton, in *Shakespearean Tragedy*, p. 147, and Eugene Waith, in "Manhood and Valor in Two Shakespearean Tragedies," *ELH*, 17 (1950), 265–266, discuss Macbeth's divided mind on the concept of manhood.

19. L.C. Knights, in *Some Shakespearean Themes* (1959: rpt. Stanford: Stanford Univ. Press, 1960), p. 134, notes the special emphasis in this play upon words that name familial and social relationships (children, servant, cousin, etc.).

20. Adams makes a similar point on p. 156 of his edition.

21. The parallel is also drawn by D.W. Harding, "Women's Fantasy of Manhood: A Shakespearean Theme," *Shakespeare Quarterly*, 20 (1969), 250–251.

22. Sanders discusses Macbeth's "manifest will to self-deception" on p. 284 of *The Dramatist and the Received Idea*.

23. Francis Fergusson, "*Macbeth* as the Imitation of an Action," in *The Human Image in Dramatic Literature* (Garden City, N.Y.: Anchor, 1957), p. 117, has suggested: "It is the phrase 'to outrun the pauser reason,' which seems to me to describe the action, or motive, of the play as a whole." See also the same author's *Shakespeare, The Pattern in His Carpet*, pp. 241–242.

24. Sanders has brilliantly analyzed Macbeth's estrangement from himself and the "construction of a new 'self' whose premise is murder" (p. 290).

25. Kirschbaum, in *Character and Characterization*, p. 59, takes a similar view.

26. Knight (p. 171) suggests that the need to play the hypocrite is the worst element in Macbeth's suffering. Cleanth Brooks, "The Naked Babe and the Cloak of Manliness," in *The Well Wrought Urn* (New York: Reynal and Hitchcock, 1947), p. 32, sees Macbeth's hatred of hypocrisy as central to the clothing imagery of the play.

27. See Fergusson, *Shakespeare, The Pattern in His Carpet*, pp. 244–245.

28 .R.A. Foakes also differs from the majority view about Macbeth's lost humanity, in "*Macbeth*," in *Stratford Papers on Shakespeare*, 1962, p. 161.

29. Ed., *Macbeth*, in *The Complete Pelican Shakespeare*, p. 1108.

HOWARD FELPERIN

A Painted Devil: Macbeth

'Tis the eye of childhood
That fears a painted devil.
—*Macbeth*, II.ii.53–54

The last of Shakespeare's major tragedies to depend primarily on a native tradition of religious drama is also the most widely and seriously misunderstood in its relation to it. Indeed, *Macbeth* might well appear to be an exception to the principle of Shakespearean revision we have educed from the earlier tragedies. In those plays, the effect of mimetic naturalization over and above the older models contained within them had been achieved precisely by revealing the moral oversimplification of those models, in sum, by problematizing them. But *Macbeth* is unique among the major tragedies in having generated nothing like the central and recurrent problems that have shaped interpretation of *Hamlet, Othello, King Lear*, and even *Antony and Cleopatra*. Certain aspects of the play have of course received more than their share of attention and are continuing matters of debate: the status of its witches and of witchcraft; its topical relation to James I; the authorship of the Hecate scenes, yet these are more pre-critical problems of background and provenance than critical problems as such. For *Macbeth*, as Shakespeare's one "tragedy of damnation," is so widely acknowledged to exist within a relatively

From *Shakespearean Representation*. ©1977 Princeton University Press, 2005 renewed PUP.

familiar dramatic tradition, that critical response to the play has become almost a matter of reflex in assimilating the play to it. This would seem to contradict the argument so far advanced that Shakespearean tragedy is fundamentally and finally unassimilable to its models, and that this unassimilability is what underlies and generates their problematic status and realistic effect in the first place. At the risk of bringing chaos into order by discovering problems where none have existed, I want now to reexamine the relation between *Macbeth* and its inscribed models in the light of the previous discussion. It may turn out that those models are not quite the ones usually said to lie behind the play, and its relation to them not the clear and settled congruity that it is generally thought to be.

The tradition within which Macbeth is almost universally interpreted is that of orthodox Christian tragedy, the characteristic features of which are already well developed as early as Boccaccio and Lydgate and are familiar to all students of medieval and renaissance literature. It typically presents the fall of a man who may be basically or originally good but is always corruptible through the temptations of the world and his own pride or ambition. This action occurs against the structure of a fundamentally ordered and benevolent universe, which is finally self-restorative despite the evil and chaos temporarily unleashed within it, since crime will [win] out and sin is always repaid. Of course the point in this essentially didactic genre is to illustrate the wages of human wrongdoing and the inexorability of divine purpose. That *Macbeth*, with its malign forces of temptation embodied in the witches, its vacillating but increasingly callous protagonist, and its restorative movement in the figures of Malcolm and Macduff, has affinities with this tradition is obvious and undeniable. The moral pattern of Shakespeare's play is not essentially different from that set forth in Boccaccio and Lydgate, and there is no lack of more immediate versions of it with which Shakespeare would have been well acquainted. He had drawn on *A Mirror for Magistrates* in previous histories and tragedies; several sixteenth-century moralities deal with the same theme; and the same pattern, though without political overtones, informs *Doctor Faustus*, a play with which *Macbeth* is often compared. Shakespeare's own early Marlovian monodrama, *Richard III*, falls squarely within this tradition of Christian tragedy, and its similarities with *Macbeth* were pointed out as far back as the eighteenth century.

Yet there is another dramatic tradition at work within *Macbeth* or, more accurately, a subgenre of this same tradition, that is at once much older than these examples and more immediately and concretely present within the play. For here, as in *Hamlet*, Shakespeare allows the primary model for his own action to remain at least partly in view. We have already seen how the cry of the elder Hamlet's ghost to "remember me" is more than a reminder to his son to avenge his death; it simultaneously conjures up the older mode of being and acting which would make revenge possible, which the action of *Hamlet* at once repeats and supersedes, and which points with all the intentionality and ambiguity of any sign toward the heart of the play's meaning. In *Macbeth*, too, the persistence of an older dramatic mode within the world of Shakespeare's play is no less explicitly recalled. Though there are many places in *Macbeth* that could serve as an entry into this older world, the two modern scholars who have consciously perceived its existence have both entered it through, so to speak, its front door, the "hell-gate" of Inverness with its attendant "devil-porter." For here too the purpose of the Porter's request, "I pray you remember the porter" (II.iii.22), is more than to extract a tip from Macduff whom he has just admitted. The reference of his remark is ambiguous, as Glynne Wickham observes, "for it can be addressed by the actor both to Macduff and to the audience. As in the porter's dream, it is in two worlds at once; that of Macbeth's castle and that of another scene from another play which has just been recalled for the audience and which the author wants them to remember."[1]

That other play, which Wickham advances as Shakespeare's "model for the particular form in which he chose to cast act II, scene III, of *Macbeth*, and possibly for the play as a whole,"[2] is *The Harrowing of Hell* in the medieval English mystery cycles. Derived from the apocryphal *Gospel of Nicodemus* and adapted in two of the oldest rituals of the Roman Catholic liturgy, it is enacted in all of the extant cycles, though details of staging and dialogue differ from one to another. Between his crucifixion and resurrection, Christ comes to hell (represented as a castle on the medieval stage) and demands of Lucifer the release of the souls of the prophets and patriarchs. In all versions, the arrival of Christ is heralded by strange noises in the air and thunderous knocking at the castle gates. In the York and Towneley plays, the gate of hell has a porter appropriately named Rybald, a comic devil who breaks the news to Beelzebub of Christ's arrival and questions David and Christ himself as to his identity. Finally, Jesus breaks down the gate of hell, routs the resisting devils and, after a debate with Satan, who tries to deny the prophecies of his godhead, releases the prophets amid prayers and rejoicing. The Coventry version of the playlet, the one that Shakespeare is almost certain to have seen, is not extant, but there is no reason to think it was substantially different from the other versions. In fact, the Pardoner in John Heywood's *The Foure PP* (1529?), is described as having been on easy terms with "the devyll that kept the gate," since he had "oft in the play of Corpus Christi ... played the devyll at Coventry," and is himself addressed as "Good mayster porter."[3] With its castle setting, bumbling porter named Rybald, "*Clamor vel sonitus materialis magnus*"[4] in the depth of night, and background of prophecy, the cyclic play of the Harrowing of Hell would have been easily evoked by the business of *Macbeth*, II.iii in the minds of many in Shakespeare's audience who still remembered the porter. Moreover, the memory of the old play would strongly foreshadow the outcome of *Macbeth* as well, since Christ's entry into and deliverance of the castle of hell also looks forward to Macduff's second entry into Macbeth's castle and triumph over the demonic Macbeth at the end of the play.

Though prefiguring the didactic superplot or counterplot of Macduff's liberation of Scotland and defeat of Macbeth, however, *The Harrowing of Hell* has little direct bearing on the main or central action of Macbeth's personal destiny within the play, aside from rather broadly associating him with Beelzebub or Satan. But there is another play, or rather pair of plays, in the mystery cycles that supply what *The Harrowing of Hell* leaves out in the action of *Macbeth*, namely *The Visit of the Magi* and *The Massacre of the Innocents*. The cycles are more varied in their dramatization of these episodes from St. Matthew than they are in the case of the deliverance from hell, particularly as to the outcome of the massacre, but all share certain elements that bear directly on Macbeth's career. In all of them, three wise men come to pay homage to a king born in Israel and descended from David, the prophecies of whose birth they rehearse to Herod. Outraged at these prophecies of a king not descended from him, which are confirmed by his own biblical interpreters, Herod plans to murder the magi and all the children of Israel. The magi escape, warned by an angel, whereupon Herod sends his soldiers out to exterminate his rival, who also escapes into Egypt. The outcome of Herod's brutality—the murders are carried out on stage amid the pleas and lamentation of the mothers—though different in each version, is in all cases heavy with dramatic irony. The Towneley play, for example, concludes with a self-deluded Herod proclaiming that "Now in pease may I stand / I thank the Mahowne!"[5] In the York and Coventry versions, the irony is more explicit, as the soldiers of the former admit under questioning that they are not sure whether Jesus was among the "brats" they have murdered, and in the latter a Messenger informs Herod that "All thy dedis ys cum to noght; / This chyld ys gone in-to Eygipte to dwell."[6] In the Chester play, Herod's own son is murdered by his soldiers while in the care of one of the women. When told the news, Herod dies in a paroxysm of rage and is carried off to hell by devils. Even more pointed and ironic is the *Ludus Coventriae* version, in which Herod stages a feast to celebrate the successful execution of his plan to consolidate his reign and succession. Its mirth and minstrelsy are interrupted with the stage-direction, "*Hic dum* [the minstrels] *buccinant mors interficiat herodem et duos milites subito et diabolus recipiat eos.*" While the devil drags Herod away, the spectral figure of Death, "nakyd and pore of array" closes the play with the inevitable moral: "I come sodeynly with-in a stownde / me with-stande may no castle / my jurnay wyl I spede."[7]

The appearance of death at Herod's feast cannot help but recall the appearance of Banquo's ghost at Macbeth's feast. For even though this motif of death at the feast of life occurs only in this one version of the Herod plays, it is a medieval topos which must have been available to Shakespeare from other dramatic or pictorial sources, if not from this particular play, since he had already employed it in Fortinbras' image at the end of *Hamlet*:

> O proud Death,
> What feast is toward in thine eternal cell,
> That thou so many princes at a shot
> So bloodily hast struck?
>
> (V.ii.353–6)

Indeed, the influence of the medieval cycles on *Macbeth* is not confined to the pair of plays already discussed but can be traced to other plays within the same cycles. Shakespeare's choric trio of witches, for example, are anticipated not only by the three kings in *The Adoration of the Magi*, but by the three shepherds and the three prophets in the play that precedes it in the Coventry and other cycles, *The Adoration of the Shepherds*. There, both the shepherds and the prophets are granted foreknowledge of Christ's birth, both discuss his prophesied kingship, and in the Chester version, both employ a form of paradoxical salutation similar to that of Shakespeare's witches:

> *Primus Pastor*: Haile, King of heaven so hy, born in a
> Cribbe...!
> *Secundus Pastor*: Haile the, Emperour of hell, and of
> heaven als...!
> *Tertius Pastor*: Haile, prynce withouthen peere, that
> mankind shall releeve...![8]

Moreover, prophecies of the birth of a potentially subversive child trouble not only Herod, but both Pharaoh and Caesar Augustus before him in the Towneley cycle. Both follow the same, self-defeating course of attempting to defy the prophecies through promiscuous slaughter. Certain details of the Towneley play of Pharaoh may even find their way, from this or other versions of the story, into some of Macbeth's most famous language and imagery. His miraculous lines on how "this my hand / Will rather the multitudinous seas incarnadine, / Making the green one red" (II.ii.60–62) may well have their humble beginning in the reported outcome of Pharaoh's equivocations with Moses, the first of Egypt's plagues:

> Syr, the Waters that were ordand
> for men and bestis foyde,
>   Thrugh outt all egypt land,
> ar turnyd into reede-bloyde.[9]

Or Macbeth's anguished outcry, "O, full of scorpions is my mind, dear wife!" (III.i.36) may echo the same soldier's account of the third plague while internalizing it: "Greatte mystis [of gnats], sir, there is both morn and noyn, / byte us full bytterly."[10] Even the plague of darkness may contain the hint for the dominant imagery of Shakespeare's play. It is not my intention to press these parallels as literal "sources," but it is important to recognize the close affinities of *Macbeth* with a series of biblical tyrant plays, all repeating essentially the same story, each of whose protagonists—Satan, Pharaoh, Caesar, Herod—is a type of tyranny within a providential scheme of history. The apparently innocent request to "remember the porter" opens up an historical context for *Macbeth* that we have only begun to explore.

What, then, is the significance of these largely neglected models as they are deliberately recalled within Shakespeare's play? Glynne Wickham sums up their contribution to *Macbeth* as follows:

> The essentials that he drew from the play [of Herod] are the poisoning of a tyrant's peace of mind by the prophecy of a rival destined to eclipse him, the attempt to forestall that prophecy by the hiring of assassins to murder all potential rivals and the final overthrow and damnation of the tyrant. ... Like Herod with the Magi, Macbeth adopts a twofold plan. He aims first at Banquo and Fleance; and, when this plan miscarries, he extends his net to cover all potential rivals and strikes down Lady Macduff and her children. The last twenty lines of this scene are imbued with the sharpest possible verbal, visual and emotional echoes of the horrific scene in Bethlehem. Young Siward's image of Macbeth as both tyrant and devil in act V, scene VIII, recalls the drunken devil-porter of act II, scene III, and thereby the two complementary images of the religious stage, Herod the tyrant and the Harrowing of Hell, are linked to one another in compressed form to provide the thematic sub-text of this Scottish tragedy. Pride and ambition breed tyranny: tyranny breeds violence, a child born of fear and power: but tyrants are by their

very nature Lucifer's children and not God's, and as such they are damned. As Christ harrowed Hell and released Adam from Satan's dominion, so afflicted subjects of mortal tyranny will find a champion who will release them from fear and bondage. This Macduff does for Scotland.[11]

The passage is worth quoting at such length because it so accurately reflects not only the indisputable elements Shakespeare takes over in *Macbeth* from the medieval tyrant plays but the doctrinal message those plays were designed to illustrate and inculcate, a moral orientation that critics much less conscious of dramatic traditions and much more "modern" and secular in outlook than Wickham also find in *Macbeth*. But to assimilate the meaning of *Macbeth* to that of its medieval models, as Wickham and most other critics of the play more or less explicitly do, is not only to make Shakespeare's play less interesting than it is but to make it say something it does not say. Such an interpretive stance is based on a misunderstanding of the way any truly great writer uses his sources and models, as well as the way Shakespeare used his own in this play.

For the resemblances of plot structure, characterization, even language between *Macbeth* and the medieval cycle plays cannot simply be ascribed to a pious attitude and a parallel intent on Shakespeare's part in relation to his models. All these resemblances arise in the first place as a result of the efforts of characters within the work to turn the action in which they are involved toward or even into a certain kind of older action, to recreate their experience in the image of certain precedents for their own purposes, purposes which cannot be immediately identified with the author's and which the play as a whole may not ratify. We have already seen this impulse at play within *Hamlet* and the previous tragedies, where Hamlet, Othello, and Lear all attempt and fail to turn the action into a version of the morality play, and it is no less present and pervasive in *Macbeth*, though here the particular medieval convention involved is a somewhat different one. For from the inception of the Scottish counterplot, Malcolm, Macduff, and the others are given to recreating present history in terms of medieval dramatic conventions. In Malcolm's depiction of him during the interlude at the English court, for example, Edward the Confessor is presented not as an historical monarch but as a type of royal saintliness, the dispenser of "The healing benediction" and possessor of "a heavenly gift of prophecy" (IV.iii.156–58). In contrast to the England blessed with such a king, Scotland has become, in Ross's account, a place "Where sighs and groans, and shrieks that rent the air, / Are made, not marked; where violent sorrow seems / A modern ecstasy (IV.iii.168–70), that is, a hell on earth that cries out for the harrowing. Its ruler becomes, in Macduff's words, "Devilish Macbeth," "this fiend of Scotland" than whom "Not in the legions / Of horrid hell can come a devil more damned" (IV.iii.55–56). In the same highly stylized and archaic vein, Malcolm proceeds to characterize himself, first as a walking abstract and brief chronicle of vices exceeding even those of the collective portrait of Macbeth, and then as an equally abstract model of virtue allied to Edward the Confessor. To seek some naturalistic basis for his highly abstract "testing" of Macduff is futile, for like Hamlet's "portrait-test," its rhetorical and theatrical overdetermination will always be in excess of any personal motive that can be offered in so far as it is inspired by old plays rather than present feeling. Malcolm, like Hamlet, must go out of his way to abstract and depersonalize himself and his world as a necessary prelude to the scenario of redress being contemplated. He and his fellows must remake Scottish history into moral allegory, thereby legitimating themselves and their historical cause by assimilating them to an absolute and timeless struggle of good against evil. Malcolm and his party must, in sum, represent themselves and their world, in precisely the terms of the play's medieval models, that is, in the name of all that is holy.

This effort to abstract themselves to older and purer roles, however, is not the exclusive prerogative of the angelic party of Malcolm and his followers and not confined to the Scottish superplot. A complementary but antithetical project is already underway near the beginning of the play in Lady Macbeth's attempt to become one with a demonic role:

> Come, you spirits
> That tend on mortal thoughts, unsex me here,
> And fill me from the crown to the toe top-full
> Of direst cruelty. Make thick my blood;
> Stop up th' access and passage to remorse,
> That no compunctious visitings of nature
> Shake my fell purpose. ...
>
> (I.iv.38–44)

Her terrible soliloquy is appropriately cast in the language of the tiring room, as if its speaker were an actress beckoning attendants to costume her and make her up for the part she is about to perform, to "unsex" and depersonalize her into yet a fourth weird sister, even to dehumanize her into the "fiend-like" creature that Malcolm styles her at the end. All her efforts are bent toward making herself into a creature who trades lightly, even whimsically, in evil, and if her soliloquy echoes something of the incantatory tone of the witches' speeches, her utterances surrounding the murder reproduce something of their levity:

> Give me the daggers. The sleeping and the dead
> Are but as pictures. 'Tis the eye of childhood
> That fears a painted devil. If he do bleed,
> I'll gild the faces of the grooms withal,
> For it must seem their guilt.
>
> (II.ii.52–56)

Her entire effort of depersonalization lies compressed within the notorious pun: an inner condition of being ("guilt") is to be externalized into sheer theatrical appearance ("gilt"), not simply to transfer it onto others but to empty it of the substance of reality and make it (stage-)manageable. Her repeated assurance that "A little water clears us of this deed" (II.ii.66) would similarly transmute the red and real blood of Duncan not simply into gilt but into something as superficial and removable as the Elizabethan equivalent of ketchup or greasepaint: "How easy is it then!" There is bad faith here of course, in so far as her transformation never loses consciousness of its own theatricality and thus never becomes complete. She would qualify herself for murder by becoming a devil, but to her devils remain only "painted," thereby disqualifying herself for murder. Lady Macbeth's attempt to theatricalize herself into a callous instrument of darkness and thereby disburden herself of the horror of the time is doomed to break down, largely because it receives no external confirmation or reinforcement from her husband—since role-playing in drama as in culture does not go on in a vacuum—who is constitutionally unable to think of these deeds after these ways.

In contrast to her fragile and ambivalent commitment to a mode of imitation which is expedient, temporary, and only skin-deep, Macbeth's commitment is to a mode of vision in which sign and meaning coincide, role and self are indivisible, and an action is not imitated but accomplished, once and for all time. It is a way of thinking and seeing much closer to that of Macduff, who describes the scene of the murder as "the great doom's image" (II.iii.74), than to that of his wife:

> This Duncan
> Hath borne his faculties so meek, hath been
> So clear in his great office, that his virtues
> Will plead like angels, trumpet-tongued against
> The deep damnation of his taking-off;
> And pity, like a naked new-born babe

Striding the blast, or heaven's cherubin horsed
Upon the sightless couriers of the air,
Shall blow the horrid deed in every eye
That tears shall drown the wind.

(I.vii.16–25)

In Macbeth's apocalyptic and allegorical projection of the deed and its
consequences, Duncan becomes the Christ-like victim, and Macbeth the
Judas-like traitor and Herod-like judge who will himself be judged. With its
winds, weeping, pleading, and trumpet-tongued angels, the imagined scene
conflates features of several typologically related cycle plays, notably those
of the Crucifixion and Last Judgment. Within a mode of vision that blurs
distinctions between intent and action, subject and object, illusion and
reality, even to contemplate such a deed is to shake and crack the "single
state of man" in which role and self were formerly united in the figure of
Duncan's trusted defender. "To know my deed," he tells his wife after the
murder, "'twere best not know myself" (II.ii.72), and for Macbeth the rest
of the play is dedicated to assimilating himself to the role he has fully
foreseen to replace his old one, to closing any gap that remains between
himself and it:

From this moment
The very firstlings of my heart shall be
The firstlings of my hand. And even now,
To crown my thoughts with acts, be it thought
    and done:
The castle of Macduff I will surprise,
Seize upon Fife, give to th' edge o' th' sword
His wife, his babes....
No boasting like a fool;
This deed I'll do before this purpose cool.

(IV.i.146–54)

A new and antithetical unity of being is born. Macbeth expounds and enacts
a philosophy of language in relation to action that brings him into line with
every previous tyrant of the medieval and Tudor stage. Tamburlaine's
insistence on the instantaneous convertibility of his words into deeds is
notorious, but the same attitude underlies Cambyses' murderous
demonstrations of his omnipotence, as well as the decrees of Pharaoh,
Herod, and Caesar that all the children shall be slain and all the world taxed.
In each case, the tyrant enacts a demonic parody of the divine power he

claims, namely the power to make the word flesh. By the end of his play, Macbeth's assimilation of himself to the dictates of the tyrant's role within the older drama being mounted by Malcolm and Macduff would seem to be complete, their dramatic visions having joined into one.

Given that the Macbeths willingly take on and play out the roles of "butcher" and "fiend-like queen" assigned to them in the apocalyptic history of Scotland according to Malcolm and Macduff, how can we contend that they are anything more than the walking moral emblems that the latter say they are, or that their play is anything essentially different from its medieval models? The answer is already implicit in the nature of their role-playing. For the fact is that, despite the different attitudes they bring to their role-playing and the different outcomes of it, Macbeth and Lady Macbeth both have to strain very hard to play out their respective roles, and neither is completely successful in doing so. Lady Macbeth cannot fully become the fiend she tries to be, and Macbeth cannot fully become the strutting and fretting Herod he thinks he is. In the case of Lady Macbeth, her eventual madness is the index of the very humanity she would negate by turning herself into a pure and untrammeled role, the residue of an untransmuted humanity that had sought boldness in drink and was checked by remembered filial ties before performing the act that should have been second nature. Madness in Shakespeare's tragedies always attests to the incompleteness of an unreinforced role-playing, that technique by which the self in its naked frailty seeks refuge from the anxiety of such extreme and disruptive actions as revenge, regicide, or abdication through the adoption of an older and simpler mode of being. In this respect, the "antic disposition" of Hamlet, the madness of Lear on the heath, and now the quiet somnambulism of Lady Macbeth are very different from the behavior of Herod, who "ragis in the pagond and in the street also"[12] when he fails to find confirmation of his absolute kingship in the prophecies, the wise men, and events themselves. For Herod does not and cannot go mad; he is mad. His "rage" is his role, and no matter how often he is traumatized, he will rebound with cartoon-like resiliency to his former outline, and rage again.

To define the truer madness that occurs in Shakespeare's tragedies, however: what is it but to be something other than role? Those who would follow Malcolm, Macduff, and the rest in equating Lady Macbeth with her fiend-like role and Macbeth with his role of butchering tyrant, and proceed to moralize or patronize them accordingly, are simply not listening:

Macduff: Turn, hellhound, turn!
Macbeth: Of all men else I have avoided thee,

> But get thee back! My soul is too much charged
> With blood of thine already.
>
> (V.vii.3–6)

Macduff's challenge proceeds programmatically out of his own role of missionary, Christ-like avenger. Yet Macbeth's response proceeds not out of his assigned and chosen role of stage-tyrant, but out of an unsuspected reserve of sympathetic and spontaneous humanity that exists beneath it, a self still fragile and unhardened in evil even at this point, against his own and Macduff's protestations and accusations to the contrary. And Shakespeare's juxtaposition of the two reveals how inadequate and inappropriate are the moral terms deriving from the didactic drama of Satan, Pharaoh, Herod, Cambyses, even Richard III, to the drama of Macbeth.

Shakespeare makes it clear that Macbeth's play is in a fundamental sense *not* their play, despite the efforts of the characters within it, including Macbeth, to conform it to an orthodox tyrant play, and the many resemblances that result. Consider, for example, the nature of the prophecies and the manner in which they are accomplished. Just as Herod had questioned the Magi (and in one version his own interpreters), Macbeth questions the Witches. He is shown in a highly archaic dumb show an emblem of a "Child Crowned, with a tree in his hand" and another of a "Bloody Child," with accompanying glosses to the effect that "none of woman born / Shall harm Macbeth" and "Macbeth shall never vanquished be until / Great Birnam Wood to high Dunsinane Hill / Shall come against him" (IV.i.80–91, 92–94). Malcolm's camouflaging of his troops with the foliage of Birnam Wood identifies him with the crowned child bearing a branch, Macduff's Caesarean birth identifies him with the bloody child, and together they do indeed overcome Macbeth, with all the irony of a violated nature having her vengeance on the man who has violated her workings in himself. Yet even as these prophecies come true, they do so with an air of contrivance and artificiality quite alien to the inevitability of those of the cycle plays. On the religious stage the prophecies had had a literal transparency that those of *Macbeth* no longer possess. No interpretive effort is necessary to reconcile what was predicted (a king is to be born who will supplant Herod) and what occurred; or the literal meaning of the prophecy (Christ will supplant Herod) and its moral meaning (good will supplant evil); or the signs in which the prophecy is expressed (a star in the sky like a "sun"; a word in a sacred text) and their significance (the "son" of God, the "word made flesh").

In *Macbeth*, by contrast, a strenuous interpretive effort is necessary to reconcile the portentous emblems and pronouncements of the witches' dumb show with their human and natural fulfillments, though we are largely unconscious of that effort when we make it. This is not simply a matter of the trickiness traditionally associated with prophecies of demonic origin. For not only are the prophecies of *Macbeth* not transparent and univocal as the prophecies of the Herod plays had been; strictly speaking, they do not even come true. It is not Birnam Wood but Malcolm's army bearing branches from Birnam Wood that comes against Macbeth at Dunsinane. Macduff may have been "Untimely ripped" from his mother's womb, making him something of a man apart, but that hardly qualifies him as one not "of woman born," the immaculate and otherworldly avenger of a fallen Scotland. It is only when we suppress their literal meaning (and our own literalism) and take the prophecies solely at a figurative level that they can be said to "come true" at all, let alone be made to illustrate the kind of moral logic we like to read out of them. In his handling of the prophecies so as to reveal their "double sense," their disjuncture of literal and figurative meanings, Shakespeare has introduced an element of parody, of fallen repetition, into his play in relation to its medieval models.

Yet this parodic discrepancy between Christian vision and Shakespearean revision which runs through the play does not in the least prevent the Scottish resurgents from blithely conducting themselves and their counterplot as if no such gap existed and the two were one and the same, even though their own elected roles and exalted design are compromised by it. We might think, for example, that Macduff's unexplained abandonment of his own children and wife to Macbeth's tyranny, though ultimately providing him with the most natural of motives for revenge, could scarcely strengthen his claim to the exalted, impersonal role of Scotland's avenger prescribed by the play's Christian model. After all, even on the medieval stage it is the epic, superhuman Christ of the Apocalypse who harrows hell, and not the more human figure of the gospels. But for the Scottish resurgents, these deeds must not be thought of after these ways. It is precisely their capacity to sublimate their naked frailties into the service of a missionary role and a divine plan that constitutes their real strength and the prerequisite for their success. Macduff's personal guilt and grief are instantly transformed, at Malcolm's prompting, into the "whetstone" of his sword in the impending divine conflict, for which "the pow'rs above / Put on their instruments" (IV.iii.238–49). As such an "instrument" of righteousness, Macduff "wants the natural touch" (IV.ii.9) in more ways than his wife imagines. His unhesitating absorption into his role is never more astonishing than when he finally presents his own nativity legend, however literally lacking it may be, as the necessary credential for defeating Macbeth, however invincible in combat he once again appears.

The same absence of self-doubt or self-consciousness in his new kingly role also characterizes Malcolm (whose single act prior to the mounting of the counterplot was also one of flight), particularly in his disposition of that "which would be planted newly with the time" (V.viii.65) after the final victory. His announced intent of rewarding his followers with promotion to the rank of earl and of punishing his foes ("The cruel ministers / Of this dead butcher and his fiend-like queen" [V.viii.68–69]) sets the seal on the new historical order of his reign as a secular imitation of divine judgment. Yet the scene is also an eerie and unsettling repetition of an earlier scene in the play. For Malcolm's language and gestures cannot help but recall those of Duncan after the victory over Cawdor and Macdonwald, a new era of freedom and love that proved only too fragile and temporary, anything but an apocalyptic triumph of good over evil. The battle toward a civilized and humane order, like all the play's battles would seem only to have been lost and won after all. The arrival of Malcolm and Macduff at Dunsinane is decidedly not the harrowing of hell or the coming of Christ, though its partisans behave as if it were.

Of course it is not really surprising that Macduff and Malcolm never come to perceive, much less feel, themselves to inhabit the gap between the heroic and archaic roles they adopt and the precarious selves that adopt them. For they are ultimately akin to such earlier Shakespearean tragic foils as Laertes and Edgar, un-self-conscious and un-self-questioning imitators of an inherited and wholly conventional way of acting, two-dimensional characters in a three-dimensional world. It makes no difference whether we say that such foils seem cardboard or cut-to-pattern because they are supporting actors or that they are doomed to be supporting actors because they are cardboard and cut-to-pattern. For it is precisely the conventionality of Laertes' rant and Edgar's mock-madness that throws into relief the dimensionality of Hamlet's and Lear's more demanding experience. We cannot accept in them an unreflectiveness, even an insensitivity that is harder to accept or understand in Shakespeare's protagonists themselves. We are not unsettled when Laertes acts like Laertes, rants for revenge and leaps into his sister's grave. The cat will mew, the dog will have his day. It is much more unsettling, however, when Hamlet acts like Laertes, betrays the very depth and sensitivity that distinguishes him from Laertes, and does the same. Similarly, no one is shocked when Macduff enters with "the tyrant's cursed head" atop a pike and apocalyptically proclaims that "The time is free" (V.viii.55), nor when Malcolm lends his blessing to the deed and the sentiment. For that judicial brutality and the ritual language that surrounds it proceed directly out of the ingenuous repetition of convention that we have come to expect from these characters and violate nothing that has been shown to exist in either of them. Macbeth's brutalities, by contrast, and the self-brutalization that makes them possible are profoundly disturbing to us, not simply because they remain so disturbing to him, and not simply because they represent, as one critic puts it, "murder by thesis"[13]—for what else is Macduff's decapitation of Macbeth?—but because they betray precisely that fullness of humanity with which Shakespeare has endowed *him* in contrast to his foils. In his strenuous effort to become the complete tyrant, to achieve the demonic equivalent of his angelic foils' unselfconscious conventionality, Macbeth must go out of his way to ignore the gap he senses between the pious and preordained view of things and the way things are, must do willfully what the others do quite naturally.

The question arises, then, why does Macbeth accept his destiny as a latter-day Herod, when he is not Herod? For no less remarkable than Macduff's unhesitating conviction that his birth carries the necessary credential for defeating him, is Macbeth's unresisting acceptance of it and the consequent slackening of his "better part of man." Why does Macbeth acquiesce to prophecies that require his cooperation to be fulfilled? The answer to these questions, I would suggest, lies in the mode of vision that we have already seen him bring to his experience before the murder of Duncan. He simply cannot do otherwise, not because his actions are compelled from without—the prophecies are not theologically binding like those of the cycle plays but psychologically self-fulfilling[14]—but because he has long since internalized his society's way of seeing and thinking. Both before and after the murder, Macbeth's is a primitive and animistic world of portents and totems, of stones that "prate" of his whereabouts, of a bell that summons to heaven or hell, of knocking that might raise the dead, of the crow turned emblem of darkness, of night that is synonymous with evil, of accusing voices and menacing visions, a world become archaic melodrama burdened with significance. This "overperception," in which distinctions between subject and object, man and nature, illusion and reality, past and present—all the potential distinctions of our modern critical and historical consciousness—are lost, is characterized in its essence by Lady Macbeth, when she reminds her husband that "'Tis the eye of childhood / That fears a painted devil," that "these flaws and starts ... would well become / A woman's story at a winter's fire, / Authorized by her grandam" (III.iv.63–66). Yet it is just such a childlike and superstitious vision that finally binds everyone else in the play, including Macbeth, into a society as traditional and cohesive as a tribe or a clan. It is the vocation of the ruling and priestly class of such a society to paint, fear, and punish the devils who endanger that cohesiveness and their own power, and this is exactly what the Scottish thanes do, from the suppression of Macdonwald and Cawdor to the overthrow of Macbeth. The act of mounting atop a pole Macdonwald's and

Macbeth's painted images, or better still their heads, is necessary as a totemic deterrent to tyranny, a public symbol of the inviolability of the social order and glaring reminder of the inevitability of the moral law that sustains it: the wages of ambition is, and always must be, death. Macbeth had been an integral part of this social order, as Cawdor had been, so it is in no way surprising to see them both attempt to conform their careers to the sacred fictions they were born into and carry around within them, Cawdor by repenting like a morality protagonist and Macbeth by remaining the arch tyrant to the end. Macbeth and Macduff understand one another perfectly, across the moral gulf that separates them, for both speak the primitive language of the tribe.

This is not to suggest that Shakespeare is simply holding up to ridicule the sacred myths, symbols, and forms that so pervade *Macbeth*. It is Marlowe, not Shakespeare, who is given to expressing an adolescent contempt for religion as something invented to "keep men in awe."[15] The play is much more than an easy demystification of the ritual forms that dominate the consciousness and condition the actions of virtually all its principles, for it shows those forms to be at once quite arbitrary and fictive in themselves but wholly necessary and "real" in the social function they serve. In this respect, the play presents a stylization not only of Shakespeare's own society, where these Christian, ritual forms still prevail, but of all societies. It would be the height of ethnocentric naivete to view the "ecstatic" or "nostalgic" community depicted in *Macbeth* as any more primitive in its constitution than later, more "enlightened" societies in which heads are no longer mounted on poles.[16] The gibbet in the eighteenth century—some of whose Shakespearean criticism does indeed condescend to his Elizabethan "barbarism,"—or the electric chair in the twentieth are designed to serve the same necessary function of deterring deviance within the community and to preserve the same necessary fiction that crime must inevitably be followed, as the night the day, by punishment. Moreover, the play depicts the impulse constitutive of every society to makes its particular social forms and institutions, which are always arbitrary insofar as they are manmade, seem as necessary as natural forms and processes themselves, indeed a logical extension of them:

> I have begun to plant thee and will labor
> To make thee full of growing.
>
> (I.iv.28–29)

> What's more to do,
> Which would be planted newly with the time—

As calling home our exiled friends abroad....

(V.viii.64–66)

My way of life
Is fall'n into the sear, the yellow leaf....

(V.iii.22–26)

Within a world that sees itself through the ritual forms of the medieval drama, in which the book of human history and the book of nature are one volume of God's making, it is almost a reflex of all its members to describe the social and historical process of meting out rewards and punishments, for all its demonstrated fallibility, in an imagery of unfailing natural process. But to dismiss this impulse as a version of nostalgic fiction or pathetic fallacy is to misunderstand the play. For like Macbeth's, Duncan's, Lennox's, and the others' investment of the natural world with human attributes, these efforts to endow the human and historical world with a serene inevitability that properly belongs only to nonhuman nature is more than fiction and less than truth, another aspect of the persistent recreation of the sacred, the remystification of the merely secular, that defines the world of the play in its essential doubleness.

It is this radical equivocation of *Macbeth* in relation to its medieval models, the double sense in which it at once recreates those models through the communal effort of its characters and reveals them to be a means of social and institutional legitimation, that makes the play so susceptible to pious mystification or ironic demystification. Of these possibilities for misinterpretation, the pious reading has of course prevailed. The play is generally regarded as a humanization and vivification, through the flesh and blood of Shakespeare's mature language and dramaturgy, of the bare skeleton of its stagy and didactic antecedents. In this view, their homiletic intent though it may be softened is not fundamentally questioned or altered in the process of benign and respectful transformation. The "good" characters are granted just enough of a depth they do not possess, and the "evil" characters are denied just enough of the depth they do possess, to flatten the play into a consistent domestication of a wholly traditional moral design. But surely it must be otherwise, for in what does Shakespeare's humanization of his sources consist but the putting into question of their conventional roles and forms? To the extent that the figures who carry around with them that older moral design as a sacred and unselfconscious trust are made to appear conventional, predictable, and bidimensional by contrast with the figures with whom they share the stage and who are restless in their roles, however strenuously they attempt to conform to them, that older moral design can no

longer be authoritative. Critics have always been responsive to the interiority
of Macbeth's struggle, but they have been reluctant to recognize that it is
achieved precisely at the expense of his status as a moral emblem or example.
Yet he becomes something much more interesting to us than any moral
emblem in the process, and not because, as the critical commonplace would
have it, evil is intrinsically more interesting than good. Macbeth is more
interesting than his prototypes and foils, not because they are good and he
becomes evil—for Herod is hardly "good"—nor even because they "are" and
he "becomes"—for his change is in many ways regressive—but because he
cannot take his nature for granted. He cannot quite rest content in an action
in which his role and his nature are determined in advance, but must
continuously reinvent himself in the process of acting them out. It is in this
that Macbeth's "modernity" consists and that his case bears directly on our
own, at least to the extent that we are as fully human as he is. In this respect,
too, he becomes a very different kind of dramatic model, a type of modernity
whose compelling interest for the playwrights who follow Shakespeare will
cause him to be imitated again and again.

The simplifications that have become doctrine in the tradition of
interpretation of *Macbeth* are the result not only of a failure to establish the
play's relation to its models in its full ambivalence, but of a failure to identify
the play's primary models in the first place. Just as *Hamlet* has less to do with
Senecan revenge drama than with native morality tradition, so *Macbeth* has
less to do with the morality play than with the tyrant plays of the biblical
cycles. Its nearest contemporary analogue is not Marlowe's *Faustus*, with
which it is often compared as a parallel study in the psychology of
damnation,[17] but *Tamburlaine* or even *Edward II*, those early Elizabethan
history plays which, like Macbeth, are modeled on the medieval tyrant plays
that are the authentic prototypes of Elizabethan historical tragedy. The
morality play is a misleading model in the interpretation of *Macbeth* insofar
as it presents a world already more cerebral and voluntaristic than the cultic
and animistic world of the cycles. It emphasizes, that is, freedom of moral
choice within a mental setting, as opposed to the communal and typological
destiny unfolded in the cycles. This misplaced emphasis on moral choice
within *Macbeth*, where it receives little of the extended deliberation accorded
to it in *Hamlet*, may well arise from the forced imposition of morality
conventions upon the play and may well underlie all the misguided adulation
of the bland and reticent Banquo and the equally misguided pity for
Macbeth. For Macbeth's choices and actions, as I have tried to show, are not
free in the way the morality protagonist's are, but are largely determined by
his own and his society's expectations soon after the play begins. The
universe of *Macbeth* is not ultimately and comically free, as it is even in those

variations of the morality (like *Faustus*) where the protagonist persists in choosing wrongly and thus qualifies as an object of tragic pity, but is conditioned by forces largely outside his control. Of course those forces are no longer the benign and providential ones embodied in the figures of God and his angels who descend from above upon the human community below. Rather, they are disruptive forces that periodically and inexplicably bubble up, as it were, from within human nature and society, as the witches who incarnate and herald them seem to do from within the earth itself. Unlike the morality protagonist, who is confronted at all points with a clear choice between moral meanings already established by generations of sophisticated theological apologetics, Macbeth, and the protagonist of Elizabethan historical tragedy generally, must struggle with meaning as it ambiguously unfolds in the world. It is only by confusing these two dramatic modes that such reassuring commonplaces as "the Elizabethan world picture" or "the great chain of being" could misleadingly have been applied as a norm in the interpretation of Shakespeare's histories and tragedies in the first place, as if the "natural condition" they present were order and the life of man could be analogized to the life of nonhuman nature. In our own struggle with the meaning of *Macbeth*, the proper identification of those models actually implicit within the play thus proves crucial and affirms once again the interdependence of literary history and interpretation.

NOTES

1. *Shakespeare's Dramatic Heritage* (New York, 1969), p. 222. Wickham's discussion of the influence of the cycle plays on *Macbeth* is reprinted in part from *Shakespeare Survey* 19, ed. Kenneth Muir (Cambridge, 1966), pp. 68–74. See also John B. Harcourt, "I Pray You, Remember the Porter," *Shakespeare Quarterly*, XII (1961), 393–402.

2. Wickham, p. 215.

3. J.M. Manly, ed., *Specimens of the Pre-Shakespearean Drama* (Boston, 1900), vol. I, p. 510.

4. *The Chester Plays, Part II* (E.E.T.S., London, 1959), p. 323.

5. *The Towneley Plays* (E.E.T.S., London, 1966), p. 180.

6. *Two Coventry Corpus Christi Plays*, ed. Hardin Craig (E.E.T.S., London, 1957), p. 31.

7. *Ludus Coventriae or The Plaie Called Corpus Christi*, ed. K.S. Block (E.E.T.S., London, 1922), pp. 176–177.

8. *The Chester Plays, Part I* (E.E.T.S., London, 1926), pp. 155–156.

9. *The Towneley Plays*, p. 73.

10. *The Towneley Plays*, p. 73.

11. Wickham, pp. 230–231.

12. *Two Coventry Corpus Christi Plays*, p. 27.

13. "It [Macbeth's atrocity against Macduff's family] is not nursed malice (they are 'unfortunate' souls), but murder for thesis, a deed in which all that makes an act recognisably human, whether moral or immoral, has been by-passed." Wilbur Sanders,

The Dramatist and the Received Idea (Cambridge, 1968), p. 270. That the impulse behind Macbeth's "thesis" of dehumanization remains "recognizably human" and hardly as alienating in its effect as Sanders claims is confirmed by the fact that he can still call his victims "unfortunate," that he adopts it precisely for its promise of destroying his human sympathies, and that he never completely achieves its aim of self-demonization. Sanders' essay, in its responsiveness to the dramatic phenomenon of *Macbeth* and resistance to the received moral ideas that surround it, represents a genuine advance in interpretation of the play despite occasional atavisms.

14. By changing their nature from the "goddesses of destinie" of Holinshed's *Chronicle* to Elizabethan witches, Shakespeare subtly but significantly curtails the weird sisters' power of determination. It is now Macbeth's actions that make the prophecies "come true" and not the prophecies that reveal a predetermined truth. Of course he will be conquered when Birnam Wood comes to Dunsinane, but only if he leaves his siege-proof castle to meet it; of course he must beware Macduff, once he slaughters his family; of course Macduff alone has the power to harm Macbeth, but only when Macbeth recognizes him as one not of woman born. On the grounding of the prophecies in a purely natural "law of retributive reaction," see the excellent discussion by Sanders, pp. 253–307.

15. Marlowe's religious views and the testimony of Thomas Kyd and Richard Baines, quoted here, are intelligently discussed by J.B. Steane, *Marlowe: A Critical Study* (Cambridge, 1964), p. 17–26.

16. The term "ecstatic" is aptly applied to Shakespeare's tragic societies by Northrop Frye, *Fools of Time* (Toronto, 1967), p. 29, and "nostalgic" by Alvin Kernan, "*The Henriad*: Shakespeare's Major History Plays," *The Yale Review*, LIX (1969), 1, 3–32, to the older, passing world of the second tetralogy. The concept is further elaborated by Maynard Mack, Jr., *Killing the King* (New Haven, 1972). It is worth noting that the object Macduff carries in the closing scene of D'Avenant's revision of the play (1674) is not Macbeth's "head" but his "sword." The substitution, part of a larger effort to render Shakespeare seemly by rendering him bloodless, works to obscure the primitive essence of the Scottish society of Shakespeare's play and the underlying similarity between Macduff and Macbeth as creatures of it.

17. See, for example, Helen Gardner, "Milton's Satan and the Theme of Damnation in Elizabethan Tragedy," *Essays and Studies*, I (1948), 42–61. The fundamental inappropriateness of morality models to *Macbeth* is also apparent from D'Avenant's version, where Macbeth is reduced to a personification of Tyranny and Ambition (at his death, the stage direction reads "Ambition (lies)", and the sharpest possible moral contrast, summed up in Macduff's closing couplet, is aimed at: "His Vice shall make your Virtue shine more Bright, / As a Fair Day succeeds a Stormy Night." The moralization of the play is carried a stage further toward absurdity in Garrick's additions to J.P. Kemble's acting copy (1795), in which Macbeth becomes a pale and frightened Faustus before his death:

> Ambition's vain delusive dreams are fled,
> And now I wake to darkness, guilt and horror;
> I cannot bear it! let me shake it off—
> It will not be; my soul is clog'd with blood—
> I cannot rise! I dare not ask for mercy—
> It is too late, hell drags me down; I sink,
> I sink;—my soul is lost for ever!—Oh!—Oh!—*Dies.*

Reprinted by H.H. Furness, ed., Variorum *Macbeth* (Philadelphia, 1873), pp. 355, 295.

ROBERT N. WATSON

"Thriftless Ambition," Foolish Wishes, and the Tragedy of Macbeth

T he crude outlines of *Macbeth* as a moral drama are visible in Elizabethan panegyrics to universal order:

> Now if nature should intermit her course, and leave altogether
> though it were but for a while the observation of her own laws ...
> if the prince of the lights of heaven, which now as a giant doth
> run his unwearied course, should as it were through a languishing
> faintness begin to stand and to rest himself; if ... the times and
> seasons of the year [should] blend themselves by disordered and
> confused mixture ... the fruits of the earth pine away as children
> at the withered breasts of their mother no longer able to yield
> them relief: what would become of man himself, whom these
> things now do all serve?[1]

A dozen years after Hooker's *"Laws of Ecclesiastical Polity"* asked these questions, Shakespeare's *Macbeth* provided some fairly conventional answers: man himself becomes a disordered mixture, with no regenerative cycles to rescue him from his mortality and no social system to deliver him from his evil impulses. The cosmic and bodily disorders that accompany Macbeth's rebellion distinctly resemble the ones predicted in the official "Exhortation

From *Shakespeare and the Hazards of Ambition.* ©1984 by the President and Fellows of Harvard College.

Concerning Good Order, and Obedience to Rulers and Magistrates":

> The earth, trees, seeds, plants ... keep themselves in their order:
> all the parts of the whole year, as winter, summer, months, nights,
> and days, continue in their order ... and man himself also hath all
> his parts both within and without, as soul, heart, mind, memory,
> understanding, reason, speech, with all and singular corporal
> members of his body, in a profitable, necessary, and pleasant
> order: every degree of people ... hath appointed to them their
> duty and order: some are in high degree, some in low, some kings
> and princes, some inferiors and subjects ... and every one hath
> need of other ... Take away kings, princes ... and such estates of
> God's order, no man shall ride or go by the highway unrobbed,
> no man shall sleep in his own house or bed unkilled, no man shall
> keep his wife, children, and possessions in quietness ... and there
> must needs follow all mischief and utter destruction both of souls,
> bodies, goods, and commonwealths.[2]

In *Macbeth* as in *Richard III*, this deadly loss of personal and natural integrity does not result (as in Hooker) from some careless indolence of the world's ordering forces, but rather (as in the "Exhortation") from a human determination to disturb the political aspect of that order. In murdering the princes who would exclude him from the throne, Richard willingly "smothered / The most replenished sweet work of Nature / That from the prime creation e'er she fram'd" (4.3.17–19). In unseating Duncan, Macbeth willingly made "a breach in nature" through which "the wine of life" was drained (2.3.113, 95). Both usurpers push back toward primal chaos a Creation that thwarts their desires, hoping to reconstruct it in the image and likeness of their aspiring minds. Ambition, in its inherent opposition to heredity and the established order, thus becomes the enemy of all life, especially that of the ambitious man himself.

But these passages, like most others cited by critics seeking to define a unified "Elizabethan world view," are taken from works expressly written in defense of England's political and theological authorities. Those authorities had a tremendous stake in maintaining order and hierarchy, and in defining them as natural and divinely ordained. If we can recognize in such passages the voice of self-serving pragmatism rather than objective philosophy, we can infer a contrary voice, the voice of the disempowered that the propaganda is struggling to refute. To understand Shakespeare's play, as to understand English cultural history as a whole, requires this sort of inference.[3] The play, like history, like the witches who are agents of them both, "palter[s] with us in a double sense" (5.8.20). Where the witches' prophecies seem to endorse ambition, but warn on a more literal and less audible level against its futility, *Macbeth* contains a silent, figurative endorsement of ambition, even while loudly and eloquently restating the principles expressed by Hooker and the "Exhortation Concerning Good Order."

The spirit of tragedy itself cuts against such single-minded, heavy-handed moralizations, striving subversively on behalf of the individual human will. Shakespeare moves from history to tragedy by clarifying and universalizing the hazards of ambition: this cautionary pattern, which was shaped by the propagandistic aspect of *Richard III*, creates its own sort of moral drama in *Macbeth*. We may view Richard with horrified admiration, but we identify with Macbeth from within.[4] Shakespeare accomplishes this, makes Macbeth eligible for the fear and pity that permit catharsis, by encoding many of our repressed impulses, many of the rash wishes society has obliged us to abandon or conceal, within Macbeth's conventionally dramatic desire to replace the king. In his soliloquy before the regicide, Macbeth acknowledges that his deed will entail all the kinds of violence civilization has been struggling to suppress since it first began: violence between the guest and the host, violence by subjects against a monarch, and violence among kinspeople. When Shakespeare wants to show society's descent into utter deprivacy in *King Lear*, the moral holocaust consists of exactly these crimes: crimes against the host Gloucester, crimes against the royal father Lear, and crimes among siblings over legacies and lovers. In fact, Macbeth's misdeed resembles the one Freud says civilization was formed to suppress: the murder of the ruling father of the first human clan because he refused to share his reproductive privileges with his filial subjects.

In the history plays, Shakespeare established Oedipal desires as a metaphor for ambition; in *Macbeth*, he exploits the metaphor to implicate his audience in the ambitious crime, by tapping its guilt-ridden urges against authority and even against reality. On an individual as well as a racial scale, the Oedipal patterns psychoanalytic critics have noticed in this play, with Duncan as a father-figure and Lady Macbeth as the sinister temptress who is both mother and wife, may be a way of making the men in the audience intuitively identify with Macbeth's wish fulfillment. For most young men, that Oedipal guilt is a perfect focal point for more general resentments like the ones that turn Macbeth against Duncan: resentments against those who have power over us, those who have things we want, and those whom we want to become. The conflicts Shakespeare is addressing here are not merely the sexual ones. As he demonstrates the deeper meanings and broader ramifications of ambition, he necessarily implies that any desire to change the given order is a scion of that sin; and such a moral inevitably collides with the basic imperatives of life. To live is to change the world, to shape the environment to meet one's needs; even before the Oedipal phase begins, every infant is profoundly involved in a struggle to learn how far that shaping can go, and how best to perform it. So what might at first have been merely analogies or resonances by which Shakespeare suggested the foundations of his cautionary political tales become, in *Macbeth*, the openings through which we enter the story and receive the tragic experience.

To make these openings more accessible, Shakespeare expands and details a motif implicit in the history plays' treatment of ambition: the "foolish wish" motif of folklore, in which a person's unenlightened way of desiring converts the power of gaining desires into a curse. Richard III and Henry IV pursue an unlineal, unnatural kingship, and that is precisely what they get, much to their distress. In *Macbeth* this motif acquires the imaginative breadth, and hence the universal applicability, that it has in fairy tales, where it usually involves a narrow-minded disruption of nature's complex balances. The stories achieve their cautionary effect by showing the logical but terrifying ramifications of having such wishes granted. King Midas, for example, acquires the golden touch only to discover that it isolates him from food, love, and family—all the joys of natural life.[5] Perhaps more strikingly relevant to *Macbeth* is the Grimm Brothers' story called "The Fisherman and His Wife." The humble man discovers a magic fish in his net and, at the insistence of his shrewish wife, obliges it to replace their hovel with a castle. The wife steadily increases her demands for splendor and power, the ocean becomes angrier with each new request, and the couple becomes more discontented after each wish is granted, until the fish finally returns them to their original humble state.

But once Macbeth has rashly "done the deed" of self-promotion at his wife's instigation, they both learn that "What's done cannot be undone" (2.2.14; 5.1.68). Bruno Bettelheim "cannot recall a single fairy tale in which a child's angry wishes have any [irreversible] consequence; only those of adults do. The implication is that adults are accountable for what they do."[6] As such tales fascinate children by providing them with metaphorically coded lessons about the conduct of their own, more basic problems, so *Macbeth* conveys its harsher lessons to us. We do not need magic fish or bloodthirsty witches to provoke us; nature doth teach us all to have aspiring minds, as Tamburlaine asserts, or at least fickle and envious minds. We desire this man's art and that man's scope, with what we most enjoy contented least. Shakespeare alerts us to the fact that, to this extent, we participate in the murderous ambition we witness on stage, creating and suffering its poetically just consequences. While the official homilies claim that rebellion contains all other sins and provokes universal alterations,[7] *Macbeth* suggests reciprocally that all other sins—indeed, all impulses toward change—partake of rebellion.

Foolish-wish stories serve to develop in the child a mechanism and a rationale of repression, a necessary device for subordinating immediate urges to long-term goals and abstract rules—necessary, because infantile desires are no less selfish, violent, and murkily incestuous than the ones propelling Macbeth. Human beings seem to share a stock of foolish wishes, and society survives on its ability to discourage their fulfillment. That may be one reason why the play (as several of its directors have emphasized) suggests that this crisis is only one instance of an endless cycle of rebellion: the play is less the story of two evil people than it is a representation of impulses—ambitious, rebellious, Oedipal—that the hierarchical structures of family and society arouse in every human life. Normal behavior resembles Macbeth's successful curbing of insurrection's lavish spirit early in the play; but deeply human motives constantly impel each person toward a comparable rebellion, differing in scale but not necessarily in basic character from Macbeth's.

In opposing the lineal succession to Scotland's throne, Macbeth and his wife foolishly wish regenerative nature out of existence, then suffer the consequences of their wishes' fulfillment. An attack on the cycle of parents and children necessarily affronts the cycles of night and day, sleeping and waking, and planting and harvesting, as well. Perhaps Rosse's warning against "Thriftless ambition, that will ravin up / Thine own live's means (2.4.28–29) seems all too obvious a moral, but it is worth remembering that Rosse here supposes that his observation refers simply to a patricide; the play obliges us to generalize it for him, into an axiom about our relationship to great creating nature as a whole. Even this grander lesson, that people should not rashly disrupt the web of nature for the sake of their individual desires, was as clearly deducible from the Elizabethan concept of a beneficent universe as from the modern concept of ecological networks. Some seventy-five years earlier, John Heywood's "Play of the Wether" ridiculed the idea of tampering with that natural system to satisfy the whims of individuals. There needs no ghost come on the stage to tell us this.

But evidently it was not obvious enough for Macbeth and Lady Macbeth, and in a sense it is not obvious enough for anyone who has ever idly wished for more light in December, more flowers in February, or less rain in April. In a fairy tale such wishes would cost us dearly, and justly; yet we cannot really feel guilty for having them. In his susceptibility to conventional human desires, and his momentary willingness to forget the reasons they must be suppressed, Macbeth is one of us. He shows us the logical extension, and the logical costs, of our own frailties. Macbeth merely encounters those frailties in a situation that magnifies them into something momentous and horrible; and he encounters them in a dramatic context that blurs the borderline between nightmarish fantasy and reality. When the witches first appear, they take us into a region where the distinction becomes foggy; when they first appear to Macbeth, they do the same for him. Their status as partly a product of his mind and partly actual witches, and their talent for self-fulfilling prophecy, confirm that liminal function. They convey him, as they convey us, into a world where one might suddenly find one's destructive impulses magically fulfilled, where crimes are "thought and done" simultaneously (4.1.149). Place any person in such a world, and who should 'scape whipping, or even hanging for murder; though we are indifferent honest, we could accuse us of such things that it were better our mothers had not borne us.[8] If we can recognize Macbeth's crime as essentially an extension of our most casual recalcitrance at the ways of natural and social order, a symbolic performance of our resentful impulses against the aspects of the world that inconvenience us, we may find it hard to hold him accountable for his sin. The Porter and Macbeth have much to say against equivocators in this play (2.3.8–36; 5.5.42), but Shakespeare himself performs a Jesuitical equivocation in conveying the play's beliefs. Everything on the play's stated level follows the orthodox line against ambition; the heresy resides where the words trail off into unspoken thoughts, Shakespeare's and ours, a heresy that (to state the case most extremely) portrays Macbeth as a martyr who dies for our sins at the hands of an order so strictly repressive that it makes the very business of living a punishable crime.[9]

The Vengeance of Regenerative Nature

The foolish-wife motif, with its overtones of poetic justice, was extremely popular among Jacobean moralists, particularly those warning young men against defying their fathers' instructions and leaving their hereditary places. Samuel Gardiner's *Portraiture of the Prodigal Sonne* declares that "there is nothing that hurteth so much as the having of our wils," and elsewhere that "a sinner may be killed with his owne poyson, even the poyson of his sinne"; several other prodigal-son tracts echo this idea.[10] Macbeth himself worries about teaching

> Bloody instructions, which, being taught, return
> To plague th' inventor. This even-handed justice
> Commends th' ingredience of our poison'd chalice
> To our own lips.   (1.7.7–12)

We can see, even if Macbeth cannot, how this axiom about regicide applies to the violations of universal order implied in that regicide, just as we could see that Rosse's remark about "thriftless ambition" could apply to any assault on sovereign nature as well as to a patricide. Henry IV's practical fear of counterusurpation thus expands into a tragic intuition about Pyrrhic victories over regenerative nature.

Macbeth and his Lady find their entire world sickened by the poisonous gall they fed to the Scottish body politic in place of its nurturant milk. Like Richard Brathwait's prodigal-son figure, Macbeth is "ill to others, worst unto himselfe."[11] He murders sleep and plunges the world into an uneasy darkness, but he and his wife suffer the worst insomnia of all, and the long night exhausts them before finding day in Malcolm's vengeful return. They attempt to steal life and patrimony from the new generation of babes, but die without a living heir. The kingdom's vegetation, like its sunlight, fades at Duncan's death, but while Macbeth's life falls "into the sear, the yellow leaf" (5.3.23), Malcolm echoes his father's metaphors of seeds and planting in reclaiming his father's throne. In a stratagem that resembles a Maying festival, Birnam Wood comes like a sudden spring to the walls of Dunsinane castle. Sun, sons, and seedlings all return together to destroy the man whose ambition has made him their enemy.

The fisherman's wife in the Grimm Brothers' story crossed into the realm of the forbidden when she demanded control over the sun and the moon; Lady Macbeth provokes and performs a similar ambitious violation. When she exults that the regicide "shall to all our nights and days to come / Give solely sovereign sway and masterdom" (1.5.69–70), we may detect an aspiration to sovereignty over those nights and days, as well as during them. Bettelheim observes that "Many fairy tales depict the tragic outcome of ... rash wishes, engaged in because one desires something too much or is unable to wait until things come about in their good time."[12] As long as Macbeth plans to let natural events gain him the throne, he thinks in terms of letting time run its diurnal course. His aside about letting chance "crown me without my stir" is immediately followed by his aside that "Come what come may, / Time and the hour run through the roughest day" (1.3.144–48). But when Duncan extends that cyclical inevitability to include the succession of son as well as sun, Macbeth attacks the balance of light and dark as well as the unity of his own identity in opposing Duncan's choice: "Stars, hide your fires, / Let not light see my black and deep desires; / The eye wink at the hand" (1.4.50–52).

In the following scene, Lady Macbeth suggests a similar pair of assaults, against light and organic identity, to aid the assault on Duncan. Her first words are read from her husband's letter about the witches: "They met me in the day of success" (1.5.1). But the witches specialize in false encouragement and secondary meanings: daylight and succession are precisely what they induce this couple to sacrifice. Lady Macbeth quickly concludes that she must eradicate the vision daylight permits, along with the nursing succession demands, in order to fulfill the witches' promise:

> Come to my woman's breasts,
> And take my milk for gall, you murth'ring ministers,
> Wherever in your sightless substances
> You wait on nature's mischief! Come, thick night,
> And pall thee in the dunnest smoke of hell,
> That my keen knife see not the wound it makes,
> Nor heaven peep through the blanket of the dark
> To cry, "Hold, hold!"   (1.5.47–54)

She will abandon her maternal role in the nursery in favor of a phallic role in the bedroom.[13] To engineer their rebirths as monarchs, she and her husband will perform a forbidden deed on the paternal Duncan, under a blanket that leaves us uncertain whether the deed is essentially sexual or essentially violent. Such a cover is useful, not only in preventing Macbeth from thinking conscientiously of his mother and Lady Macbeth of her father (1.5.16–18; 2.2.12–13), but also in making us think about Shakespeare's symbolic pattern, which blends incest with parricide, and insemination with Caesarean section, in the forbidden act of self-remaking.

These requests for a crime-facilitating darkness soon lead to inadvertent predictions that the crime will actually forestall the progress of night into day.[14] As they test each other's susceptibility to the idea of regicide, Lady Macbeth asks when Duncan will leave their castle. When Macbeth answers, "To-morrow, as he purposes," she exclaims, "O, never / Shall sun that morrow see!" (1.5.59–61). She means that Duncan will not live to go forth—*that* day will never come, we might say—but by saying it indirectly, she seems to imply that the murder will deprive future days of sunlight. Duncan, generally a solar figure,[15] is the light that will not see the morrow, and that the morrow will not see.

The archetypal crime against the healthy progress of night and day for the Renaissance was also the archetypal crime of filial ambition: Phaethon's disastrous usurpation of Phoebus' solar chariot.[16] Phaethon's premature seizure of his father's place neatly conflated two sorts of rebellion: the attempt to unseat the sun-king, and the Oedipal attempt to take the father's mount, against his strictest prohibition and before developing the abilities to manage or even survive the attempt. The story's moral is clear enough, and Shakespeare alludes to it to moralize his own cautionary tale: such ambitions, whether they are the seditious ones of a subject or the sexual ones of a son, threaten the universal order by which humanity survives, and the rebel must be sacrificed to preserve that order. After Duncan is murdered, Rosse reports that the royal horses "turn'd wild in nature, broke their stalls, flung out, / Contending 'gainst obedience, as they would make / War with mankind" (2.4.16–18). Like Phoebus' horses, they mirror the unruliness of the son who has stolen their reins, and thereby threaten the entire human race. Lennox's report that "the night has been unruly" (2.3.54) may therefore suggest to us more than that disorderly events have occurred during the nighttime hours: since Macbeth—one of "Night's black agents" (3.2.53)—has usurped the sun's royal chariot, darkness refuses to yield to day as the natural order dictates. In the speech preceding his comment on the unruly horses, Rosse remarks,

> By th' clock 'tis day,
> And yet dark night strangles the travelling lamp.
> Is't night's predominance, or the day's shame,
> That darkness does the face of earth entomb,
> When living light should kiss it?
> *Old Man*   'Tis unnatural,
> Even like the deed that's done.   (2.4.6–11)

Their association of the sun's misconduct with a regicide (and, they are soon told, a patricide) invites us to adduce Phaethon's archetypal crime, which unites and moralizes Macbeth's various violations of nature.

Banquo's literal and figurative resistance to the onset of darkness parallels his resistance to the temptations of regicide. As Duncan falls asleep in Macbeth's castle, Banquo notes uneasily the very blackness Macbeth and his wife eagerly invoke: "There's husbandry in heaven, / Their candles are all out" (2.1.4–5). He seems to echo this observation shortly before he, too, is murdered. His offhand remark to Fleance that "it will be rain tonight" suggests that he sees a dark, blank sky. In the form of his torch, he tries to keep daylight alive against this darkness; he has, as he promised Macbeth, "become a borrower of the night / For a dark hour or twain" on his journey (3.1.26–27)—the opposite movement to Macbeth's rush to nightfall. Macbeth's murderous ambition, as Rosse's remark suggested, again "strangles the travelling lamp"—this time the travellers' torch rather than the travelling sun. Macbeth intends to snuff out the final light of the old order, and relatedly the final obstacle to his new identity as a royal patriarch,

by killing Banquo and Fleance in another artificial darkness that hides the
deadly hand from the conscientious eye:

> Come, seeling night,
> Scarf up the tender eye of pitiful day,
> And with thy bloody and invisible hand
> Cancel and tear to pieces that great bond
> Which keeps me pale! Light thickens, and the crow
> Makes wing to th' rooky wood;
> Good things of day begin to droop and drowse,
> Whiles night's black agents to their preys do rouse.   (3.2.46–53)

Macbeth now seems to be working for night as much as night is
working for him. Day will suffer in this assault precisely what the First
Murderer reports that Banquo suffers: wounds that constitute "a death to
nature" (3.4.27). Banquo and Fleance represent the final force of daylight,
the last gleam of hope: as the murderers close in on them, one comments that
"the west yet glimmers with some streaks of day" (3.3.5). As their knives
come down on Banquo, they answer his prediction of rain with, "Let it come
down!" (3.3.16), as if the rain blotting the starlight and the knives taking his
life were the same "it." Like Othello, they put out the light, and then put out
the light:

> *Third Murderer* Who did strike out the light?
> *First Murderer*   Was't not the way?   (3.3.19)

But it was not. Fleance, prophesied to be the source of a new royal
succession, escapes because the murderers have followed Macbeth's self-
benighting policy to its misguided extreme by striking out the torch. By
completing the nightfall, Macbeth and his "black agents" invite the next day
to begin. Macbeth had told those agents that Fleance, like his father, "must
embrace the fate / Of that dark hour" (3.1.136–37). As so often in this play,
the "double sense" of words returns to haunt Macbeth: the luminous father
(3.3.14) and his son embrace the dark hour as dusk and dawn embrace
midnight. In *Macbeth*, the generational cycle and the solar cycle are like two
clock-faces with a single dial. The striking out of the final light, like the
stroke of midnight, announces the start of a new cycle. Nature regenerates
itself miraculously from this terrible moment of nullity, as when Macduff
rises to life after the terrible pause between his mother's death and his own
birth. From the dire stillness of no light or life at all, a new light and a new
life emerge. Rosse tells Lady Macduff, "Things at the worst will cease, or else

climb upward / To what they were before" (4.2.24–25); in *Macbeth*, the sun or son always rises up again—except within the Macbeth household, which made itself an enemy of such resurrection. Some time passes before the renewed forces make themselves felt, but from the moment of Fleance's escape, we sense that they own the future. Macduff can still ask rhetorically of his country, "When shalt thou see thy wholesome days again?"; but Scotland's new sun king provokes a compelling if vague answer: "The night is long that never finds the day" (4.3.105, 240). This aptly echoes the lesson Macbeth forgot: "Time and the hour run through the roughest day" (1.3.148). Macbeth's has become a "distemper'd cause," and only at his death can it be declared that "The time is free" (5.2.15, 5.9.21).

As soon as Banquo's light has been put out, Macbeth and his wife become stagnant in time and benighted at noon. Macbeth calls Banquo's ghost a "horrible shadow" which has "overcome us like a summer's cloud"; trying to recover his temporal bearings that same night, he asks his wife, "What is the night?" and she replies, "Almost at odds with morning, which is which" (3.4.105–26). Her somnambulism is also a confused battle between a day-action and a night-action, and though "she has light by her continually, 'tis her command" (5.1.22–23), it cannot bring back the previous day's sun, nor give her a place under the new one. As Lady Macbeth wanders through the night in futile pursuit of a previous day, Macbeth wanders into a series of undefined tomorrows. But he, too, finds that his crime against the regenerative cycles has compelled him to exchange life for a "brief candle" (5.5.23); his figurative exchange resembles her literal one, and both represent the fool's bargain involved in the creation of their unnatural royal selves. That bargain may be moralized as Montaigne moralizes the resort to garments: "like those who by artificial light extinguish the light of day, we have extinguished our own means by borrowed means."[17]

When Birnam Wood springs up in Scotland's new dawn, a sort of heliotrope to the new generation's royal sun, Macbeth shrinks away from it: "I gin to be aweary of the sun" (5.5.48). Daytime itself, as he inadvertently willed it, becomes his oppressor, joins the war against him. Young Siward, part of that new generation, assures Malcolm at the battle that "the day almost itself professes yours, / And little is to do" (5.7.27–28). Siward may simply mean that Malcolm's forces have nearly "won the day," to use a common phrase. But the active phrasing suggests that daytime itself seems almost to fight on Malcolm's behalf in an alliance with regenerative nature that leaves little to be done by the actual military force. In *Richard III* Richmond was urged by the ghosts of Richard's enemies to "win the day," and shortly thereafter we learned that the sun itself was refusing to shine on Richard's army, literally foreshadowing his defeat (5.3.145; 276–87). The

same pattern underscores the character of Macbeth's defeat. He battles
Malcolm's sunlight forces as an agent of the "black, and midnight hags"
(4.1.48), and as surely as the sun rises, his brief dark kingship falls.

If Macbeth's suppression of daylight is a symbol, a tactic, and a
punishment of his usurpation, then so is his attack on sleep. Having foolishly
trapped himself in an endless night, he compounds the error by wishing away
night's regenerative aspect. Insomnia, as I have said, is a fitting concomitant
of ambition in Shakespeare: Henry IV must strive constantly to remain above
his hereditary level, whereas Falstaff, who has sunk about as low as a human
being can in the chain of being, as if it were a hammock, sleeps deeply at the
very moment he is threatened with arrest. In *Macbeth* the correspondence
between wakefulness and ambition takes on a greater importance and
complexity.

Though Macbeth and Banquo are kept awake on the murder night by
the same ambitious fantasy, the differences are crucial. Macbeth remains
awake to overcome his political limitations, the same insomnia Henry IV
suffers; Banquo remains awake to overcome his moral limitations, precisely
the insomnia Falstaff spares himself. The distinction between these two
responses to temptation resembles the distinction by which Milton's Adam
consoles Eve for her own dreams of disobedient aspiration toward the
Father's power:

> Evil into the mind of God or Man
> May come and go, so unapprov'd, and leave
> No spot or blame behind: Which gives me hope
> That what in sleep thou didst abhor to dream,
> Waking thou never wilt consent to do.   (*Paradise Lost*, 5, 117–21)

Banquo is such an innocent, telling Fleance:

> A heavy summons lies like lead upon me,
> And yet I would not sleep. Merciful powers,
> Restrain in me the cursed thoughts that nature
> Gives way to in repose!   (2.1.6–9)

Ten lines later we learn that he "dreamt last night of the three Weird sisters."
The bad dreams, here as in Hamlet's "bounded in a nutshell" speech
(2.2.254–59), are the fantasies of patricide, regicide, and incest that seem to
haunt the whole world. No sooner are Banquo's words out than a vast image
out of *spiritus mundi* troubles his sight: his partner in the sinister prophecy,

also walking late. Banquo, apparently returning from seeing Duncan safely to bed (2.1.12–15), with any regicidal fantasies newly repressed, encounters Macbeth as a Doppelgänger, a Second Coming of his evil impulses. Macbeth is the waking figure of the cursed dream Banquo would be having were he asleep; Banquo might remark, as Leontes does in *The Winter's Tale*, "Your actions are my dreams" (3.2.82).

The notion that Macbeth is like any of us, only doomed to live in a world where one's dreams and desires become reality, is clearly bolstered by this moment, where we see Banquo horrified by the appetitive dreams the witches have aroused in him, then see his alter ego, stirred by the same force, condemned to live those dreams. Macbeth is again a version of the rash wisher in fairy tales: dreams are generally wish-fulfillments that evade the judging and censoring faculties, faculties that remain alert in us and in Banquo, crying "Hold, hold!" while we watch Macbeth stalk his desires. Freud cites approvingly "the old saying of Plato that the good are those who content themselves with dreaming of what others, the wicked, actually do."[18] Our identification with Banquo cannot completely reassure us about our moral worth because we are forced to realize how fine and even fortuitous the distinction is between Banquo's soul and Macbeth's. No one who has ever awakened with relief from a dream of evil-doing should feel any easy superiority to Macbeth at this decisive moment in his fall.

Half-asleep from exhaustion, Banquo watches the beginning of his regicidal nightmares acted out by Macbeth, who is crossing the stage in the opposite direction. Macbeth then watches distantly his own predatory advance, as we often watch ourselves in dreams; he announces that "wicked dreams abuse / The curtain'd sleep" (2.1.50–51). Macbeth has somehow *become* Banquo's bad dream, and Duncan's sleep seems to be tortured at this same moment by that same nightmare, which is closing in on him as a reality. The three characters are fatally jumbled together, as are the waking and dreaming states of consciousness. One result is that, after the regicide, Macbeth becomes both its perpetrator and its victim in an endless half-waking nightmare. As in the tortured sleep of Henry IV, the memory of committing a regicide and the prospect of serving as king work together against one's peace of mind; indeed, as Richard III discovers before Bosworth Field, they combine into symbolically appropriate nightmares of self-slaughter, the internal civil war implicit in ambition. Richard, in fact, foreshadows Macbeth's problems in another, more intriguing way. His nightmares, too, become reality; his dreams of defeat in battle come true under a sky that has stubbornly refused to turn to day. In the waking hours, when actions have real consequences, he is trapped in a repetition of the previous night. Macbeth, having lived out Banquo's evil dreams and fulfilled

Duncan's, finds the boundary disappearing for him as well, finds it impossible to escape his nightmare either by sleeping or by waking. Awake, he is visited by terrifying ghosts, moving forests, deceptive riddles, prophetic and symbolic visions—the sorts of things that most people encounter only in dreams. But his dreams seem to be only an extension of his waking deeds and his waking fears. He would rather disrupt the universe than have himself and his wife sleep

> In the affliction of these terrible dreams
> That shake us nightly. Better be with the dead,
> Whom we, to gain our peace, have sent to peace,
> Than on the torture of the mind to lie
> In restless ecstasy. Duncan is in his grave;
> After life's fitful fever he sleeps well.
> Treason has done his worst; nor steel, nor poison,
> Malice domestic, foreign levy, nothing,
> Can touch him further.   (3.2.18–26)

For their purposes, in fact, Duncan sleeps too well. By breaking the cycle that would normally have awakened him, they have inherited and perpetuated the nightmares of regicide which Macbeth imagined were tormenting Duncan's final hour. The implication is that the fear of a traitor bearing steel or poison wrenches Macbeth from his own sleep these nights. When the now dangerous world comes pounding on Macbeth's door, he says, "Wake Duncan with thy knocking! I would thou couldst!" (2.2.71). He wants the solar sovereign to rise again, bringing the new day's sun with him, thereby rescuing Macbeth on two levels from his nightmarish situation by revealing that he merely dreamed his evil deed. But cyclical renewal is precisely what Macbeth unwittingly forfeited when he abused "the curtain'd sleep":

> The death of each day's life, sore labor's bath,
> Balm of hurt minds, great nature's second course,
> Chief nourisher in life's feast.
> *Lady Macbeth*   What do you mean?
> *Macbeth*   Still it cried, "Sleep no more?" to all the house;
>   "Glamis hath murther'd sleep, and therefore Cawdor
>   Shall sleep no more—Macbeth shall sleep no more."
> (2.2.35–40)

The voice consigns him to sleeplessness by the same set of names the Witches used to assign him to ambition. When he asks them for reassurance against Macduff, so he may "sleep in spite of thunder," their answer is immediate and ominous: thunder, and the apparition of "a Child crowned, with a tree in his hand" (s.d. at 4.1.86). The forces of generational and seasonal rebirth unite against his craving for rest—"the season of all natures," as Lady Macbeth all too aptly defines it.[19]

Insomnia, like the other cyclical failures Macbeth and his wife cause, briefly afflicts all of Scotland. To restore "sleep to our nights," Macduff must leave his native body politic for England, "to wake Northumberland" (3.6.31–34); but no such cure is available for the nightmares and somnambulism that erode the bodies unnatural of the king and queen. The Doctor and the Waiting Gentlewoman "have two nights watch'd" to observe Lady Macbeth's "slumb'ry agitation," but are then free to tell each other "Good night" and flee to their own restful worlds. The Doctor calls it "a great perturbation in nature, to receive at once the benefit of sleep, and do the effects of watching," but we may suspect that Lady Macbeth's perturbation of nature has entailed the opposite, an appearance of sleep with none of its regenerative qualities (5.1.1–79). She is propelled through an endless night by a driving nostalgia for the moment before the ambitious crime that rendered her both literally and symbolically ineligible for rest. Her sleepwalking thus complements her hand-washing: both represent a futile effort to erase the consequences of a deed that murdered sleep both in Duncan and in her.

Shakespeare portrays Macbeth's crimes, from first to last, as costly violations of the procreative cycle. Dr. Isadore Coriat, one of the play's first psychoanalytic critics, identifies the Witches who instigate these offenses as "erotic symbols, representing, although sexless, the emblems of the generative power in nature. In the 'hell broth' are condensed heterogeneous materials in which even on superficial analysis one can discern the sexual significance."[20] But superficial analysis dismisses too easily the discordant aspects of that emblem. These bearded women provoke Macbeth to mix the sexual elements ruinously, as they provoked him to mix the elements of the other natural cycles that must be polarized to be regenerative: night with day, dreaming with waking, and fall with spring. Under their influence he misuses his generative powers in such a way that he undermines the hereditary order, rendering his sexuality as barren and distorted as their own.

The Oedipal crimes constitute a man's ultimate offense against his hereditary nature, and the most insidious mixture of the generational cycles, which must remain distinct to remain healthful. Since so much has been written about the Freudian implications of *Macbeth*, however, this chapter will examine only those aspects of the Oedipal situation that relate to ambitious revisions of identity. Macbeth conspires with the temptress to "do the deed" that will make him king, or remake him as king. Norman Holland outlines the standard psychoanalytic axioms about the play: "Macbeth acts the role of a son who replaces the authority of his father by force and substitutes himself. The motive for this father murder is Lady Macbeth, the 'demon woman' who creates the abyss between father and son."[21] Since Gertrude is the prize of Claudius' crime, Hamlet holds her partly responsible for that crime; Richard III entraps the Lady Anne by a trickier version of the same deduction. Freud argues that the woman's passive role gradually became misinterpreted in "the lying poetic fancies of prehistoric times" until the mother became an active instigator.[22] Lady Macbeth seems to offer herself as the sexual prize of Macbeth's regicide, and threatens to become the murderous mother rather than the seductive mother if he refuses the task (1.7.56–59).

But, from my point of view, the reading of the crime as essentially ambitious rather than essentially sexual squares better with the situations the psychoanalysts describe. What Lady Macbeth actually provokes in her husband is an ambitious deed; the analogy to the Oedipal situation may be a resonance rather than a primary but veiled meaning. In offering to become either the seductive mother or the murderous one, she is reminding him that it is in his own power to decide whether to create this new royal self or to destroy it in its infancy. His success in creating it will be a measure of his sexual capacity, but that sexual provocation remains at the distance of a metaphor, and is intimately linked to the goal of a new birth rather than to any goal of sensual gratification. Occam's Razor seems to cut against the traditional Freudian reading in this case. Sexuality is Lady Macbeth's means to an ambitious end in the play's superficial psychology, and it would be fitting for the same transaction to apply on the play's deep figurative level. If psychoanalytic critics argue that "Macbeth's killing of Duncan represents hatred and resentment of a fatherlike authority" and that "Lady Macbeth embodies or projects Macbeth's ambitious wish," as Holland summarizes it,[23] then the tensions seem more applicable to the hazards of ambition than to the "family romance" as such. Duncan is not Macbeth's actual father, but plays the paternal role in limiting the legitimate range of Macbeth's aspiration; the play makes it clear that Duncan is not a restrictive authority except in holding his preeminence and in promising it to another heir before Macbeth. Lady Macbeth is not Macbeth's actual mother, but plays the maternal role in offering to "embody" an ambitious new self for him.

Several critics have suggested that the murder of Duncan is figuratively a rape, or that the murder is only the offspring, or the projection onto Duncan, of a sexual crime between Macbeth and his Lady.[24] Rather than making either the violent or the sexual aspect of the "deed" merely a metaphor for the other, however, my thesis makes them mutually dependent: this is a rape with procreative purposes, and it entails ripping the hereditary body politic untimely from its haven in Duncan's body. (The revelation of Macduff's Caesarean origins is, in this sense, another example of Macbeth's crime functioning as a rash wish that unwittingly invites its own punishment.) But this sinister seduction turns out to be a dismal failure. One critic equates the spirits of drink that the Porter says inspire but hinder sexual activity with the spirits that appear to Macbeth as witches: for each man, "The spirits that seem to make him potent actually render him impotent."[25] The sexual situation is again not merely parallel to the political situation, but intimately linked to it: the attempt to conceive a new self becomes instead a loss of the original birth, and the effort to seize sovereignty over the process of procreation and lineage is steadily revealed as a forfeiting of all procreative abilities and lineal aspirations. Macbeth is left with a "barren sceptre" (3.1.61): the ambitious abuse of his sexual powers has ruined those powers. His castration, like that of Oedipal sons, is the final result of indulged Oedipal impulses; his impotence, like that of fisher-kings in myth, leads necessarily to his expulsion from rule.

The phallic character of Macbeth's crime is clear enough, however one chooses to interpret it. Led by a dagger, he advances toward Duncan's bedchamber "with Tarquin's ravishing strides" (2.1.55). Newly convinced by his wife to assert his sexual manhood by this deed, to become the "serpent" striking up through the "innocent flower" (1.5.64–65), Macbeth claims to "bend up / Each corporal agent to this terrible feat" (1.7.79–80); and when conscientious fear renders him impotent to act, she says, "You do unbend your noble strength" (2.2.42). When she mocks him for lacking the "manhood" to finish that task, she chooses to call him "infirm of purpose" (2.2.49). The murder is described by everyone, including the perpetrators, as a "deed" or "act"; but these euphemisms for the horror that "tongue nor heart cannot conceive nor name" (2.3.64–65) refer to sexual deeds or acts as often as murderous ones in Shakespeare.[26] This convergence of the two acts suggests the mixed crime of Oedipus; since the direct result is the creation of an exalted but sinister Macbeth, it may refer to the aspect of the Oedipus story that focuses on pride and identity, rather than the aspect that focuses on sexual psychology for its own sake.[27]

The regicide is not the first time Macbeth had violently "conceived" an exalted new self and hewed its Caesarean path to life through another's body. Scotland is conventionally described as a mother throughout *Macbeth*, and only a few lines into the play we see Macbeth emerge as her heroic child. Using his "brandish'd steel" to make himself "valor's minion," he "carv'd out

his passage" to Macdonwald and "unseam'd him from the nave to th' chops."
A "passage" was a standard term in Renaissance medicine for "the necke of
this wombe" at the base of the uterus.[28] Richard II uses the same term when
he strives to "tear a passage through the flinty ribs / Of this hard world, my
ragged prison walls" for his rebirth in "a generation of still-breeding
thoughts" (5.5.6–21), and Shakespeare will use it again to describe
Coriolanus' determination to chop "his passage" through "Rome gates,"
which (as I will argue) become the symbol of his mother's womb through
which any viable rebirth must pass.

Macbeth's first rebirth, however, is a defense of Duncan's paternal
privileges rather than an assault on them. Disdaining the sinister allure of the
"rebel's whore" Fortune—a version of the Oedipal temptress—Macbeth and
Banquo confirm their identities as "children and servants" to Duncan's
throne (1.4.25). But once the prospect of creating heroic new identities with
their swords has presented itself, the loyal soldiers become susceptible to the
lure of the sinister Witches, who offer them a rebirth that evades rather than
affirms their hereditary subordination. The witches are Jocasta-figures,
avatars not only of the temptress-figure Lady Macbeth with whom they share
a provocation and a sexual ambiguity, but also of that sinister temptress
Fortune, with whom they share a name: etymologically as well as
mythologically, "the three Weird Sisters" are the women of fortune.
Furthermore, witches and midwives were strongly identified with each other
in sixteenth-century England, particularly in accusations that midwives
induced birth to give the child a soul, then consecrated that soul to Satan by
ritualistically killing the infant before it could be baptized.[29] The parallels
between this accusation and the witches' instigation of Macbeth's rebirth,
death, and damnation are certainly speculative, but also intriguing. Once it
becomes clear that his first rebirth has not granted Macbeth a place in the
royal lineage, he determines to use the same figurative technique that made
him Duncan's loyal son to become Duncan's rebellious son. As with Prince
Hal, Shakespeare undoes the dreamwork of a boy's father-saving fantasy,
revealing the latent father-killing fantasy that was lurking symmetrically
behind it. The witches perform the same psychoanalytic function, for
Macbeth and for us, encouraging him to recognize the inevitable Oedipal
conflict arising from his role as Duncan's child and servant, and thereby to
recognize the perverse psychological mechanism connecting his loyal deeds
with his "horrible imaginings."

The witches' prophecy is what sets the play's tragic aspect in motion,
and it does so by luring Macbeth away from the normal cycle of generation.
The prophecy seems to announce an equitable distribution of glory to the
two triumphant soldiers: rule to Macbeth and succession to Banquo. But, as

Lucien Goldmann suggests, the tragic hero generally finds that his gods "speak to him in deceitful terms and from afar off, the oracles which he consults have two meanings, one apparent but false, the other hidden but true, the demands which the Gods make are contradictory, and the world is ambiguous and equivocal."[30] The hidden truth in the riddling prophecy, arising from the fog of the "foul and fair" day on the heath, is that the two promised forms of glory are mutually exclusive. A cause-and-effect relationship lurks unrecognized in the witches' division of the spoils: since Macbeth will seize a paternal identity that does not belong to him hereditarily, he will be forbidden to father a lineal successor. The prophecy that confronts Macbeth is therefore an Oedipal prophecy—specifically, a warning about filial rebellion and the castration that avenges it—as Lévi-Strauss argues all riddles are.[31] Such a riddle tempts man toward the fatal violation it describes, sends him in pursuit of self-destruction through a desperate and deluded attempt at self-preservation. The "paradoxical impression that Macbeth gives of being morally responsible for his own destruction even though he is so heavily fated to destroy himself that the lines of his destiny can be read by prophecy"[32] may be partly resolved by recognizing the unwitting act of choice that invites his fated barrenness. His fatal error, like that of Oedipus, is a failure to notice the cautionary aspect of the prophecies affixed to the gloriously inciting aspect; the contrastingly cautious Banquo avoids that Oedipal (and figuratively castrating) mistake. Banquo, the acknowledged enemy of Macbeth's "genius" or generative force (3.1.48–69), may safely partake of the crown by growing into it through generation rather than transforming himself forcibly into a figure of royal stature. As Edward Forset wrote in the same year that Shakespeare wrote *Macbeth*, "when wee be disposed to alter any thing, we must let it grow by degrees, and not hast it on too suddenly."[33] The flesh of Banquo's flesh eventually grows into the kingly robes that hang so loosely on Macbeth's artificial person.

Lady Macbeth is quicker than her husband to recognize that murdering Duncan will entail murdering the procreative order. The fisher-king Duncan basks in the natural fecundity that he half-perceives and half-creates in the couple's home. Banquo explains Duncan's enjoyment of this castle in suggestive terms:

> This guest of summer,
> The temple-haunting martlet, does approve,
> By his lov'd mansionry, that the heaven's breath
> Smells wooingly here; no jutty, frieze,
> Buttress, nor coign of vantage, but this bird

Hath made his pendant bed and procreant cradle.
Where they most breed and haunt, I have observ'd
The air is delicate.   (1.6.3–10)

Just as Lady Macbeth has already begun replacing this martlet with a raven,
and the domesticated jutties with battlements (1.5.38–40), so has she begun
to replace this nurturant sexuality with its antithesis. Her plea that the spirits
"unsex me," according to a recent study, contains a specific request that her
menstrual cycle be intermitted:[34]

Make thick my blood,
Stop up th' access and passage to remorse,
That no compunctious visitings of nature
Shake my fell purpose.   (1.5.43–46)

Even her request that the spirits "take my milk for gall" suggests that the
reborn Macbeth (like the reborn Coriolanus) can be nurtured into life only
by fluids opposite to "the milk of human kindness" by which he was
originally formed and fed (1.5.48, 17).

Freud understood this couple's loss of progeny as essentially such a rash
wish, a barren instruction returning to plague the inventors: "It would be a
perfect example of poetic justice in the manner of the talion if the
childlessness of Macbeth and the barrenness of his Lady were the
punishment for their crimes against the sanctity of geniture."[35] The
inconsistencies concerning Lady Macbeth's children, despite L.C. Knights's
famous argument, actually makes Freud's point all the more convincing.[36] If
the children were concretely presented to us, Shakespeare would be obliged
to provide a literal cause for their parents' poetically just lack of an heir. That
would likely both alter the polarity of our sympathies and conceal the
important symbolic cause behind a crudely physical efficient cause. This is
opportunism on Shakespeare's part of the sort Knights describes, where the
play works as something other than a realistic story, but if (as Knights urges)
we ignore the apparent disappearance of the children, if we refuse to think of
Lady Macbeth as a procreative creature, then we lose the moral import of
that disappearance. Macduff's reasons for abandoning his family to slaughter
remain somewhat unclear, perhaps for same didactic purpose.[37] By including
only the comment that this Caesarean figure "wants the natural touch"
(4.2.9), Shakespeare suggests that the products of disordered procreation are
deprived of heirs by a jealous natural order. Since it requires Duncan's death,
Macbeth's royal rebirth thriftlessly ravins up his own life's means (2.4.28–29);
since Caesarean operations were virtually always fatal to the mother in the

Renaissance,[38] Macduff's birth entails the same unwitting offense. By refusing us a complete factual explanation for either man's loss of progeny, Shakespeare focuses our attention on the defect they share and the nemesis it provokes.

This shared unnaturalness and childlessness enables Macduff to cure the disease that threatens the nation's procreative health. Macbeth's crimes against Malcolm's "due of birth" and against "nature's germains" in general have blighted Scotland's fertility (3.6.25; 4.1.59). The threatened kingdom is, as Macduff says, truly a threatened "birthdom" (4.3.4). In reply, Malcolm portrays himself as merely another agent of that blight, a creature of indiscriminate lust in conceiving children, and hardly better than Lady Macbeth in nursing them thereafter: he will "pour the sweet milk of concord into hell" (4.3.98). This causes Macduff to wonder whether there can be any hope for Scotland's regeneration,

> Since that the truest issue of thy throne
> By his own interdiction stands accus'd
> And does blaspheme his breed? Thy royal father
> Was a most sainted king; the queen that bore thee,
> Oft'ner upon her knees than on her feet,
> Died every day she liv'd.   (4.3.106–11)

What this speech emphasizes is generational continuity: Malcolm's royal virtues should follow from his hereditary rights, almost as if orderly succession were virtue itself. The quality Macduff eulogizes in Malcolm's mother is her daily exchange of death and life, a pattern associable with the regenerative virtues of sleep, "the death of each day's life" as it is called at the time of Duncan's murder (2.2.37). This figuratively posthumous mother merges with Macduff's literal one into the notion of Scotland as such a mother:

> Alas, poor country,
> Almost afraid to know itself! It cannot
> Be call'd our mother, but our grave; where nothing,
> But who knows nothing, is once seen to smile.   (4.3.164–67)

Macbeth's Caesarean rebirth has infected the entire nation with his nullified and self-alienated condition, and precludes any more natural births in the future. "Cruel are the times when we are traitors, / And do not know ourselves," the choral Rosse tells Lady Macduff moments before she and her babes are slaughtered (4.2.18–19). Disruptions of succession converted individual mothers and the mother-country into tombs in *Richard III* (4.1.53; 4.4.138, 423) and *Richard II* (2.1.51, 83), and now the same transaction threatens Scotland's future.

But eventually Scotland, like Macduff, is rescued from the dead maternal womb and begins a new generation of life. Macduff's role as the spearhead of this vengeful revival becomes an emblem of the fact that Macbeth is destroyed by the unlineal, unnatural provenance of his own royal identity. Macbeth is able to achieve his bloody rebirth only by performing a regicide; Macduff is able to perform his regicide, according to the prophecies, only because of his Caesarean origins. Macduff is, in this sense, the fulfillment of Macbeth's foolish wish to replace natural succession with abrupt violence. Macbeth again resembles Richard III, in serving as the sacrifice by which his nation restores its damaged lineal health, and Macduff is a suitable blade-wielding hierophant. When a society must purge a sin that has injured its fertility, it generally sacrifices a figure onto whom all the sin is projected, often a temporary mock-king; the executioner is generally a liminal figure who partly reflects or partly contracts the victim's particular taint.[39]

A group of paradoxically mighty infants resume the process of generation as Macbeth's enemies.[40] From the corrupt jumble of nature's germains in the witches' cauldron arise miraculously two such symbols of procreation's determination to survive and destroy the barren tyrant. The crowned babe, suggesting the rightful heir Malcolm, and the bloody babe, suggesting the Caesarean child Macduff, represent several things on other levels: the inheriting children Macbeth cannot have, the potential heirs Macbeth has sought to kill, the Oedipal children who typically abuse the father who was himself an Oedipal criminal, and the wounded regenerative order as a whole.[41] For Macbeth as for Richard III, the failure to eradicate all such heirs, and relatedly the failure to terminate all such cycles, generates a nemesis that returns to destroy him. As in Greek and Christian myths, at least one heir escapes the tyrant's defensive Slaughter of the Innocents, and the army that defeats Macbeth consists of "Siward's son, / And many unrough youths that even now / Protest their first of manhood" (5.2.9–11). Once again Macbeth has succeeded only in interrupting a cycle he sought to override completely, and when it resumes he finds himself trapped in an unnatural generational isolation (5.3.24–26), with no child of his own to succeed him.

Macbeth is not only the bad ruler of Freudian myth, who deprives others such as Macduff and Banquo of their reproductive rights; he is also the bad ruler of fisher-king myths, whose own reproductive impotence causes his nation's crops to fail. The repression and vengeful return of human generation in the play is closely paralleled by a repression and return of the seasonal forces of vegetative life. The parallel has several revealing precedents:

> The first religious poet of Greece, Hesiod ... tells us that when men do justice [their crops flourish and] "their wives bear children that are like their parents." So, on the other hand, when a sin has been committed—such as the unconscious incest of Oedipus—all Nature is poisoned by the offence of man. The land of Thebes "Wasteth in the fruitless buds of earth, / In parchèd herds, and travail without birth / Of dying women."[42]

The Oedipal archetype, apparently from the very first, has been associated with a punitive collapse of nature's various regenerative cycles. In *2 Henry IV*, the haunted country is England rather than Thebes, but the ghosts are similar. Gloucester mentions "unfather'd heirs and loathly births of nature. / The seasons change their manners, as the year / Had found some months asleep and leap'd them over" (4.4.121–24). A few lines later, Prince Hal confirms the Oedipal character of this disturbance by stealing his sleeping father's unlineal crown. This blight began, according to the Gardener, when Richard II allowed the "prodigal weight" of "unruly children" to ruin a tree, and allowed "the noisome weeds" to "suck / The soil's fertility from wholesome flowers" (*Richard II*, 3.4.29–45). The natural order is only temporarily salvaged when Hal conquers France in deference to his forefathers, thereby acquiring a new world of vegetative and procreative fertility. The more lasting solution is the return of Richmond, who supposedly unites and renews the White and Red Roses.

The same correspondences appear in *Macbeth*, where the savior returns accompanied by his nation's foliage, and by young men determined "to dew the sovereign flower and drown the weeds" on their "march towards Birnam" (5.2.30–31). When Duncan arrives at Macbeth's castle, he is associated not only with the martlet's procreative aspects, but also with its role as a "guest of summer" (1.6.3). Conversely, Macbeth describes his usurping reign by adjacent metonymies that suggest vegetative and procreative sterility respectively: "Upon my head they plac'd a fruitless crown, / And put a barren sceptre in my gripe, / Thence to be wrench'd with an unlineal hand, / No son of mine succeeding" (3.1.60–63). He returns to the witches hoping for a revision of this prophecy, but the visions they conjure only serve to reinforce it. As early as 1746, John Upton perceived the brutally literal level of these portents:

> The armed head represents symbolically Macbeth's head cut off
> and brought to Malcolm by Macduff. The bloody child is
> Macduff untimely ripp'd from his mother's womb. The child with
> a crown on his head, and a bough in his hand, is the royal
> Malcolm, who ordered his soldiers to hew them down a bough
> and bear it before them to Dunsinane.[43]

Having been lured by the witches across the threshold from reality into a
fairy tale where words and imagination have an absolute efficacy, Macbeth
overlooks this literal level of the portents, as he and other rash wishers
overlook the literal level of their wishes; "the letter kills," as theologians
warned, and the literal components of these apparitions emerge to kill
Macbeth. Of course the armed head "knows thy thought," if it is actually his
own head; it is an "unknown power" only to the extent that his own
conscientious imagination is (4.1.69). The bloody babe is so overdetermined
as a symbol that it resists any careful reading. The child's bough is all too
easily interpreted as a symbol of regenerative nature, the rightful heir's
sceptre that will replace Macbeth's "fruitless" one.

Yet there is a level on which this symbolic reading of Malcolm's return
remains valuable, because even the literal advance of Birnam's branches
symbolizes the unified nature that engulfs its betrayer. Dunsinane Castle, as
a prize of Macbeth's ambition, represents on one level all of man's futile stays
against his moral limitations. It symbolizes for Shakespeare what
Ozymandias' statue symbolized for Shelley, and the advancing branches are
the equivalent of Shelley's centuries of sandstorms. In the form of Birnam
Wood, the balance of nature springs back against the kingly enclave man has
manufactured against it; the wood, on this level, represents the endlessly
persistent forces that erode humanity's efforts to make the world conform to
its desires and reflect its consciousness. To build the castle in the primeval
forest, to establish human sovereignty, land was cleared; eventually nature
will reforest that land. The fact that civilization rapidly deforested Scotland
in the era of the historical Macbeth makes the symbolism all the more
plausible and evocative.[44] The camouflaged advance on Dunsinane provides
an accelerated emblem for the futility of humanity's ambitious projects, an
ethical lesson presented by a sort of time-lapse photography.

Several critics have commented that this advance resembles a Maying
festival, in which the young people carry green branches to chase out the
tyrannical winter.[45] Such an association, however subliminal, would serve to
reinforce our sense that we are witnessing nature's cyclical victory over its
barren enemies. What I am suggesting is that Shakespeare has grounded his
warning against ambition in a parable applicable to the entire history of

human civilization, and not just to the cycle of any given year, just as the confrontation between Hal and the Lord Chief Justice in *2 Henry IV* is applicable to much more than the reformation of a single unruly son. Shakespeare thus reinforces the power of the specific confrontations, and at the same time reminds us of their universal relevance; the hazards of ambition are an essential component in human experience, all human experience.

The shift in the moral balance from the history plays to *Macbeth*—the shift that makes *Macbeth* a tragedy—is visible in the difference between these two primal confrontations. We may not be entirely delighted with Hal's submission to the Lord Chief Justice and his banishment of Falstaff, but we sense that it is a choice we have all made, and that it is finally not only compatible with our humanity, but necessary for its survival. But, inasmuch as Macbeth's ambition may represent the essential projects of humanity, the very essence of our identity as *homo faber*—the creature who shapes his environment, with words and other tools, to his desires—the destruction of Macbeth by that fated moving wood can please us as humane justice on only the most superficial level. Conventional goodness is victorious, but it defeats an evil that Shakespeare invites us to recognize as a plausible extension of the things that make us human, and its weapons are the instruments of our oppression as well as our salvation. Shakespeare may have suggested all the natural concomitants to the political hierarchy in the history plays to remind people of the deep sinfulness and foolishness of attempting to overthrow that hierarchy; he may simply have been dramatizing the Elizabethan propaganda typified by the passages quoted earlier from Hooker and from the "Exhortation Concerning Good Order." But at some point Shakespeare recognized the logical counterpart to the argument that rebellion can arise only from a failure to recognize the seamless and providential character of the world's order. To dislike anything about nature is to lose sight of the essential principle defending the sovereign's authority over the will of his individual subjects. If all levels of the established order are so intricately linked, then repercussions may travel upward from lesser violations of that order, as well as downward from greater ones. If political ambition entails a parallel distortion of every other natural system, then we are all implicated in an array of crimes including regicide by our casual individual resentment of some inconvenient bad weather, and by our imperative resistance as a species to the landscape and the climate, a resistance palpably evinced by our houses and garments.

The notion that human beings are necessarily ambitious has substantial precedents in Renaissance philosophy. Petrarch argues that the specific need for shelter and clothing authorizes humanity's more general aspirations to surpass its given condition. As opposed to the lower animals, who "are allotted whatever is given them at birth and no more," man's naked frailties indicate that God wants him to achieve and acquire "as much as he is able in his acute genius to attain by living and thinking."[46] Similarly, to Bovillus, as Ernst Cassirer explains it,

> freedom simply means that man does not receive his being ready-made from nature, as do the other entities, nor does he, so to speak, get it as a permanent fief; but rather that he must acquire it, must *form* it through *virtus* and *ars* ... If he falls prey to the vice of inertia—the medieval *acedia*—he can sink down to the level at which only naked existence remains to him ... The man of nature, simple *homo*, must become the man of art.[47]

In *Macbeth* Shakespeare gives us glimpses of the dark converse of this glorious art, the grand transformation. What if man's greatest and most characteristic quality is trapped in a world where it can express itself only as sin, or at least where its natural activity will be perceived and punished as a violation of natural law by a jealous paternal God? This was the belief of the Gnostics, who felt that some higher God had planted a spark of his own divinity in each person, but that we have been trapped into a natural world inimical to that divine essence by a lower and envious God-the-Father. To the Gnostics, according to Hans Jonas,

> It is almost by exaggeration that the divinity of cosmic order is turned into the opposite of divine. Order and law is the cosmos here too, but rigid and inimical order, tyrannical and evil law, devoid of meaning and goodness, alien to the purposes of man and to his inner essence, no object for his communication and affirmation.

> The blemish of nature lies not in any deficiency of order, but in the all too pervading completeness of it. Far from chaos, the creation of the demiurge, unenlightened as it is, is still a system of law. But cosmic law, once worshiped as the expression of a reason with which man's reason can communicate in the act of cognition, is now seen only in its aspect of compulsion which thwarts man's freedom.[48]

The cosmic order thus appears in its aspect of *heimarmene*, a Fate morally congruent with Mosaic law and opposed to the human essence, rather than *pronoia,* a true Providence. From such a viewpoint, Macbeth's steadfast opposition to, and destruction by, a unified system of nature would mark him as a martyr rather than a sinner.

Even his diseases, from the Gnostic perspective, are the proper tactics for opposing the Archons (the gods who rule this world) rather than punishments imposed by those Archons; this is revisionistic history on a grand theological scale. Macbeth's abstention from procreation, and his intimately related program of "uprooting" the heirs of others, recalls part of the formula dying Gnostics recited to escape the Archons, a sort of perverse last confession: "I have not sown children to the Archon but have uprooted his roots." To the Gnostics, the Mosaic God's injunction to "be fruitful and multiply" was an evil trick designed to entrap more of the divine sparks in his labyrinth. Even Macbeth's murder of sleep in himself and in others squares with the Gnostic project of awakening humanity from a sleep imposed by the Archons through a soporific poison that made us passive to this world's evils and forgetful of our true, more exalted home. Ambition is equated with insomnia in Gnosticism as it is in Shakespeare, but for the Gnostics that would have been an endorsement rather than a condemnation. The Gnostic is saved, not damned, by the Call from the supernatural agency that answers to an inner potential, as the witches' call answers to Macbeth's prior ambitions.

There are also elements here of the family romance, and of the decomposition motif by which that romance expresses itself in fairy tales as well as in psychotic delusions: a Gnostic's ambitions, apparently rebellions against the Father, are actually justified as fulfillments of his true heritage from the lost higher Father who rules the greater realm.[49] The genetic identity is an obstacle to fulfillment for the Gnostics, and not a truly divine dictation of identity. In Valentinian Gnosticism, the Oedipal archetype emerges when the mother conceals the truly divine spark from the lower God-the-Father, and tricks him into leaving it "implanted in the human soul and body, to be carried there as if in a womb until it had grown sufficiently to receive the Logos."[50] This Mother carries within her the seed by which the son reconceives himself, and she hides him (as Zeus and Moses were hidden) to protect him from the father's jealous and fearful wrath until the boy is strong enough to rebel successfully and thus reunite with her. To this extent, the Oedipal components of Macbeth's crime correspond to the Gnostic program.

The world of Macbeth thus moves closer to the world of Marlowe's Faustus, whose effort to find something above the mundane that answers to his aspiring mind becomes mired in the limits of the physical universe. The lower God has taught us to perceive as Satanic the voices—Macbeth's

Witches, Faustus' Mephistopheles—that urge us to fulfill the transcendent within us; he has also learned how to imitate the grandeur of such voices when he chooses, for the purpose of luring us more deeply into the worldly labyrinth. When the witches implicitly laugh at Macbeth's defeat, as when the gods silently laugh at the defeat of Coriolanus (5.3.183–85), we may easily and chillingly sense that a spiteful conspiracy has triumphed over the ambition that is intrinsic to our humanity. What makes this even more horrifying is the recognition that this conspiracy has triumphed in the name of a "nature" we had been taught to revere as our mother, and to believe functioned in perfect harmony with our needs.

Nevertheless, on the play's primary level, the return of Birnam Wood to Dunsinane serves the human good as well as the natural order. A virtuous new human generation accompanies these moving branches, and is protected by them. Malcolm restores to Scotland the same combination of blessings that the flower-strewing Perdita brings into the artificial winter of Sicilia, making her as welcome "As is the spring to th' earth" (5.1.152). Macbeth cannot embrace this renewed vegetation as Leontes does, because in this adult fairy tale nature returns not in forgiveness, as a gift, but in vengeance, as a weapon. When the cycle he has briefly suppressed resumes its natural flow, Macbeth is stranded outside it. Even while this new spring burgeons, he becomes the yellowed creature of autumn, and "ripe for shaking" (5.3.23; 4.3.238). As the Gardener remarks about Richard II, "He that hath suffered this disordered spring / Hath now himself met with the fall of leaf" (3.4.48–49).

Time, which Macbeth would not trust to bring the prophecies to fruition, thus becomes his enemy. For him, as for Tennyson's Tithonus, the fact that the cycles of days, seasons, and generations continue all around him only makes his own steady decay more painful. Macbeth finds himself on a linear course into winter, while his wife retreats into a ritualistic repetition of yesterdays, until he loses her entirely:

> She should have died hereafter;
> There would have been a time for such a word.
> To-morrow, and to-morrow, and to-morrow,
> Creeps in this petty pace from day to day,
> To the last syllable of recorded time;
> And all our yesterdays have lighted fools
> The way to dusty death. Out, out, brief candle!
> Life's but a walking shadow. (5.5.17–24)

With the loss of his wife, Macbeth's hopes for diurnal or generational renewal disappear. In this Shakespeare seems to be building on a Jacobean commonplace. Richard Brathwait's *The Prodigals Teares* suggests the same associations: "I know Lord, that the candle of the wicked ... shalbe soone put out ... his faire and fruitfull fieldes laid waste, his treasures rifled, his pastures with all his hierds dispersed, and his children utterly rooted out and extinguished."[51] Nehemiah Rogers' prodigal-son tract provides a similar analogue to Macbeth's resigned conclusion that "life's but a walking shadow," asserting that any existence devoid of spiritual growth and regeneration is "but a shadow of life."[52] Macbeth's phrase also alludes ominously, unwittingly, to his earlier characterization of Banquo's ghost as a "horrible shadow" (3.4.105). Both Banquo's shade and Birnam Wood return as the ghosts of the natural life his royal aspirations have murdered, and as the fathers of the natural renewal he has failed to kill.

Macbeth's resigned conclusion, however, becomes a literal as well as a figurative truth. This speech is closely bracketed by revelations about the movement of Birnam Wood. Specifically, less than forty lines before Macbeth dismisses life as a walking shadow, Malcolm tells his soldiers each to "hew him down a bough, / And bear't before him, thereby shall we shadow / The numbers of our host" (5.4.4–6). In its emblematic march on Dunsinane, in other words, life actually *is* a walking shadow. Malcolm's stratagem, Macbeth's verbal metaphor, and Shakespeare's visual emblem, all agree on that point. Macbeth has not foreseen either Malcolm's military tactic or Shakespeare's artistic device, but most important, he has again failed to perceive the literal as well as the figurative meaning of a phrase, a phrase that subsequently becomes all too prophetic. The world, like the Witches, palters with him in a double sense (5.8.20). His very resignation to the hollowness of life actually invites life's true power to rise up against him, in a bitterly ironic reshaping of his own metaphor; again Macbeth becomes the fairy-tale figure whose unenlightened words return to haunt him. This complicated play on the notion of the walking shadow recapitulates in small the tragedy's central transaction. Macbeth's lack of faith in the natural cycles led to the rash wish that deprived him of cyclical regeneration; here, his lack of faith in life leads to a rash observation that unwittingly invites his death at hands of Malcolm's forces.

Cut off from his natural roots, Macbeth becomes a lifeless head on a pike (5.8.26), while Malcolm, festooned with green branches, takes his place. A contemporary of Shakespeare proposes a similar fate for his own murderous, incestuous, and overreaching protagonist:

> God would not permit him to enjoy that wealth, which to purchase had made him violate the lawes both divine, and humane, and prophane the most Sacred bonds that are in nature; [but] he that just labours, and lawfull industries, gathers up any

thing shall see his goods prosper like a tree planted neere the
current of waters, which brings forth fruite in its season.[53]

The wages of sin are death, and the reward for cancelling the bonds of nature
is at best an absence of life.

Malcolm, nominated as the new fisher-king by the procreative order
itself, promises to reward his loyalists and to undertake all the tasks "which
would be newly planted with the time" (5.9.30–31). This represents a return
to natural continuity, not only in the character of the metaphor he employs,
but also in the history of that metaphor. He assumes his hereditary place
while using the same figuration his father used at the start of the play to
thank *his* loyalists. As nature is a metaphor for heredity in this play, so is it a
hereditary metaphor. With the big war that made ambition virtue
successfully concluded, Duncan told Macbeth,

> I have begun to plant thee, and will labor
> To make thee full of growing. Noble Banquo,
> That hast no less deserv'd, nor must be known
> No less to have done so, let me infold thee
> And hold thee to my heart.
> *banquo*   There if I grow,
> The harvest is your own.   (1.4.28–33)

The Witches know better than the egalitarian Duncan: Banquo shall be
"lesser than Macbeth, and greater" (1.3.65) when his grains grow and
Macbeth's do not, and this exchange suggests the reasons for that distinction.
By accepting Duncan's vegetative metaphor, Banquo acknowledges his
dependence on Duncan's fertility, and thus becomes eligible for the role as
"the root and father / Of many kings" that the Witches promised him
(3.1.5–6). By agreeing to surrender his fruits to the throne, he reserves a
place for his scions on the throne.

Macbeth, in contrast, describes his "duties" as Duncan's "children"
rather than as Duncan's "harvest," as if he expected his Caesarean deeds to
win him a place in the royal family (1.4.24–25). That expectation becomes
more obvious a few lines later in his violent response to Duncan's naming of
Malcolm as heir to the throne.[54] Macbeth must pretend to accept what is
duly planted with the time, while secretly undermining it as the traditionally
parricidal serpent:

> *Lady Macbeth*   To beguile the time,
> Look like the time; bear welcome in your eye,

> Your hand, your tongue; look like th' innocent flower,
> But be the serpent under't.   (1.5.63–66)

Macbeth thus subverts the harvest Duncan promises. As soon as the regicide has been performed, the Porter, pretending to welcome the newly damned to hell, first hypothesizes his guest as "a farmer, that hang'd himself on th' expectation of plenty" (2.3.4–5). This paradoxical farmer destroyed himself because a healthy, orderly harvest and reseeding thwarted his selfish speculations: Macbeth's hope that the death of a royal line will legitimize his unnatural succession parallels the farmer's hope that scarcity will drive up the price of his hoarded grain. This correlation gains conviction from the similarly damning flaws of the Porter's other guests, who are all "caught out by overreaching themselves."[55] So, of course, is Macbeth, whose ambition has converted the blessings of nature into a curse.

Macbeth's attack on Banquo, like his attack on Duncan, arises from the extension of the planting metaphor into generational continuity. Banquo confronts the Witches with characteristic confidence in the natural order:

> If you can look into the seeds of time,
> And say which grain will grow, and which will not,
> Speak then to me, who neither beg nor fear
> Your favors nor your hate.   (1.3.58–61)

Moral philosophers from Pelagius to Pico to Ralegh to Iago have used the selective cultivation of seeds as a metaphor for the legitimate range of self-improvement, self-cultivation.[56] Shakespeare, rather more conservative in his view of human aspiration, has Banquo leave not only the seeding, but also the choice of which seeds will grow, in the hands of God alone. He may therefore become "the root and father" of a new royal family tree (3.1.5). Macbeth has sacrificed his otherworldly hopes for worldly glory, only to find that he has no one to whom he may bequeath his costly acquisition; D'Amville, in Tourneur's *The Atheist's Tragedy*, makes much the same complaint, after a similar set of violations (4.2.36–39). But Shakespeare manipulates the vegetative metaphors to make the unity of divine and natural rules more vivid. Macbeth specifically complains about ruining his soul "to make them kings—the seeds of Banquo kings!" (3.1.69), unaware that his primal violation of nature necessarily entailed a loss of succession as well as virtue. This fear of seedlings, plausibly a premonition of the attack on his castle by shoots from Birnam Wood, compels Macbeth to strike down Duncan and Banquo in the hope that their scions, Malcolm and Fleance, will then be destroyed. He has not reckoned, with the proverbial truth Ben

Jonson expresses in his *Discoveries*: "Severity represseth a few, but it irritates more. The lopping of trees makes the boughes shoote out thicker."[57]

Precisely that truth is driven home to Macbeth, on both the figurative and the literal levels, when Birnam Wood begins its advance. But until it does, Macbeth supposes himself secure, because he has again failed to connect a figurative level with a literal one. His confidence that he can uproot these family trees is based on a literal reading of the Witches' prophecy that he cannot be defeated until the trees of Birnam move, which he supposes is impossible:

> That will never be.
> Who can impress the forest, bid the tree
> Unfix his earth-bound root? Sweet bodements! good!
> Rebellious dead, rise never till the wood
> Of Birnam rise, and our high-plac'd Macbeth
> Shall live the lease of nature, pay his breath
> To time and mortal custom. (4.1.94–100)

Either roots can be extirpated or they cannot; but because a family tree is a metaphor and a Birnam tree is real, Macbeth characteristically fails to see the contradiction in his hopes. Having broken the lease of nature, he can hardly expect to enforce it in his own defense; time and mortal custom, which he sought to subdue to his will, subdue him instead. All that remains of Macbeth's natural foundation, all that grows to fill his oversized royal robes, is what he sees disturbing his wife's rest: "a rooted sorrow" (5.3.41). For her as for the barren women of the history plays, sorrow is the only thing that retains a regenerative basis. Macduff, too, was cut off at the root, but according to Rosse, he retained some feeling for "the fits o' th' season" (4.2.17), understood the principle of cyclical growth. Macbeth evidently does not: the plants he lops off inevitably send up new shoots, culminating in the forest that envelops his castle. At the end of the play the impotent fisher-king is a lifeless head on a wooden pole, like an old tree that has dropped no seedlings, disappearing one spring in the eternal forest, vengefully excluded by the regenerative cycles his ambition sought to suppress.

NOTES

1. From *Sermons or Homilies Appointed to be Read in Churches in the Time of Queen Elizabeth of Famous Memory* (London: C & J Rivington, 1825), pp. 114–115.

2. Richard Hooker, *Of the Laws of Ecclesiastical Polity* (1594), Everyman's Library (London: J. M. Dent, 1907), p. 157.

3. Harry Berger, Jr., "The Early Scenes of *Macbeth*," *ELH* 47 (1980), 1–5, detects

subversive notes in the play's ostensible endorsement of the natural and political orders, and suggests that repeated insurrections against those orders may be an inevitable product of the social structure.

4. For other explanations of this identification, see Robert B. Heilman, "The Criminal as Tragic Hero: Dramatic Methods," in *Aspects of Macbeth*, ed. Kenneth Muir and Phillip Edwards (Cambridge: Cambridge University Press, 1977), pp. 26–38; Ivor Morris, *Shakespeare's God* (London: George Allen and Unwin, 1972), p. 310; and Muir, "Introduction" to the Arden *Macbeth* (London: Methuen, 1951), pp. l and lvi. For another comparison of Richard III's and Macbeth's talionic punishments, see E. M. W. Tillyard, *Shakespeare's History Plays* (London: Chatto and Windus, 1951), pp. 315–318.

5. Alexander Ross, *Mystagogus Poeticus* (London, 1648), p. 288, made King Midas a figuration of "the folly and madnesse of some mens wishes, who pray many times for that which proves their destruction."

6. Bruno Bettelheim, *The Uses of Enchantment* (New York: Random House, 1977), p. 72.

7. "An Homily Against Disobedience and Wilful Rebellion" in *Sermons*, pp. 630–631, argues that "he that nameth Rebellion nameth not a singular or only sin, as is theft, robbery, murther, and such like ... all sins, I say, against God, and all men heaped together nameth he, that nameth Rebellion."

8. *Hamlet*, 2.2.529–30, 3.1.121–23. Compare Aristotle's argument that culpability attaches to intentions only when they are accompanied by acts, with Christ's warning that any man who lusts after a woman in his heart is committing adultery, and that any man who hates his brother is committing murder (Matthew 5:21–28). The potential destructiveness of efficacious thought has been largely the realm of fairy-tale and science-fiction writers: see Jerome Bixby's "It's a Good Life," in which the power belongs to an irresponsible boy, and Ursula LeGuin's *The Lathe of Heaven*, in which the power belongs to dreams that change into nightmares.

9. The doctrine of equivocation depends (like Macbeth's fate) on blurring the distinction between the outwardly expressed and the merely thought. A Jesuit might avoid self-incrimination, without breaking a holy oath to tell the truth, by speaking words acceptable to his inquisitors, but continuing mentally, audibly only to God, with additional words that brought the spoken words into line with his actual heretical beliefs or disloyal intentions. See Lawrence Danson, *Tragic Alphabet* (New Haven: Yale University Press, 1974), pp. 132–135; Muir, "Introduction," pp. xvii–xxi; and Steven Mullaney, "Lying Like Truth," *ELH* 47 (1980), 39–40.

10. Samuel Gardiner, *Portraiture of the Prodigal Sonne* (London, 1599), pp. 33, 111; Nehemiah Rogers, *The True Convert* (London, 1620), p. 77, writes that "God doth often punish sin in it owne kinde"; see also Richard Brathwait, "The Prodigals Glasse," in Patrick Hannay, *A Happy Husband* (London, 1618), sig. 15v; John Newnham, *Newnams Nightcrowe* (London, 1590), p. 5; Thomas Ingeland, *The Disobedient Child*, in *The Dramatic Writings of Richard Wever and Thomas Ingeland*, ed. John Farmer (London: Early English Drama Society, 1905), pp. 68–69; and Shakespeare's *Rape of Lucrece*, line 128.

11. Brathwait, "Prodigals Glasse," sig. 17. 12. Bettelheim, *Enchantment*, p. 70.

13. Wilbur Sanders, *The Dramatist and the Received Idea* (London: Cambridge University Press, 1968), p. 268, remarks on the phallic attributes of Lady Macbeth's fantasy here.

14. Caroline Spurgeon, *Shakespeare's Imagery* (1935; rpt. Boston: Beacon Hill, 1958), pp. 329–331, remarks on night's suppression of daylight, but treats it as an allegory of evil's suppression of good, rather than as a significant violation of cyclical nature. Political

rebellion similarly provokes night to rebel against its obligation to yield to day in Thomas May's 1631 translation of Lucan's *Pharsalia*, book 6, sig. K6v.

15. D.A. Traversi, *An Approach to Shakespeare*, 2nd ed. (New York: Doubleday, 1956), p. 159, observes "the light which radiates from the royal figure of Duncan." See *Richard II*, 3.3.63, 179; *Merchant of Venice*, 5.1.94; and *Henry VIII*, 1.5.56, for examples of this standard metaphor.

16. A similar conflation occurs in the myth of Icarus; see Ross, *Mystagogus*, pp. 87, 361. Charles Masinton, *Christopher Marlowe's Tragic Vision* (Athens, Ohio: Ohio University Press, 1972), p. 130, suggests that Marlowe portrays "the primal sin" of "characters who destroy or disregard their heritage ... and try instead to become monarchs of realms that do not belong to them. They are jealous of the light, but in trying to usurp the glory of the sun they burn their wings and fall to their deaths." Much the same moral, and the same mythic referents, could be adduced to Macbeth's fall.

17. Michel de Montaigne, "Of the custom of wearing clothes," in *The Complete Essays of Montaigne*, trans. Donald M. Frame (Stanford: Stanford University Press, 1975), p. 167.

18. Sigmund Freud, A *General Introduction to Psychoanalysis*, trans. Joan Riviere (New York: Permabooks, 1953), p. 153.

19. Sir William Cornwallis, *Essayes* (London, 1606), sig. 18r, comments that "sleepe is to me in the nature that Dung is to Ground"; Rogers, *True Convert*, p. 299, describes sleep as the life-giving "dew of nature" for both soul and body.

20. Quoted by Norman Holland, *Psychoanalysis and Shakespeare* (New York: McGraw-Hill, 1964), p. 220.

21. Ibid., p. 221; see also his p. 225.

22. Sigmund Freud, in the Standard Edition of his *Works*, trans. James Strachey, XVIII (London: Hogarth Press, 1955), 136.

23. Holland, *Psychoanalysis and Shakespeare*, p. 219; see also Irving Ribner, "*Macbeth*: The Pattern of Idea and Action," *Shakespeare Quarterly* 10 (1959) 150.

24. See for example Dennis Biggins, "Sexuality, Witchcraft, and Violence in *Macbeth*," *Shakespeare Studies* 8 (1975), 255, 264–266.

25. Coppélia Kahn, *Man's Estate* (Berkeley: University of California Press, 1981), p. 178.

26. Eric Partridge, *Shakespeare's Bawdy* (London: Routledge and Kegan Paul, 1968), mentions some examples in his entries under "act" (p. 56) and "do it" (p. 95).

27. The Oedipal character of the crime is suggested in other, more allusive ways, mostly by the guilty couple themselves. On the night of the regicide (2.2), Lady Macbeth is almost paralyzed by Duncan's resemblance to her father, and by the typical Oedipal fear that "Th'attempt and not the deed / Confounds us"; she then warns her brooding husband as Jocasta warned hers: "Consider it not so deeply" (2.2.9–29). But Macbeth, reading his sins in his palms, cries out, "What hands are here? Hah! They pluck out mine eyes"; "To know my deed," he adds, "'twere best not know myself," which is at least as true for Oedipus as it is for Macbeth. The witches also resemble Jocasta in admonishing Macbeth to "Seek to know no more" about the riddling prophecy by which he rose to power, and the ominous prophecy, linked in unspoken ways to the first one, by which he is fated to fall. When he insists on and receives an answer, he finds it "does sear mine eyeballs" (4.1.103–13). Macbeth is thus well-suited to teach Scotland's young men "What 'twere to kill a father" (3.6.3–20).

28. Richard Jonas, *The Byrth of Mankynde* (trans. from Eucharius Roesslin, *De partu hominis*), rev. and ed. Thomas Raynold (London, 1545), I, fol. 9v; cited by Jenijoy La Belle, "'A Strange Infirmity': Lady Macbeth's Amenorrhea," *Shakespeare Quarterly* 31 (1980), 382.

29. Thomas R. Forbes, *The Midwife and the Witch* (New Haven: Yale University Press, 1966, p. 127 and passim.

30. Lucien Goldmann, *The Hidden God*, trans. Philip Thody (London: Routledge and Kegan Paul, 1964, p. 44.

31. Claude Lévi-Strauss, *The Scope of Anthropology*, trans. Sherry Ortner Paul and Robert A. Paul (London: Jonathan Cape, 1967, pp. 35–39.

32. Willard Farnham, *The Medieval Heritage of Elizabethan Tragedy* (Berkeley: University of California Press, 1936, p. 407; cf. Sanders, p. 282.

33. Edward Forset, *A Comparative Discourse of the Bodies Natural and Politique* (London, 1606), p. 64.

34. La Belle, in *Shakespeare Quarterly* 31: 381–386; as she points out, this disruption of the menstrual flow "is tantamount to murdering infants—albeit unborn," and thus "destroys the lineal flow," making Lady Macbeth analogous to Rosse's Scotland, not the mother of a new generation but instead its grave. The rebirth of Macbeth, then, entails a biological event that reveals how opposed ambitious alterations are to natural fertility.

35. Sigmund Freud, *Collected Papers*, trans. Joan Riviere et al. (London: Hogarth Press, 1934), IV, 330; see also Holland, *Psychoanalysis and Shakespeare*, p. 66, on the ways "other analysts, notably Ludwig Jekels," develop Freud's idea; and Janet Adelman, *The Common Liar* (New Haven: Yale University Press, 1973), p. 7.

36. L.C. Knights, "How Many Children Had Lady Macbeth?" rpt. in *Modern Shakespearean Criticism*, ed. Alvin B. Kernan (New York: Harcourt Brace, 1970, pp. 45–76. Edgar Allan Poe's short piece on "The Characters of Shakespeare" makes an argument similar to Knights's.

37. Sanders, *Dramatist*, p. 263, describes Macduff's responsibility for his own loss of family as unmistakable yet oddly undefined. Holland, *Psychoanalysis and Shakespeare*, p. 222, reports one psychoanalytic reading in which "Macduff proves again, in the logic of the unconscious, that 'the bad son makes a bad father.'"

38. Harvey Graham, *The Story of Surgery* (New York: Doubleday, 1939), p. 375.

39. For a discussion of such sacrificial practices, particularly as they relate to tragedy, see René Girard, *Violence and the Sacred*, trans. Patrick Gregory (Baltimore: Johns Hopkins University Press, 1977), passim. Macduff may also serve as society's pristine agent against the threat of Oedipal rebirth embodied by Macbeth. Victor Calef, "Lady Macbeth and Infanticide," *Journal of the American Psychoanalytic Association* 17 (1969), 537 n. 10, points out that his Caesarean birth leaves Macduff miraculously free from the taint of having entered his mother's genital passages even once. See also Holland, *Psychoanalysis and Shakespeare*, p. 227.

40. Cleanth Brooks, "The Naked Babe and the Cloak of Manliness," rpt. in Kernan, *Modern Shakespearean Criticism*, pp. 385–403, discusses the peculiar strength of these babes. Cf. Philostratus the Elder, *Les Images ou Tableaux de Platte Peinture*, trans. B. de Vigenère (Paris, 1629, p. 480, which captions a drawing of "Hercules Among the Pygmies" with a moral applicable to *Macbeth*: "C'est un mal heur extreme / De s'ignorer soymesme, / Un Geant triomphant / Est bravé d'un enfant."

41. Holland, *Psychoanalysis and Shakespeare*, p. 219.

42. Francis M. Comford, *From Religion to Philosophy* (New York: Longmans, Green and Co., 1912, p. 5. Brathwait's "Prodigals Glasse," sig. 17v, uses the family-tree metaphor to warn about a similar cluster of dangers.

43. John Upton, *Critical Observations on Shakespeare* (London: G. Hawkins, 1746, p. 39 n. 17.

44. This massive deforestation regained momentum when the exhaustion of English

forests led the iron smelters to Scotland, where they built their first large furnace at the same time Shakespeare was writing *Macbeth*. See R.N. Millman, *The Making of the Scottish Landscape* (London: B.T. Batsford, 1975), pp. 48–49, 63, 86–87, 101.

45. M. Karl Simrock, *On the Plots of Shakespeare's Plays* (London: Shakespeare Society, 1850), first suggested this identification, and Jekels used it in his "The Riddle of Shakespeare's *Macbeth*" (1943), rpt. in *The Design Within*, ed. M.D. Faber (New York: Science House, 1970), pp. 235–249.

46. Quoted by Charles Trinkaus, *"In Our Image and Likeness"* (London: Constable, 19700, 194.

47. Ernst Cassirer, *The Individual and the Cosmos in Renaissance Philosophy*, trans. Mario Domandi (New York: Harper and Row, 1964), pp. 90–91; see similarly Trinkaus, *"In Our Image,"* I, xxii. Joan Webber, *The Eloquent "I"* (Milwaukee: University of Wisconsin Press, 1968), p. 10, sees an analogous principle emerging in Anglican prose: "To turn oneself into art is only to become more fully realized." Even the Puritans, though less sympathetic to art as a moral tool, developed an ethic of perpetual self-recreation; Michael Walzer, *The Revolution of the Saints* (Cambridge: Harvard University Press, 1965), p. 311, observes that "The old order was imagined to be natural and eternal," but that for the Puritan revolutionaries, virtue and social health must be "the product of art and will, of human doing."

48. Hans Jonas, *The Gnostic Religion* (Boston: Beacon Press, 1963), pp. 250, 328.

49. Trinkaus, *"In Our Image,"* I, 184, describes a similarly divided father-figure in the theology of Philo Judaeus, who "believes man's creation was shared by God with ... lower creators [who] gave man his lower and potentially sinful portions."

50. Jonas, *Gnostic Religion*, p. 195; on abjuring procreation, see p. 168, also pp. 59, 145; on mistrusting sleep, see pp. 44–45; on the Call away from the mortal self and toward "rebirth" through the Mother-Wisdom, see p. 45. This concept of human alienation from nature was certainly active in Shakespeare's time. Jonas, p. 323, discerns a version of Gnosticism in Descartes' view of man: "As he shares no longer in a meaning of nature, but merely, through his body, in its mechanical determination, so nature no longer shares his inner concerns. Thus that by which man is superior to all nature, his unique distinction, mind, no longer results in a higher integration of his being into the totality of being, but on the contrary marks the unbridgeable gulf between himself and the rest of existence." In fact, this mental Call away from sleep and away from the hereditary self has revealing analogues in English Romantic thought. Harold Bloom, "The Internalization of Quest-Romance," in *Romanticism and Consciousness*, ed. Bloom (New York: Norton, 1970), p. 6, speaks of "a baffled residue of the self, determined to be compensated for its loss of natural assurance, for having been awakened from the merely given condition that to Shelley, as to Blake, was but the sleep of death-in-life." The point is not that these Romantics were secretly Gnostics, or that Shakespeare was; the point instead is that certain metaphors have repeatedly presented themselves to great fiction-makers over the centuries when they have sought to describe an intuited need for transmundane fulfillment, to articulate that need's moral ambiguities, and to explain the peculiar burdens of self-consciousness it evokes.

51. Richard Brathwait, *The Prodigals Teares* (London, 1614), p. 70.

52. Rogers, *True Convert*, p. 289.

53. John Peter Camus, *Admirable Events*, trans. S. du Verger (London, 1639), p. 223.

54. As the ambiguities about Lady Macbeth's children and Macduff's motives serve Shakespeare's orthodox moral, the slight ambiguity about the propriety of Malcolm's nomination helps sustain the contrary, subversive moral. It leaves unclear, without imputing any wrongdoing to Duncan, whether Macbeth's resistance constitutes an

unjustified and suicidal defiance of a unified natural and political order, or a noble assertion of individual rights. For the debate about the proper succession, see Elizabeth Neilsen, "*Macbeth*: The Nemesis of the Post-Shakespearian Actor," *Shakespeare Quarterly* 16 (1965), 193–199; and Michael Echeruo, "Tanistry, the 'Due of Birth' and Macbeth's Sin," *Shakespeare Quarterly* 23 (1972), 444–450. On the significance of Banquo's "harvest" reference, see Berger, in *ELH* 47:21.

55. Muir, note to 2.3.15 in the Arden *Macbeth* (pp. 61–62).

56. Pelagius, quoted in *The Anti-Pelagian Works*, II, 19, 58, in *The Works of Aurelius Augustine*, vol. XII, ed. Marcus Dods (Edinburgh, 1885): "we have implanted in us by God a possibility for acting in both directions. It resembles, as I may say, a root which is most abundant in its produce of fruit. It yields and produces diversely according to man's will ... Nothing good, and nothing evil, on account of which we are deemed either laudable or blameworthy, is born with us, but is done by us." Pico, the most prominent advocate of self-perfectibility in philosophy, as Pelagius is in theology, uses the seedling metaphor similarly. His "Oration on the Dignity of Man," trans. Elizabeth Forbes, in *The Renaissance Philosophy of Man*, ed. Cassirer et al. (Chicago: University of Chicago Press, 1948), p. 225, declares, "On man when he came into life the Father conferred the seeds of all kinds and the germs of every way of life. Whatever seeds each man cultivates will grow to maturity and bear in him their own fruit." Sir Walter Raleigh, *The History of the World*, ed. C.A. Patrides (London: Macmillan, 1971), p. 130, writes that "God gave unto man all kinde of seedes and grafts of life ... whereof which soever he tooke pleasure to plant and cultive, the same should futurely grow in him, and bring forth fruit, agreable to his owne choyce and plantation."

Iago tells Roderigo that "'tis in ourselves that we are thus or thus. Our bodies are our gardens, to the which our wills are gardeners" (*Othello*, 1.3.319–26). Banquo, in treating even this selectivity as an impious resistance to a divine order, seems closer to Philo's Stoic attitude toward ambitious projects, as Jonas, *Gnostic Religion*, p. 279, describes it: "Rather than modes of self-perfection, they are temptations by the fact that they can be taken as such ... 'Since it is God who sows and plants the goods in the soul, it is impious of the nous to say, I plant.' Alternatively, the soul may renounce the claim to its own authorship and acknowledge its essential insufficiency—and this ... general attitude ... is *itself considered as 'virtue,'* although it is the denial of there being any virtue of the self." Although Shakespeare makes it clear that the seed of Macbeth's ambitious crime lies dormant in Banquo, the decision as to which man will perform it, like the decision "which grain will grow, and which will not," seems more a mystery of divine election than an act of individual will.

57. Ben Jonson, *Discoveries*, in *Ben Jonson*, ed. C.H. Herford and Percy and Evelyn Simpson (Oxford: Clarendon Press, 1947), VIII, 599.

KAY STOCKHOLDER

'Blanket of the Dark':
Stealthy Lovers in Macbeth

M acbeth storms the barricade Othello attempted, seizes the woman with whose help he crowns himself king of the nightmare realm on the margins of which Hamlet delayed. By defining himself as husband, Macbeth becomes conscious of the emotions and associations that other protagonists avoided. In the process he creates a polarity between domestic and social harmony and sexual passion. Rather than being the source of procreation and love, Macbeth's relation to his wife is fulfilled in the murder of Duncan, who represents for Macbeth legitimate authority, gentle fathering, maternal nurturing, social accord, and childlike trust. His murder constitutes a psychological holocaust that is also the climax of Macbeth's erotic passions.

Macbeth is not only pervaded by dreamlike occurrences, but Macbeth experiences himself in a dreamlike state. As a consequence of the different level of dreaming involved, this play more explicitly than others involves connections between internal and external experience. The introductory sequence of action parallels the full sequence of earlier plays in which the protagonist comes to experience as emotions what previously he confronted as external circumstance. But most of the action reverses that process to render a figure transforming his own dreamlike state into what he later confronts as external reality.[1]

The world Macbeth inhabits contains, besides himself, only three

From *Dream Works: Lovers and Families in Shakespeare's Plays.* ©1987 University of Toronto Press.

defined figures, two of whom he eliminates in short order. The remaining figures with whom he peoples his world, all in some degree shadowlike, fall into two categories. Those relatively realistic but thinly characterized fissures who extend from Banquo and who slowly become inimical to Macbeth represent royal authority. The other more dreamlike figures extend from Lady Macbeth to seduce Macbeth into the depths of nightmare. They include the witches, Hecate, and, in the imagery, the country itself as well as the owls, rooks, ravens, and all the extensions of Lady Macbeth's language that compose almost the entire lurid landscape on which Macbeth moves, more real to him than the pallid remnants of the more present-oriented figures.

We encounter Macbeth in a state of transition, indicated by the male figures who acclaim him as 'Valour's minion' (I.ii.76) in images of violence and blood and those who couple his name with that of the traitor thane of Cawdor. Both Cawdor's treason and the blood of battle are associated with Macbeth's role as husband when he is called 'Bellona's bridegroom.' The drama of Macbeth's emerging redefinition of himself is enacted when Duncan gives Cawdor's title to Macbeth while he reflects that 'There's no art / To find the mind's construction in the face: / He was a gentleman on whom I built / An absolute trust' (I.iv.11–14). Macbeth momentarily resists donning the 'borrowed robes' of Cawdor's treachery, but his inner readiness generates the witches' prophecies. In the 'horrible imaginings' that appear to his inner eye instead of images of the 'imperial theme,' he reveals that his desire to kill Duncan, only vaguely suggested before, has suddenly coalesced into an identification of himself with Cawdor's treachery.[2] Cawdor's defection was as mysterious to him as is the image of Duncan murdered by his own hand that fills his inner vision and obscures what previously constituted both his external reality and his self-definition, so that now 'nothing is but what is not.'

Macbeth's previous and fading self-definition appears in his characterization of and relation to Duncan. Duncan as king occupies a paternal realm, which Macbeth emphasizes when he says, 'our duties / Are to your throne and state, children and servants; / Which do but what they should, by doing everything / Safe toward your love and honour' (I.iv.24–7). Duncan's paternal role, which Lady Macbeth emphasizes when she says that the sleeping Duncan reminds her of her father, also appears in Duncan's praise of Macbeth's heroism: 'The sin of my ingratitude even now / Was heavy on me,' and 'More is thy due than more than all can pay' (I.iv.15–16, 21). Duncan's lament that he cannot adequately reward Macbeth becomes ironic when Duncan in the next breath names Malcolm as successor to the throne. In a subtle way Macbeth casts himself as a slighted 'worthiest cousin' rather than eldest son. In doing so he expresses his feeling that he is unworthy of the mantle of authority, and he fuels a sense of grievance that derives from his having interpreted as betrayal his ambition for paternal authority and the maturity it represents. Hearing himself praised as his country's saviour is then a strategy by which he justifies the betrayal that is already taking shape.[3] Already hidden within the initial configuration is the image of himself as a 'dwarfish thief' in the process of acquiring a 'giant's robe' (V.ii.21–2).[4]

However, the paternal image that excites Macbeth's divided feelings carries distinctly maternal colouring, in a way that makes more explicit Hamlet's merger of maternal and paternal figures. In praising Macbeth, Duncan says, 'I have begun to plant thee, and will labour / To make thee full of growing,' and wishes to 'bind us further to you' (I.iv.28–9, 43). Even while Macbeth reflects on his 'black and deep desires,' Duncan associates himself with nurturing and food: 'he is full so valiant, / And in his commendations I am fed; / It is a banquet to me' (I.iv.51, 54–6). The association of Duncan with nurturing fertility is elaborated when he approaches Macbeth's castle: 'This castle hath a pleasant seat; the air / Nimbly and sweetly recommends itself / Unto our gentle senses' (I.vi.1–3). While Macbeth plans to murder Duncan as king and father, he surrounds him with an aura of creaturely warmth.

The only figure with whom Macbeth identifies is Banquo. They are companions in battle, in encountering the witches, and in earning Duncan's praises. Macbeth completes the isolation of himself and Lady Macbeth when he moves Banquo into Duncan's orbit by associating him with the images of children from which he begins to remove himself. After the witches vanish Macbeth observes that Banquo's 'children shall be kings,' and immediately upon learning that he is thane of Cawdor he says, 'Do you not hope your children shall be kings' (I.iii.86, 118). Macbeth's association of Banquo with children also associates him with Duncan, who, after having promised to make Macbeth 'grow,' has more intimate words for Banquo: 'let me enfold thee, / And hold thee to my heart' (I.iv.31–2). Banquo becomes for Macbeth a figure fused with Malcolm as a more legitimate successor than he to the mantle of authority, when Banquo adds to Duncan's praises of Macbeth's castle his observation that

> The temple-haunting martlet, does approve,
> By his loved mansionry, that the heaven's breath
> Smells wooingly here: no jutty, frieze,
> Buttress, nor coign of vantage, but this bird
> Hath made his pendent bed, and procreant cradle:
> Where they most breed and haunt, I have observ'd
> The air is delicate.   (I.vi.4–10)

His association of Macbeth's castle, within which Macbeth and Lady Macbeth plan a different kind of birth, with images of fertility and tender nurturing contrasts this external image of Lady Macbeth to her interior, which she describes in a different bird image when she says, 'The raven himself is hoarse / That croaks the fatal entrance of Duncan / Under my battlements' (I.v.38–40). Macbeth generates the two opposed images of femininity; he espouses the latter but distantly expresses in Banquo's words haunting regret for the realm of nurture, fidelity, affection, and procreation, which is for him in opposition to his marital intimacy with Lady Macbeth.

Having defined his desires for becoming father and king as illegitimate, Macbeth has reversed the classical Oedipal paradigm in which the son in order to marry the mother wishes to kill the father. Rather, he has married the mother, and included the implied sexuality in the project of killing the father. Becoming Bellona's bridegroom meant for him forgoing Banquo's 'bosom franchis'd, and allegiance clear' (II.1.28), and eating of the 'insane root, / That takes the reason prisoner' (I.iii.84–5), so that he may with her aid enter, as Hamlet did not, the Vulcan's stithy of his own imagination.

Macbeth's attitudes towards women appear first in the figures of the witches and Hecate. As non-realistic figures they represent emotions from past configurations that have not been integrated into present circumstances. The sense of depth in this play derives largely from these figures and the resonant imagery that surrounds them and spreads to other figures. Unlike most plays, *Macbeth* contains no reference to any circumstance or event prior to the action we witness, but the sense of pastness is suggested by the entranced or dreamlike state into which the witches draw Macbeth. In their first appearance, remote from himself, Macbeth reveals the feelings he has aroused in himself in the process of casting himself as husband. Their plan to waylay him expresses his fear of women's devious strategies, and the surrounding 'fog and filthy air' expresses his moral confusion in which 'fair is foul, and foul is fair.' He casts himself as the object of women's nefarious designs, and in interpreting these women, most unseductive in appearance, as preternatural, he reveals the gap between his self-conception and the seductive desires that have generated these fateful figures. In the image of the 'blasted heath' on which they appear Macbeth associates women with all that is the reverse of the gentle nurturing suggested in the images with which Banquo and Duncan describe the exterior of Macbeth's castle.[5] That the first and second appearances of the witches sandwich the voices that declare his martial heroism suggests that these bubbles of the earth are the opposite side of the coin on which is stamped his self-image as bloodily heroic.

The meaning of the witches for Macbeth unfolds later in the action as more associations cluster around them. Through their relation to Hecate they are associated with murder, but more important, despite his initial revulsion, Macbeth links them to the sensuous images with which he anticipates murdering Banquo when he says,

> Ere the bat hath flown
> His cloister'd flight; ere to black Hecate's summons
> The shard-born beetle, with his drowsy hums,
> Hath rung Night's yawning peal, there shall be done
> A deed of dreadful note.   (III.ii.40–4)

These images of the night creatures that are radically opposed to legitimate daylight activities evoke a kind of dark ease that overwhelms and cancels the moral horror that is the overt content. Macbeth savours the theoretically horrifying deed when he continues, 'Light thickens; and the crow / Makes wing to th'rooky wood; / Good things of Day begin to droop and drowse, / Whiles Night's black agents to their preys do rouse' (III.ii.49–52). The language with which he invokes Hecate associates sensuous darkness with moral outrage ('Fair is foul and foul is fair') and adds a more specifically sexual note when 'Night's ... agents' rouse their prey. These lines that precede Banquo's murder show Macbeth swooning into an anticipation of erotic violence that he interprets as supernaturally induced.

In the witches and Hecate Macbeth evokes a distanced and diabolically defined version of an offended mother. Hecate scolds the witches like erring daughters, Macbeth's sisters rather than his mother, and sounds like a neglected and resentful parent when she rebukes them for having favoured 'a wayward son, / Spiteful, and wrathful; who, as others do, / Loves for his own ends, not for you' (III.v.11–15).[6] In Hecate's words Macbeth expresses his sense of himself using women for his own ends, and of them in reprisal manipulating him through an equivocal seduction that will 'palter with us in a double sense, / That keep the word of promise to our ear, / And break it to our hope' (V.viii.20–2). All of the images that compose these remote actualizations of feminine figures are also associated with Lady Macbeth.[7] These unrealistic and dreamlike forms in their wavering reality and supernatural attributes depict emotional components from a past or infantile level out of which Macbeth assembles the more present figure that he espouses in his wife. Her figure merges with theirs when she awaits Duncan as the witches did Macbeth, and calls upon the spirits that 'tend on mortal thoughts' to

> unsex me here,
> And fill me, from the crown to the toe, top-full

Of direst cruelty! make thick my blood,
Stop up th'access and passage to remorse;
That no compunctious visitings of Nature
Shake my fell purpose, nor keep peace between
Th'effect and it! Come to my woman's breasts,
And take my milk for gall, you murth'ring ministers,
Wherever in your sightless substances
You wait on Nature's mischief! Come, thick Night,
And pall thee in the dunnest smoke of Hell,
That my keen knife see not the wound it makes,
Nor Heaven peep through the blanket of the dark,
To cry, 'Hold, hold!'   (I.v.39–53)

The images of 'thick night' and 'dunnest smoke of Hell' recall the earlier 'fog and filthy air,' and the croaking raven is the first of the crows, owls, bats, and rooks that reach deep into the later murky depths. Lady Macbeth's desire that 'direst cruelty' should fill her 'from the crown to the toe' recalls the figure that Macbeth 'unseam'd ... from the nave to th'chops' (I.ii.22), and 'make thick my blood' leads to the images of blood that flow through the play. More explicitly than the witches, she opposes herself to the nurturing that defines Duncan. Banquo will grow in Duncan's bosom, but no nourishment will flow from her breasts, and in wanting freedom from any 'compunctious visitings of Nature,' she relates herself to the barren infertility of the 'blasted heath.'[8]

Her scorn of the weak, milky-natured nurturing aspect of Macbeth, which is associated with the benign and foolishly trusting Duncan, extends through associated images to infants and mothers. She separates children from the sexuality that generates them by relating sexuality to her murderous desire that Duncan, who reminds her of her father, should pass beneath her battlements. The raven that will herald him, along with bats, beetles, rooks, is associated with owls when Lady Macbeth says during the murder, 'It was the owl that shriek'd, the fatal bellman, / Which gives the stern'st goodnight' (II.ii.3–4). Lady Macduff, blaming Macduff for leaving his family unprotected, says, 'for the poor wren / The most diminutive of birds, will fight / Her young ones in her nest, against the owl' (IV.ii.9–11). Macbeth himself becomes the child-killing owl when Macduff says, 'O Hell-kite! All? / What, all my pretty chickens, and their dam, / At one fell swoop?' (IV.iii.219–21). Ross and the Old Man include in the portents on the night of the murder 'A falcon, towering in her pride of place, / Was by a mousing owl hawk'd at and kill'd' (II.iv.12–13). Since a falcon image underlies Macbeth's invocation, 'Come, seeling Night / Scarf up the tender eye of pitiful Day /

And with thy bloody and invisible hand / Cancel, and tear to pieces, that great bond / Which keeps me pale!' (III.ii.47–50), the falcon killed by the mousing owl comes to represent a fusion of regal pride with infantile tenderness and pity. Though a prideful falcon may seem an unlikely image for an infant, it coheres with Macbeth's image of pity, like a new-born babe, riding the blasts. These clustering images, which are implied in Lady Macbeth's croaking raven, fuse infanticide into the aura of erotic violence in which Duncan's murder is anticipated.

Lady Macbeth's denied maternity is associated with perverse sexuality— through another cluster of images that relates her to the witches, and casts Macbeth as child to her. On the witches' second appearance, one says that she has been 'killing swine' (I.iii.2), and when Macbeth wishes to consult the witches' masters the witch says to pour in their cauldron 'sow's blood, that hath eaten / Her nine farrow' (IV.i.64–5). Lady Macbeth, when planning the murder with Macbeth, says that when Duncan's attendants are 'in swinish sleep / Their drenched natures lie, as in a death, / What cannot you and I perform upon / Th'unguarded Duncan?' She calls them 'spongy officers' (I.vii.68–71, 73), and while she awaits Macbeth's return she says, 'The surfeited grooms / Do mock their charge with snores' (II.i.5–6). Her scorn is a bit unjust, since it was she who 'drugged their possets,' but the image of swinish sleep merges with that of drunkenness. She associates swinishness with drink and sleep, and connects the grooms to her revulsion at Macbeth's softer nature when she rebukes him, 'Was the hope drunk, / Wherein you dress'd yourself? Hath it slept since' (I.vii.35–6). When she says that Duncan's resemblance to her father stopped her hand, she responds lovingly to that maternally tinged father image, but that image merges with those of the swinish grooms who arouse her murderous revulsion, so that she can without difficulty smear their faces with Duncan's blood. Through Lady Macbeth, Macbeth expresses his fear of woman's scorn for male passivity, seen as swinishly sodden.

A more specific form of the implied sexual impotence is evoked through the Porter, who is a version of Hamlet's grave-diggers. Though more remote from Macbeth's consciousness than is the grave-digger scene from Hamlet's, like the grave-diggers, the Porter's grotesque comedy makes explicit what is elsewhere vaguely implied when the Porter says, 'Much drink may be said to be an equivocator with lechery: it makes him, and it mars him; it sets him on, and it takes him off; it persuades him, and disheartens him; makes him stand to, and not stand to: in conclusion, equivocates him in a sleep, and, giving him the lie, leaves him' (II.iii.30–5). The parallels between equivocating drink, the equivocating witches, and Lady Macbeth's equivocating femininity as expressed in the opposing images of her castle relate Macbeth's experience of feminine duplicity to male impotence, explicitly associated in the Porter's words with the drunken swinishness of the sleeping grooms. That image completes an emotional circle in which Macbeth defines women as cruel and mocking, fears them therefore, joins them in order to safeguard himself and to use them against paternal authority, in the process wedding aggression to eroticism and becoming impotent in ordinary ways. As a consequence, he fears even more the mocking voices of women.[9]

Lady Macbeth also shares her ambiguous sexual definition with the witches, whose beards cast doubt on their sex, and with Duncan, who carries feminine attributes. She asks to be unsexed, and she imagines herself in a sexually dominant role when she wants to 'pour my spirits in thine ear, / And chastise with the valour of my tongue / All that impedes thee from the golden round' (I.v.26–8), and in her attribution to Macbeth of the 'milk of human kindness' that she denies in herself. Her language binds in a single cluster images of denied nurturing, barrenness, cruelty, and role reversal, and joins that cluster to an aura of sexualized violence when she desires that Heaven not 'peep through the blanket of the dark' to see the wound made by her 'keen knife.' Her words, ringing in the same register as Macbeth's, 'let that be, / Which the eye fears, when it is done, to see' (I.iv.52–3), gather and focus the implications that have already shadowed his figure.

In Lady Macbeth Macbeth has wedded himself to a figure on whom he projects his own eroticized violence, with all the related ideas that are suggested by the imagistic associations that condition the language of the entire play. But he also projects onto her the spurs 'to prick the sides of [his] intent' (I.vii.26), so that he may experience himself in part as passive to women's force ('he loves for his own ends / Not for you'). Despite the many images and structural forms that relate Lady Macbeth to the witches and Hecate, she is on a different dream level from the other feminine figures. Like a dream figure who appears identical to one in waking life, she carries a full sense of present reality. Macbeth, at whatever cost, has generated a female figure who complements his own, and has succeeded in envisioning a mutually loving relationship, though the nature of the shared enterprise that defines their love also carries back to the more dreamlike experiences from which these dark lovers and childless parents have arisen.[10] As their relationship takes shape it also brings to a more presently defined adult level the full implications of the surrounding suggestiveness. Therefore I will consider some of the passages already discussed in that more adult context in order to see how the associations from a deeper past, suggested by the more fantastic configurations, shape Macbeth's love for his wife.

The letter Macbeth writes to Lady Macbeth in its suggestive brevity reveals an intimacy that substantiates the lovingness expressed in its close: 'This have I thought good to deliver thee (my dearest partner of greatness) that thou might'st not lose the dues of rejoicing, by being ignorant of what greatness is promis'd thee' (I.v.10–14). Their loving intimacy is further suggested by her instant intuition of Macbeth's excited fear, and her similar assumption that circumstances alone will not fulfil the witches' prophecy. As Macbeth immediately envisioned Duncan's murder rather than himself enthroned, so she will 'catch the nearest way.' She surrounds the projected murder with perverse sexual intimacy, and associates her genitals with cruelty when she imagines Duncan entering her castle. She turns impulses of 'compunctious tenderness' to 'murthering ministers,' and evokes tender sexual feelings, associates them with mothering, and negates them even as they arise when she asks them to 'take my milk for gall.' She equates Duncan's murder with rejecting both her own normal sexuality and mothering. Macbeth expresses his desire to kill Duncan through the image of her cruelty, giving her the 'keen knife' that will make the death wound beneath the 'blanket of the dark' in the atmosphere of an intimate sexuality. A vague image of a sexual act begins to form, in which the hostility Macbeth feels for the paternal Duncan imbues his imagination of woman's violence. But he also associates himself with Duncan remotely when Lady Macbeth describes his nature as full of the 'milk of human kindness,' so that the anticipated murder includes an image of himself as passive victim of her sexualized violence.[11]

When Macbeth enters this aura of perverse sexuality she tells him that, having been transported by his letter beyond the ignorant present, she feels 'the future in the instant.' The previously denied procreative power now generates images of power in her allusion to his new title, which promises him the throne. Macbeth defines his love within his wife's unspoken thought when he responds, 'My dearest love, / Duncan comes here to-night' (I.v.57–8): The mutually intuitive understanding of their exchange drains the impact from Macbeth's vacillating demur 'We will speak further' (I.v.71). The accord of her mind to his shows that in writing to her he relied on her resolve to steady his, a naturalistic extension of what the images have suggested, and so in his passivity to her he can 'wrongly win' that which he would not 'play false' to attain.

Their relationship to each other provides a rhythm by which each excites the other to the point of action. The first movement occurred in Macbeth's sending the letter, in Lady Macbeth's response, and in his collusive reaction to her. The second begins when Macbeth for a moment enters a meditation, like that of Hamlet, on this 'bank and shoal of time' between life and death. Like Hamlet, he shrinks from the dreams that may arise in the 'undiscover'd country' (*Hamlet*, III.i.79) of the 'life to come' that he cannot jump. But Macbeth has defined himself as Claudius rather than Hamlet, and so envisions himself as victim rather than instrument of the 'even-handed justice [that] / Commends th'ingredience of our poison'd chalice / To our own lips' (I.vii.10–12). That thought rouses his more filial feelings as Duncan's 'kinsman and his subject,' as well as his host. The image of himself as host arouses his protective feelings so that he envisions himself guarding the gentle Duncan, who has 'borne his faculties so meek.' From that double image of gentleness violated is born the image of 'Pity, like a naked new-born babe, / Striding the blast,' riding the winds in vengeance against him, before which he falls back from his 'vaulting ambition.' But even as he generates an image of a natural child, he turns it against himself, for he has already chosen his Gertrude and eliminated any Ophelia against whom to unpack his heart with words.

As previously Macbeth came, as though called, at the end of Lady Macbeth's soliloquy, now she comes, as though called, to do in fact what she and Macbeth had anticipated she would. By chastising 'with the valour of my tongue / All that impedes thee from the golden round' she draws his enraptured vision into his ordinary reality and daily life, where 'Time and the hour runs through the roughest day' (I.iii.148). He initiated the integration of the past to the present level of his reality in writing the letter. She overcomes the impeding pity by equating his murderous desire to his sense of manliness, and his pity, with all its accumulated associations, to cowardice, and by implication in view of the swinish grooms, to sexual impotence. In her Macbeth generates the voice he needs to join his desire, first experienced through the witches, to his 'own act and valour' (I.vii.40). He permits himself a fleeting resistance, looking for an alternative equation between manliness and seemliness, but her words carry his deeper impulses when she argues that Macbeth's pledge to her is more binding than a mother's love for her child. Given the strong metaphorical equation generated throughout the play of the kingdom to a family, in asserting that Macbeth's pledge to her supersedes his bonds to kind and country, she opposes the love between herself and Macbeth to the encompassing scale of creaturely accord that extends from sucking infants to social harmony. When she says 'From this time / Such I account thy love' (I.vii.38–9) she defines their love as a world apart from ordinary reality, like that between Romeo and Juliet. However, in the idyllic romance of the earlier play the violence appeared as external to the lovers. That violence, seeping into the love of Hamlet and Ophelia, Desdemona and Othello, kept them apart. Here it invades and defines love, rendering it inimical to familial and social harmony when Lady Macbeth confirms Macbeth's purpose by saying,

> I have given suck, and know
> How tender 'tis to love the babe that milks me:
> I would, while it was smiling in my face,
> Have pluck'd my nipple from his boneless gums,
> And dash'd the brains out, had I so sworn
> As you have done to this.   (I.vii.54–9)

In generating Bellona for his bride Macbeth has expressed his hatred and fear of his own child self—weak, vulnerable, in his eyes despised by woman as swinishly ineffectual. Therefore Lady Macbeth's image of destroying her child does not repel him, but rather persuades him to murder the gentle Duncan. He implicitly associates her image of the sucking babe with Duncan's murder when he responds, 'if we should fail?' He completes their secret collusion in acknowledging the role he has assigned her in saying, 'thy undaunted mettle should compose / Nothing but males' (I.vii.74–5), and prepares to take her keen knife into his hands when he advises her as previously she had him: 'Away, and mock the time with fairest show / False face must hide what the false heart doth know' (I.vii.82–3).

As he approaches the murder the two levels of Macbeth's awareness draw together. Defining the airborne dagger as a 'false creation / Proceeding from a heat-oppressed brain' (II.i.38–9), he gives it a reality midway between the dagger Lady Macbeth imagines herself wielding, and the dagger with which he will kill Duncan. Pointing to Duncan's room, it preludes the murder, and then stained with 'dudgeon gouts of blood,' it marks a transition from the past to the future, and a stage in the process by which Macbeth congeals free-floating emotion into images of reality. As he follows the dagger to Duncan's bedroom the perverse sexuality that has been dimly associated with the murder comes closer to his awareness:

> Now o'er the one half-world
> Nature seems dead, and wicked dreams abuse
> The curtain'd sleep: Witchcraft celebrates
> Pale Hecate's off'rings; and wither'd Murther,
> Alarum'd by his sentinel, the wolf,
> Whose howl's his watch, thus with his stealthy pace,
> With Tarquin's ravishing strides, towards his design
> Moves like a ghost.   (II.i.49–56)

Having stilled the compunctious visitings of nature, Macbeth with deep self-reflectiveness defines himself as a wicked dream that disturbs both Duncan's and his own 'curtain'd sleep.' The logic of the sentence then becomes discontinuous, but in the sequence he identifies with Hecate and offers the murder to the celebrating witches. Abandoning the female identification, he personifies himself as Murder, but that image elides with that of 'Tarquin's ravishing strides.' The passage moves from a negative female image of witchcraft and Hecate to a negative male image of Murder represented as a wolf's howl, a distant image that suddenly transforms into the more immediate one of Tarquin. But Tarquin was not pacing towards a murder, as is Macbeth, but rather towards the rape of Lucrece. Macbeth's sudden identification with Tarquin associates the dagger penetrating Duncan to sexual penetration of a woman.[12]

The total configuration is composed of two sets of fused images. Macbeth's image of himself as a wicked dream contains both female and male ranges, and the sleeping Duncan fuses beneficent paternal with feminine and maternal associations. With his self-image fused with the image of Hecate, Macbeth gets revenge on the unmanly, swinish paternal figure 'drenched in sleep,' who 'loves for his own ends, not for you,' while as Tarquin he interprets his dagger as a bloody phallus with which he violently penetrates the equivocating and seductive woman, and revenges himself on the passive paternal figure loved by the woman, as well as on this version of his own unmanly self. In a remote Oedipal configuration Macbeth's erotic drive towards the mother has blended both with his fear and horror of it and with rage at the interfering father, so that Macbeth in a single configuration expresses the active and passive ranges of his desire, since, identified with Duncan, he is also penetrated. But in espousing the active range he opens the wound in images of father, nurturing mother, and more remotely the children associated with her, the sexual woman, and those aspects of his own emotional capacities represented by those figures. 'Who would have thought the old man to have had so much blood in him?'

Neither our eyes nor Macbeth's peep through the blanketed dark to the invisible bedroom in which Macbeth and Lady Macbeth consummate their love. But what Macbeth does not wish to see or be seen, he wishes both to hear and to be heard. For having envisioned the sexuality implied in his association of women with malicious manipulation, illegitimate authority, and violence, he calls into action representatives of the legitimate authority he has violated. Through them he both maintains his self-definition as evil—for he can be evil only in terms of some concept of virtue—and generates the agents of his own punishment.

The punitive powers that will finally overwhelm him are first dimly heard in the knocking at the Porter's gate, the sound of which links the interior of Macbeth's castle where Macbeth hears it to the exterior where the Porter describes all equivocating professions being drawn into the interior hell. In this remote form Macbeth defines his castle as an underworld that draws into itself the surrounding social world. In a reverse movement he then envisions the devastation from the bedroom encompassing the cosmos when Macduff says, 'up, up, and see / The great doom's image!—Malcolm! Banquo! / As from your graves rise up, and walk like sprites / To countenance this horror!' (II.iii.76–9). That image of doomsday joins with Lady Macbeth's 'hideous trumpet [that] calls to parley / The sleepers of the house' (II.iii.80–1), both of which were implicit in Macbeth's earlier vision of Duncan's virtues pleading 'like angels, trumpet-tongu'd against him.'

Hamlet associated Gertrude's sexuality with doomsday in images of the risen dead and of heaven's face 'thought sick' at witnessing Gertrude's 'act.' In a complex image Macbeth calls for his own punishment in evoking the Judgement Day, but also associates it with images of birth when Ross describes the 'obscure bird' that 'prophesying with accents terrible / Of dire combustion and confus'd events, / New hatch'd to th'woeful time ... Clamour'd the live-long night' (II.iii.56–9). As well, he associates himself with a birth of another kind when he says that 'Augures, and understood relations, have / By magot-pies, and choughs, and rooks, brought forth / The secret'st man of blood' (III.iv.122–5). That combination turns the doomsday image into one of the death of himself as a swinish swiller in the milk of human kindness and the birth of himself first as a usurping tyrant and then as a fiend. He also generates the opposing forces by which he can so define himself, thereby preserving in his world a vision of the good, protective paternal force, figured first in the images of the avenging babe and later in the avenging paternal figures whose forces are gathering. As well, in a remote form he satisfies perverse desires by distancing them into images of a country deprived of food, sleep, and peace. Secretly colluding with the avenging forces of legitimate authority by the self-defeating ways in which he pursues those creature pleasures, he also gradually separates himself from Lady Macbeth, even as he is reborn as the man she wanted him to be.

In Macbeth's new state his barren sceptre and fruitless crown deny the childlike and creaturely feelings that he fears. In what he defines as a means to restore natural pleasures, he repeats in externalized and remote ways the infanticide that deprived him of them. Having failed to kill Fleance, and having Hecate's assurance that no man 'of woman born' can kill him, he murders Macduff's wife and children. Since their murder in no way secures the peace of mind for which he says he commits it, the action becomes an image of his perverse relation to domestic tenderness. At the same time children become messengers of reprisal, from the image of pity as an avenging babe, to the bloody child who gives him false security, and the crowned child who shows him Banquo's progeny.[13] Consciously in search of relief from the 'affliction of these terrible dreams, / That shake us nightly' (III.ii.17–20), and the 'restless ecstasy' of his nights with Lady Macbeth, he generates images that simultaneously extend and punish his initial perverse act. In order to eat and sleep in safety he murders Banquo, but brings his ghost back to destroy the ceremonial banquet about which Lady Macbeth says, 'to feed were best at home; / From thence, the sauce to meat is ceremony; / Meeting were bare without it' (III.iv.34–6), a punning image that merges the familial and the social realms. Under the guise of seeking peace Macbeth turns his country into an extended image of the original murder. The daggers that killed Duncan are recalled when Lennox says the country weeps and bleeds as 'each new day / A gash is added to her wounds' (IV.iii.40–1), Ross says that it 'cannot / Be call'd our mother, but our grave' (IV.iii.164–66), and Macbeth's determination to eat and sleep in peace is echoed in Macduff's quest in England for succour that will 'Give to our tables meat, sleep to our nights, / Free from our feasts and banquets bloody knives' (III.vi.33–5).

As Macbeth transforms his inner turmoil into images of a waste-land kingdom he also gradually redefines himself in his relation to Lady Macbeth. The collusive intimacy between them fades almost immediately after Duncan's murder, for as Macbeth espouses her image of him as an unthinking man of action he redefines her in a more conventional feminine role. The altered relationship appears in Macbeth's secrecy about his plan to murder Banquo, and in her secrecy about her fears. He projects onto her figure the reflectiveness that previously defined him when she says that all has been for nought 'Where our desire is got without content; / 'Tis safer to be that which we destroy, / Than by destruction dwell in doubtful joy' (III.ii.5–7). But she denies her anxiety by dismissing his when he envies Duncan who 'After life's fitful fever' sleeps well, and he savours the secrecy of his planned murder when he tells her to 'Let your remembrance apply to Banquo' (III.ii.30). Both withdraw from their 'restless ecstasy' with each other to 'make our faces vizards to our hearts / Disguising what they are' (III.ii.34–5). He approaches his plan indirectly, saying 'O! full of scorpions is my mind, dear wife! / Thou know'st that Banquo, and his Fleance, lives.' When she responds that 'in them Nature's copy's not eterne' (III.ii.36–9), he secretly obtains her validation of his unspoken plan. She addresses him as 'gentle, my lord,' and he her as 'love,' but in calling her 'dearest chuck' and withholding knowledge from her he reestablishes the conventional protectiveness of men towards women. The banquet scene depicts in association with each other Macbeth's separation from his wife, his isolation of himself from the realms of creaturely and social pleasures, and his redefinition of himself as a man of action when he says, 'Strange things I have in head that will to hand, / Which must be acted, ere they may be scann'd' (III.iv.138–9). In Banquo's ghost he experiences for the last time an emotionally laden image of his inner state, an image that occasions the last rebuke for lack of manliness he will hear from Lady Macbeth.[14] He dismisses the ghost as an 'unreal mock'ry,' and starts to empty himself of his resonant inwardness and deep desires, which will remain in his consciousness only remotely when he attributes them to Lady Macbeth, from whom he will have separated himself.

This is the last scene in which Macbeth and Lady Macbeth appear together. Thereafter he allows the presently oriented image of woman defined in Lady Macbeth to sink into the inward sea of blood as he leaves it behind. Simultaneously he revivifies the more distant images of women and families, sups 'full of horrors' at Hecate's cauldron rather than at the banquet table, and then, having made the 'firstlings of [his] heart ... the firstlings of [his] hand,' kills another image of the family in Macduff's wife and children.

Just as before the regicide he had anticipated the avenging forces that would pursue him, so after it he anticipated the emptiness that would follow from externalizing his emotions into images of a devastated mother country. Earlier, after Duncan's murder, he was the better able to dissimulate for being able to say truthfully that, 'There's nothing serious in mortality; / All is but toys: renown, and grace is dead; / The wine of life is drawn' (II.iii.91–3). Later he says without dissimulation, 'I have liv'd long enough: my way of life / Is fall'n into the sere, the yellow leaf' (V.iii.22–3), and finds himself confronted simultaneously with the avenging armies and with news of his wife's 'thick-coming fancies / That keep her from her rest,' an image that attributes to her the 'thick night,' thickening blood, and light that previously they had shared. As he dons his manly armour he equates the disease that troubles his wife with the English who trouble his country when he asks, 'What rhubarb, cyme or what purgative drug, / Would scour these English hence? Hear'st thou of them?' (V.iii.55–6). In the conflicting images of Lady Macbeth and of the battle Macbeth expresses his now divided and disowned feelings. When Macbeth feels confidence that 'Our castle's strength / Will laugh a siege to scorn,' the cry of women, as though in mockery, is heard from within that castle—the centre now of disease and corruption. In response he asserts his dry indifference in an image that completes the motif of nourishing food, milk, and human warmth, when he says, 'I have supp'd full with horrors:/ Direness, familiar to my slaughterous thoughts, / Cannot once start me' (V.v.13–15). Macbeth associates his incapacity to feel with his separation from Lady Macbeth in the announcement of her death that immediately follows.

Her death signifies his final retreat from his nightmare of love:

She should have died hereafter:
There would have been a time for such a word.—
To-morrow, and to-morrow, and to-morrow,
Creeps in this petty pace from day to day,
To the last syllable of recorded time;
And all our yesterdays have lighted fools
The way to dusty death. Out, out, brief candle!
Life's but a walking shadow; a poor player,
That struts and frets his hour upon the stage,
And then is heard no more: it is a tale
Told by an idiot, full of sound and fury,
Signifying nothing.   (v.v.17–28)

Since he is preoccupied with reassuring himself of his imperviousness to death in battle, he rejects the knowledge of his own mortality already implied in his wife's death. As well, since she dies immersed in the inner world of fantasy that he has escaped, he tries to dismiss the news of her death with affectless dry weariness when he says, 'She should have died hereafter.' As a strategy to avoid the impact of her death in the present, his mind moves first to the future, and then to the past. But when he has emptied the present of significance, the future stretches ahead, 'To-morrow, and to-morrow, and to-morrow,' partaking of the present emptiness, the 'petty pace' that he presently feels. In that state of mind the prospect of escaping death in battle and living forever can give no joy when all recorded time is composed of the insignificant syllables of meaningless action. But the phrase 'creeps in this petty pace' suggests that infant state that he has violated first in himself and then in the world. With that suggestion his mind swings from the future to the past. He no longer responds to the horror of that past; only the sense of meaninglessness remains that he has already projected onto the future. All those 'yesterdays' from infancy to the present, at one time alight with desire, now appear illusory, leading to a 'dusty death' that is indistinguishable from his former vision of his future. Therefore he wants to extinguish the candle that, by illuminating the past, reveals the meaning of Lady Macbeth's death. He sees instead his inner condition writ large when he calls life 'but a walking shadow,' whereas he is now the walking shadow, the bloodless form of himself without the content of passion. The image of the moving shadow suggests one of the stage, but since the candle has been blown out, it is a darkened stage, a scene like Duncan's bedroom that Macbeth both wants and fears to see. Just as sound replaced sight earlier, so he now hears in the dusty darkness the player who 'struts and frets' upon the 'bloody stage' that he himself has generated, and which, Ross says, the heavens threaten. In turn, this suggests an image of Duncan's bloody bedroom, coloured by Macbeth's desires and revulsion, guilt and rage on which he does not wish to look again. So threatening is his projection of what he might see if he allowed himself to look that he takes a further and final means to distance himself from the vision. He transforms the image of the stage to the less immediate one of a tale; but a tale is told to a child. Despite himself, Macbeth evokes the image of a child, but denies what that child might reveal by attributing the tale to an enlarged and grotesque version of a child—an idiot. In this way he eradicates the meaning of his past, present, and future. But thereby hangs another tale of the process by which Macbeth, in fearing to see the images that reveal the emotional content of his actions, transforms life into a tale 'signifying nothing.'[15]

Before Macbeth encounters the witches, one of them says that, having been refused chestnuts, she will pursue through the ports of the world the 'rump-fed ronyon's' sailor husband in a sieve;

> I'll drain him dry as hay:
> Sleep shall neither night nor day
> Hang upon his penthouse lid;
> He shall live a man forbid.
> Weary sev'n-nights nine times nine,
> Shall he dwindle, peak and pine:
> Though his bark cannot be lost,
> Yet it shall be tempest-tost.   (I.iii.18–25)

Macbeth associates himself with that image when he conjures the witches and Hecate to foretell the future 'though the yesty waves / Confound and swallow navigation up; / Though bladed corn be lodg'd, and trees blown down' (IV.i.53–5), and the witches' images prefigure the feelings he later experiences. But the last two lines seem contrary to the play's end, since by any ordinary account Macbeth, called a fiend by Macduff, would seem as damned as man can be. But amid the increasing vilification in which he approaches his death, he also generates purified images of authority. Macduff is not of woman born, and children are referred to in images of wrens, eggs, and nestlings that remind one of those in *Hamlet*. They also are not of women born, and Malcolm evokes and dissociates himself from all of Macbeth's crimes, specifically declaring himself 'unknown to woman' (V.iii.126). Birnam wood, a disembodied female image detached from the 'rooky wood' in which Banquo dies, moves towards Macbeth's embattled tower in which Lady Macbeth lies dead. While on the one hand he claims his wife, though within the sense of evil that comes with the voices who couple them—'this dead butcher and his fiend-like Queen' (V.ix.35)—on the other he sees his head, like Cawdor's earlier, on a stick, without blood, passion, or body. That final stage image seems to flow from Macbeth's earlier words, 'They have tied me to a stake; I cannot fly, / But bear-like I must fight the course' (V.vii.1–2). One might say that in these words he initiates a process by which he denies his body, merges it with the stake to which he feels bound, and completes the process in the image of his bodiless head on a pole. One might speculate further, though it is perhaps far-fetched, that Macbeth's last vision of himself foreshadows Prospero, who has detached himself from his bodily passions, which are contained in the figure of Caliban, and who exercises total control of his domain through his books. Such a speculation gains some credence from the witches' assurance that the sailor's bark cannot be lost, though it can be tempest-tossed.

NOTES

1. In '*Macbeth*: Drama and Dream,' *Literary Criticism and Psychology*, ed Joseph P. Strelka (University Park: Pennsylvania State University Press, 1976), 150–73, Simon O. Lesser relates the play's dreamlike quality to the murder of the sovereign, the symbol of order in the state and psyche, which touches infantile anarchic desires (172). F.P. Rossiter in *Angel with Horns and Other Shakespeare Lectures*, ed Graham Storey (New York: Theatre Arts Books, 1961), implies an analogy to dreams in saying that the play's meaning resides in its plot, rather than in what characters say about it (229).

2. J.I.M. Stewart states in *Character and Motive in Shakespeare* (London: Longmans, Green, 1949) that Macbeth is compelled by the 'crime and not the crown' (93).

3. In line with Freud's comment on the poetic justice of the Macbeths' being childless, Ludwig Jekels in 'The Riddle of Shakespeare's *Macbeth*,' *The Design Within*, ed Melvin Faber (New York: Science House, 1970), thinks the play advocates being a good son in order to be a good father (243).

4. The image also suggests that beneath Macbeth's fair exterior is a self-image like that of Richard III. In *A Psychoanalytic Study of the Double in Literature* (Detroit: Wayne State University Press, 1970) Robert Rogers argues that Lady Macbeth is both a double for Macbeth and a mother-figure, a configuration that represents Macbeth's failure of individuation (51). Wagner sees her as Macbeth's 'phallic prop' (248).

5. Marjorie Garber in *Coming of Age in Shakespeare* (London: Methuen, 1981) relates Lady Macbeth's barrenness to the barren world that Macbeth creates around him (153–4).

6. Despite the general agreement that this scene is not in Shakespeare's 'usual style,' the sequence of the Hecate scenes parallels that of the two witch scenes, and accords with the previous emotional patterns. Here, as elsewhere, it is conceivable that the style reflects Shakespeare's drawing back from the images of terror he generates, leaving figures uninformed by language that flows from full imaginative evocation, even allowing for the interpolation of Middleton's songs.

7. Dennis Biggins in 'Sexuality, Witchcraft and Violence in *Macbeth*,' *Shakespeare Studies* 8 (1976) 255–77, widens and deepens the significance of the relation between Lady Macbeth and the witches by pointing out that traditionally witches were presumed to be lustful, sexually perverse, and sexually dominant. He also thinks of the murder as a kind of rape.

8. Jenifoy La Belle in '"A Strange Infirmity": Lady Macbeth's Amenorrhea,' *Shakespeare Quarterly* 31 (1980) 381–6, on the basis of medical terminology of the time, argues that Lady Macbeth literally wants and gets her menstruation stopped, and later suffers the physiological and emotional consequences in the barren sceptre and blood images that substitute for the natural flow (384–5). In 'Lady Macbeth and Infanticide, or How Many Children Had Lady Macbeth Murdered?' *Journal of the American Psychoanalytic Association* 17 (1969) 528–48, Victor Kalef writes that Lady Macbeth's childlessness both punishes her and is part of the crime (539). Vesny Wagner in '*Macbeth*: "Fair is Foul and Foul is Fair,"' *American Imago* 25 (1968) 242–57, states that Macbeth's hatred of his mother leads to his being pursued by children.

9. In 'Macbeth: Imagery of Destruction,' *American Imago* 39 (1982) 149–64, Joan M. Byles argues that Macbeth's actions are not only in proportion to his guilt, as Freud suggested, 'but rather to the threats on his manhood they represent' (155). Coppélia Kahn in *Man's Estate* (Berkeley: University of California Press, 1981) relates images of milking babes in both *Macbeth* and *Coriolanus* to their protagonists' denial of infantile vulnerability that leads to a dehumanized masculinity (154).

10. D.S. Kastan in 'Shakespeare and the Way of Womenkind,' *Daedalus* 11 (1982) 115–30, reads *Macbeth* in terms of the contemporary ideal of equal partnership in marriage. Lady Macbeth 'champions an ideal of manhood that excludes compassion' (124).

11. In 'The Babe That Milks: An Organic Study of *Macbeth*,' *The Design Within*, 251–80, David B. Barron sees incomplete masculinity rendering Macbeth helpless in a 'nightmare world of women' (265).

12. Richard Wheeler in *Shakespeare's Development and the Problem Comedies* (Berkeley: University of California Press, 1981) says Duncan's dead body becomes a 'new Gorgon,' both male and female, murdered, raped, and castrated (145). Madelon Gohlke in '"I Wooed Thee with My Sword": Shakespeare's Tragic Paradigms,' *The Woman's Part*, 150–70, says that here as in *Othello* murder is a loving act, and love a murdering one (156).

13. In 'The Naked Babe in the Cloak of Manliness,' *The Well Wrought Urn* (London: Dobson, 1968), 17–39, Cleanth Brooks first called attention to the significance of Macbeth's war with children.

14. Carolyn Asp in '"Be Bloody, Bold and Resolute": Tragic Action and Sexual Stereotyping in Macbeth,' *Studies in Philology* 78 (1981) 153–69, blames the sexual stereotyping of society for Macbeth's narrow definition of his masculinity, and for his consequent alienation (156).

15. In *The Dynamics of Literary Response* (New York: Oxford University Press, 1968) Norman Holland gives a penetrating reading of the core fantasy of this speech as though it were an independent poem (106–14). I depart from him in that I relate the speech to the past of the text, rather than to the character's hypothetical past.

CHRISTOPHER PYE

Macbeth *and the Politics of Rapture*

.

I

To glimpse the woven relation between theatricality, knowledge, and power in *Macbeth*, we need to look first, not to the king, but to his inverted image. *Macbeth* is about an instance of regicide, and the play articulates in particularly succinct form the reversionary justice which informs the age's understanding of treason. Macbeth speaks of his own condition:

> But in these cases,
> We still have judgement here; that we but teach
> Bloody instructions, which, being taught, return
> To plague th'inventor: this even-handed Justice
> Commends th'ingredience of our poison'd chalice
> To our own lips.   (I. vii. 7–12)

In its very vagueness about the precise source of this "Justice," the passage suggests the ideological range the logic of the redounding transgression was capable of assuming: Macbeth speaks at once of a psychic, a juridical, and a theological mechanism of correction.

One could argue that this reversionary justice has a very clear source in *Macbeth*: repression. Certainly no play could be more intent on lyrically evoking the machinery of psychic blockage. But repression can structure the

From *The Regal Phantasm.* ©1990 Christopher Pye.

entire range of social, not just psychic, codes in the play only because of a
contradiction in its workings which raises uncertainties about whether this
really is a psychological mechanism at all. In the course of *Macbeth* the traitor
blinds, divides, and betrays himself utterly. One knows the traitor as the one
who does not know himself: "Cruel are the times when we are traitors and
do not know ourselves" (IV. ii. 18–19). Traitors are divided things, even to the
extent of not knowing they are traitors. And yet, if the traitor betrays himself
thus, that is sign enough of guilt and shame. Suspended between psyche and
psychomachia, the traitor reveals the recoils of conscience precisely to the
extent that he is not of a piece:

> Who then shall blame
> His pester'd senses to recoil and start,
> When all that is within him does condemn
> Itself for being there?   (V. ii. 23–6)

The equation between ignorance and guilty acknowledgement implicit
in this version of psychic justice has the felicitous effect of ensuring that
treason proves itself precisely to the extent that it denies itself. It also allows
repression to assume an ordering function well beyond the psyche of the
traitor. A casual failure of recognition takes on ethical resonance—

> MACDUFF: See who comes here.
> MALCOLM: My countryman; but yet I know him not.
> MACDUFF: My ever gentle cousin, welcome hither.
> MALCOLM: I know him now. Good God betimes remove
>   the means that make us strangers!
>   (IV. iii. 159–61)

—and, if the traitor's mind can be read as a psychomachia, an abstract entity
such as the political state can be read as if it were a guilty mind: "Alas, poor
country, / Almost afraid to know itself" (IV. iii. 164–5).

Indeed, by the end of *Macbeth*, the workings of repression seem to
exceed the individual characters of the drama altogether. Our sense toward
the close that, like his uncanny somnambulist queen, Macbeth sees and does
not see, that he somehow knows what he does not know, depends less on the
psychology of the character—a caricatural tyrant by now—than on the
elevation of repression's incriminating returns into a structural principle.
The more Macbeth seals himself off in his castle and sees all before him as
little more than "walking shadow[s]," the more we feel that he knows, and
even solicits, his fated end—"I 'gin to be aweary of the sun" (V. v. 24, 49).

The effect arises because material barriers—fortifying walls, the "leavy screens" behind which the adversaries approach—seem to have taken on the force of psychic exclusions. As much as anything, treason's proper end is fulfilled in the movement of the play itself into the dimensions of psychomachia.[1]

At the same time, by the close of the play, repression's mobile limit can be seen to structure our own relation to the drama. The relationship between the unseen and masterful troops massed behind their screens and the drained tyrant become the "show and gaze o' th' time" reflects our own relationship to a play which has become increasingly a parade of shadows. By the end, repression's bar can be seen to organize an entire ethics of theatrical knowledge and power. The more we assume the powerful position of the unseen, and all-seeing, gazer firmly barricaded on the far side of theater's limit, the more we are checked by an uneasy intuition that it is only ourselves we see reflected in the spectral drama unfolding before us.

We will return to trace the dynamics of power at the conclusion of *Macbeth* more precisely, but I wanted to begin by sketching as directly as possible the relationship between the play's overt political concern—treason— and its form as a theatrical representation, and to suggest how much issues of knowledge and power in the play depend upon a paradoxical version of the limit, one which, like Lady Macbeth's disquieting gaze, retains at once the force of an outward bar and the enigmatic reserves of psychic repression, and which gives the play itself a curiously inward and outward form.[2] Ultimately, I want to argue that *Macbeth*'s political force inheres in that combination of exorbitancy and containment. If the ethically weighty drama of regicide seems oddly willing to give itself over to apparently limitless interpretive uncertainties, it is because in the specular form of that equivocation—the distinctly theatrical way the play turns its empty, solicitous gaze back on us— the play conserves and renews the structures of law and transgression upon which absolutist power is grounded. In the play, that calculated extravagancy crystallizes in an experience culturally affiliated with the newly realized formative capacities of theater itself—the experience of rapture.

II

The ambiguities of repression are evident throughout *Macbeth*, in the schematics of action toward the close, but also in its most luridly evocative poetic flights:

Be innocent of the knowledge, dearest chuck,
'Till thou applaud the deed. Come, seeling Night,

> Scarf up the tender eye of pitiful Day,
> And, with thy bloody and invisible hand,
> Cancel, and tear to pieces, that great bond
> Which keeps me pale!—Light thickens; and the crow
> Makes wing to th' rooky wood;
> Good things of Day begin to droop and drowse,
> Whiles Night's black agents to their preys do rouse.
> Thou marvell'st at my words: but hold thee still;
> Things bad begun make strong themselves by ill.
>
> (III. ii. 45–55)

Macbeth's address to the queen before Banquo's murder epitomizes much of the poetry of the play in the distinctive forms of its equivocations: a sense of anonymity in the voice, produced especially by the multiplying of personified agents, combined with an odd self-consciousness, evident in the speaker's concluding glance toward the kind of effect he is producing; more generally, a sense of evoked terror not altogether distinct from the Gothic pleasures of the act of evoking.

Such uncertainties tend to be resolved either by recourse to psychology—these are the conflicted desires of the regicide—or, in the opposite direction, by recourse to literary formalism—these are the stylized horrors of the Senecan mode. But here as elsewhere in the play, the equivocality of the poetry can be understood in terms of the radical nature of the repression Macbeth is invoking. What is "that great bond / Which keeps [Macbeth] pale"? "Banquo's lease on life," some glosses suggest. But how can "seeling Night" accomplish the deed itself? Instead, we might read Macbeth's "great bond" as his own bond of humanness; Macbeth invokes the self-forgetfulness he needs to enact the deed. In order to get at the instabilities of the address, we need to entertain the possibility that there is no difference between these two readings. If the horror the passage describes seems hard to distinguish from its own opacity, that may be because the "seeling," or bonding, of the eye it invokes is indistinguishable from the event it seals from view.

That sort of blurring between event and response, familiar from *Richard II*, recurs with more insistence in *Macbeth*, and may seem particularly susceptible to moralization in a play about regicide. Treacherous tyrants, who must blind themselves to their own deeds, enact upon themselves the violence they have enacted against others. But *Macbeth* is remarkable precisely for the extent to which it resists too immediate a recourse to moralization. Consider the moment Macbeth, fresh from the act, gazes at his blood-soaked hands.

> MACBETH: This is a sorry sight.
>> LADY MACBETH: A foolish thought to say a sorry sight.
>>> (II. ii. 20–1)

Macbeth's impressive affectlessness can be taken as the measure of repression's success. However, amid all the charged suggestions of fragmentation and madness in the scene, what catches our attention—and Lady Macbeth's—is the spectacular banality of Macbeth's response. A foolish thought crosses the mind—could he simply be "innocent of the knowledge"? The exchange raises the fleeting, and truly unsettling, suspicion that there is no dread secret animating *Macbeth*'s hyperbolic, attenuated masks.

There is a crime, of course. But a crime whose chief characteristic is epistemological uncertainty, in part because we see too little—we do not see the event itself—but equally because we see too much. David Wilbern has shown that the fateful act can be read as an instance of patricide, matricide— Duncan is given maternal, "nurturing," characteristics—rape—Macbeth moves "with Tarquin's ravishing strides" toward the fatal bedchamber—and thus incest, and, taking Lady Macbeth's characterizations of the act into account, infanticide: something, in other words, for the whole family.[3] For the spectator, the first vivid signs of the crime crystallize its vastly overdetermined, and indeterminate, nature. We hear a voice off-stage, perhaps a familiar one:

> MACBETH [*within*]:   Who's there? What, ho?
> LADY MACBETH: Alack! I am afraid they have awak'd,
>> And 'tis not done; th'attempt and not the deed
>> Confounds us.—Hark!—I laid their daggers ready;
>> He could not miss 'em.—Had he not resembled
>> My father as he slept, I had done't.
>>> [*Enter Macbeth*]
>>> My husband!
>>> (II. ii. 8–13)

Who exactly was she expecting? We are not sure. Having taken Macbeth's call for the aroused cry of his intended victims, Lady Macbeth might expect the king's entry at this point. That intuition is heightened by the stunningly timed announcement of her identification between the king and her father. The bald Oedipality of the pronouncement has the effect of conflating Lady Macbeth and Macbeth, but also of blurring, by way of the all-too-apparent desires of the castrating woman, the distinction between the king and her husband. That affiliation need not be mediated through the woman, however. Macbeth's own cry—"who's there? What ho?"—is enough to prompt a vague sense that the regicide has somehow become the victim. Out of this welter of confused identifications, Macbeth's reappearance, his arms soaked in blood, tempts us to seize upon the phantasmal possibility that killer and victim are one and the same. "What bloody man is that?" Duncan asked at the opening of the play of an anonymous messenger returning from an equivocal scene of violence masked, as Harry Berger points out, in blood indiscriminately his adversaries' and his own (I. ii. 1).[4]

For all its apparent ambiguity, such a resolution of the bloody figure of treason is bloodily resolute. A confused array of identifications coalesce under a degree of interpretive pressure into a familiar, even reassuring, sign: treason betrays itself. The play's blazoned equivocations tempt that sort of moral and thematic resolution—I am thinking of Harry Berger's subtle reading of all the accounts of redounding violence in the opening passages of the play as so many indications of a society at odds with itself.[5] But in an almost tendentious way, Macbeth also turns that reversionary violence back outward on its interpreters.

Consider Macbeth's riddling tag-line at the close of the murder scene: "To know my deed, 'twere best not know myself" (II. ii. 72). Commentators have struggled to get the line to conform to a recognizable logic of repression. " 'If I am to come to terms with what I have done, I shall need to avoid self-scrutiny'(?) or 'if not being lost in my thoughts means seeing clearly what I have done, I'd better remain lost in my thoughts'(?)" runs the Riverside gloss. The Arden edition marshalls the full array of psychologizing variants: "If I must look my deed in the face, it were better for me to lose consciousness altogether" (Clarendon), "Better be lost in thought than look my deed in the face" (Wilson), "It were better for me to remain permanently 'lost' in thought, i.e. self-alienated, than to be fully conscious of the nature of my deed" (Muir). What each of these readings avoids looking directly in the face is the line's literal sense: "To know the deed, I must not know myself." The line suggests that in a radical sense the crime is indistinguishable from its disavowal—that that is the sole condition of its appearance. What is rather difficult to confront in that version of the line is precisely how directly it turns the face of treason on us. "Hark! more knocking. / Get on your night-gown, lest occasion call us, / And show us to be watchers" (II. ii. 68–70). Lady Macbeth is referring to the danger of being found awake on the night of the crime. But her parting lines in the scene recall us to Macbeth's blandly spectatorial relationship to his own act. If treason inscribes the doer in the role of mere onlooker, weirdly "innocent of the knowledge" of the deed, what does that suggest about those of us who imagine ourselves to be merely "watchers" and thus innocent indeed?

Reflexivity is hardly a clandestine characteristic of *Macbeth*. The play returns insistently to the dangers of being caught "watching." "I have two nights watch'd" says the doctor at the start of Lady Macbeth's sleepwalking scene; "and still keep eyes upon her" he says at the close, underlining our own captivated relationship to a figure whose haunting gaze has the power to "mate" the mind and "amaz[e] the sight" of those who gaze on her (v. i. 74, 75). But the play's glances out toward us may be most effective precisely when they assume more banal and deflationary forms. When Lady Macbeth remarks as she leaves to return the daggers to the death chamber, "If he do bleed, / I'll gild the faces of the grooms withal, / For it must seem their guilt," her words are able to prompt a degree of editorial anxiety or embarrassment, again centering on the vexed issue of repression (ii. ii. 54–6). "The grim pun is ... a sign of the immense effort of will needed by Lady Macbeth to visit the scene of the crime. Those who find it distasteful should read more genteel authors."[6] The real effect of this sort of obtrusion of the apparently arbitrary signifier at just the wrong point—an eviscerating conversion of guilt into hollow gilt—seems to be the solicitation of an "immense effort of will" on our own part to reinvest the moment with its appropriate agonistic charge. Does *Macbeth* subvert an economy of guilt, then? No, no more than it simply does away with the logic of repression. Instead, in a fairly systematic way, the play compels the theater-goer to experience or enact what every traitor experiences or enacts—a shameful lack of shame.

III

We can begin to understand how moments of interpretive uneasiness manage to retain a regulative and ideologically inscribing force in *Macbeth* by dwelling on the distinctive and quite visible ways the play dramatizes the real effects of imaginary speculations From what we have seen in previous chapters, it is hardly surprising that the play most centrally preoccupied with regicide should also be the most intent on systematically unsettling the relationship between thinking and doing. The political resonance of that issue is suggested by the fact that it was also a concern that preoccupied King James. At the time of the play's composition, the king had been actively involved in debates at Oxford on whether the imagination could produce real effects, as H.N. Paul has shown.[7] In the play itself, the account of the "king's touch"—a transparent gesture in the direction of the play's royal auditor—explicitly offers an inverted, benevolent form of the daemonic contagion associated with treason. However, the most significant form of imaginative exorbitancy in *Macbeth* involves the experience of rapture.

Macbeth's rapt response to the witches' prophecies represents the most
sustained instance of the culture's obsession with the dangers, or sublimities,
of merely thinking on treason.

> [*Aside*] Two truths are told,
> As happy prologues to the swelling act
> Of the imperial theme.—I thank you, gentlemen
> [*Aside*] This supernatural soliciting
> Cannot be ill; cannot be good:—
> If ill, why hath it given me earnest of success,
> Commencing in a truth? I am Thane of Cawdor:
> If good, why do I yield to that suggestion
> Whose horrid image doth unfix my hair,
> And make my seated heart knock at my ribs,
> Against the use of nature? Present fears
> Are less than horrible imaginings.
> My thought, whose murther yet is but fantastical,
> Shakes so my single state of man,
> That function is smother'd in surmise,
> And nothing is, but what is not.
> BANQUO: Look, how our partner's rapt.
>
> (I. iii. 127–43)

For Macbeth, the ethics of this prophetic solicitation depends less on its
matter than on its form. It cannot be ill because it has given an "earnest of
success / Commencing in a truth." It cannot be good, because of the "horrid
image" it conjures, but more because of the unnatural way it compels him to
"yield to the suggestion," "smother[ing]" "function" in "surmise." Why are
"present fears" less than these "horrible imaginings"? Not simply because
they are more mysterious than what is present and visible, Macbeth's words
suggest, but because they elide presence altogether in a limitless surmise:
"Nothing is / But what is not."[8] Lady Macbeth reiterates that form of
surmise in a more exultant mode when she reads Macbeth's letters describing
the encounter: "The letters have transported me beyond / This ignorant
present, and I feel now / The future in the instant" (I. v. 56–7). The line hints
at the inherent relationship between treason and prophecy.

Like other accounts of treason, Macbeth's set-piece aside raises the
question of whether there *is* a dread deed beyond the dread it solicits.
Macbeth does make mention of the act, but in an ambiguous form: "My
thought, whose murther yet is but fantastical." Is this the murder he thinks
of, or the murder of thought Macbeth enacts in his self-eluding rapture? The

performative nature of thinking on treason is suggested throughout *Macbeth*, and accounts for the play's own headlong course. "Strange things I have in head, that will to hand, / Which must be acted, ere they may be scann'd" (III. iv. 138–9). As often as not, that precipitousness will be presented as if it arose from the need to remain blind to the deed: "Let not light see my black and deep desires; / The eye wink at the hand; yet let that be / Which the eye fears, when it is done, to see" (I. iv. 51–3). The nature of the traitor's surmise suggests, however, that the invocation of repression merely represses the more troubling possibility that the deed can only be enacted in that blind and headlong way.

Still, something does seem to come to Macbeth's mind, or his eye, when he thinks on treason. What is the "horrid image" that "unfix[es] [the] hair" of the imaginer? The sight of the murdered king, but in a "gory-locked" form which only heightens our uncertainties about the source of regicide's terrible effects. "O horror, horror, horror! Tongue nor heart cannot conceive, nor name thee! ... Approach the chamber, and destroy your sight / With a new Gorgon," Macduff exclaims, fleeing the scene of the king's death (II. iii. 62–3, 70–1). The "new Gorgon" haunts the play in a variety of avatars, but always representing a distinctly specular form of threat. The "horrid image" returns as Banquo's ghost—

> Avaunt, and quit my sight! ...
> Thy bones are marrowless, thy blood is cold;
> Thou hast no speculation in those eyes,
> Which thou dost glare with.
>
> (III. iv. 935)

—and again in Lady Macbeth's eerie somnambulism: "A great perturbation in nature, to receive at once the benefit of sleep, and do the effects of watching! ... My mind she has mated, and amaz'd my sight" (V. i. 9–10, 75). What gives the Gorgon its dreadful power? Not just the fact that it presents "death itself"—there would be some comfort in locating death so surely. Rather, the fact that it at the same time reflects any who speculate on it. To fall beneath the Gorgon's empty gaze is to confront the altogether hair-raising possibility that one is oneself already an empty, haunted thing.

The inwardness of Macbeth's rapt surmise would seem to distinguish it from these more ghastly, or perhaps more bracing, forms of speculation. In fact, though, the new Gorgon does come into view as Macbeth speaks. The play rather emphatically draws attention to Macbeth's rapt condition. During the initial encounter with the witches, Banquo declares, "He seems rapt withal," and now, after the news of the fulfillment of the first prophecy,

Banquo again fixes attention on his companion's state: "Look, how our partner's rapt." What does rapture look like? Macbeth stands on stage, his eyes open, staring fixedly at nothing, offering the first sight of the new Gorgon's haunted gaze. A few moments before, the royal messenger's report of Macbeth "in the stout Norweyan ranks, / Nothing afeared of what thyself didst make, / Strange images of death," produced the ironic impression that the avenger's greatest fear might be frightening himself to death (I. iii. 95–7). Now, with rapture, that redounding logic assumes the more radical form of a temporal ellipsis: Macbeth fears the "strange image of death" he makes of himself out of fear. In a vivid way, then, Macbeth's specular transport enacts, rather than reflects, the dread event around which the drama turns.

Macbeth's rapture is most provocative for the explicit way it aligns these performative effects—part and parcel of the age's notion of treason—with theater itself. When Macbeth begins his aside, "Two truths are told, / As happy prologue to the swelling act / Of the imperial theme," one has the distinct impression that, transported beyond "this ignorant present," Macbeth has also become transported beyond a theatrical boundary and somehow assumed the role of chorus to his own drama.[9] The effect bears on the peculiar combination of prophetic foresight and irreducible blindness that seems to be the traitor's fate. But the boundary-crossing nature of Macbeth's transport also makes us recognize that the "horrid image" that reflects and transfixes is simultaneously the image of our own rapt, and empty, theatrical absorption. Riddling the distinction between the viewer and the "horrible shadow[s]" and "unreal mock'r[ies]" that haunt the stage, Macbeth's rapture represents treason as the theater-goer's own fatal, and thoroughly captivated, "speculation."[10]

Macbeth's rapture can be seen to confirm the suspicion of the anti-theatrical polemicists that there is something inherently subversive—indeed, treasonous—about theater. For Stephen Gosson, as for others, theater's terrible power to "effeminate"—"shake (the) single state of man"—consists in its border-crossing potentials:

> The divel is not ignorant how mightily these outward spectacles effeminate, and soften the hearts of men, vice is learned with beholding, sense is ticked, desire pricked, and those impressions of mind are secretly conveyed over to the gazers, which the plaiers do counterfeit on the stage ... They that come honest to a play, depart infected.[11]

"Death," Anthony Munday proclaims, "breaketh in" at the eyes. For Gosson, that fatal speculation has a familiar form: those who "so looke, so gaze, so gape upon plaies" amount to "men that stare at the head of *Medussa* and are turned to stone."[12]

At the same time, perhaps as much as any other aspect of the drama, Macbeth's "rapture" aligns the play with spectacles of state. Anticipating the increasingly realized possibilities of specular fascination in Shakespeare's final masque-like plays—the "transport[s]" and benevolent "madness" provoked by Hermione's "statue," for instance—Macbeth's rapture should also be viewed in relation to the contemporaneous development of the royal masque itself.[13] In those spectacles, vision can assume an equally groundless and phantasmatic form. Jonathan Goldberg points out the etherializing reflexivity of a masque such as the *Vision of Delight*, where the audience looks with wonder at a figure of Wonder, and where the Chorus marks the climax of specular abandonment in the viewers' wish that "their bodies all were eyes."[14]

Macbeth's rapt surmise extends the thematics of equivocation to include the play's own status as a political representation. But, more than that, rapture ensures that the play's most radical equivocations remain limited to a regulated play between law and transgression, betrayer and king. To get at rapture's ability to maintain this controlled exorbitancy at the boundaries of the stage, we need to consider the way it draws together two of *Macbeth*'s central preoccupations: sight and sexuality.

IV

In *Macbeth*, imaginative activity has an explicit sexual charge. The queen's haunting gaze "mate[s]" the mind, and Macbeth's rapture, etymologically connected to "rape," is cast as a form of unmanning—a "shak[ing]" of the "single state of man." The sexual nature of the threat posed by the "horrid image" Macbeth conjures becomes clear when the Gorgon appears in the form of Banquo's ghost, both in the exchange between wife and husband— "Are you a man?" "Ay, and a bold one, that dare look on that / Which might appall the Devil" (III. iv. 57–9)—and in the obliging bathos of the ghost's departure:

> Hence, horrible shadow!
> Unreal mock'ry, hence!
>   [*Ghost disappears*]
>   Why so; being gone,
> I am a man again.

(III. iv. 105–8)

The obtrusion of the spectre of castration in *Macbeth* might be understood in relation to the explicit connections the play establishes between political and sexual inversion.[15] While the fatal deed threatens to "unmake" the man, that same sexual unmaking reveals the woman in all her unnatural, phallic potency: "Come, you Spirits / That tend on mortal thoughts, unsex me here, / And fill me from the crown to the toe topful / Of direst cruelty!" For Lady Macbeth, unsexing is the willful prerequisite for, not the dire consequence of, conceiving or performing the act. But we should look more closely at her invocation to the murderous "spirits," for it suggests that castration troubles, rather than sustains, the opposition between the aggressive woman and passive man precisely to the extent that it troubles the distinction between purpose and effect.

>   Come, you Spirits
> That tend on mortal thoughts, unsex me here,
> And fill me, from the crown to the toe, top-full
> Of direst cruelty! make thick my blood,
> Stop up th'access and passage to remorse;
> That no compunctious visitings of Nature
> Shake my fell purpose, nor keep peace between
> Th'effect and it! Come to my woman's breasts,
> And take my milk for gall, you murth'ring ministers,
> Wherever in your sightless substances
> You wait on Nature's mischief! Come, thick Night,
> And pall thee in the dunnest smoke of Hell,
> That my keen knife see not the wound it makes,
> Nor Heaven peep through the blanket of the dark,
> To cry, 'Hold, hold!'
>
>   (I. v. 40–54)

A "stop[ping] up" of the passage to remorse that severs the relation between "fell purpose" and its "effect," "unsexing" amounts to a form of self-willed repression in Lady Macbeth's account. But the purposiveness of Lady Macbeth's desire is undercut by the fact that here, as at other moments in the play, such blockage remains difficult to distinguish from the act it conceals and enables. Is the "wound" she vows to commit under cover of darkness the murder or her own unsexing? The uncertainty is heightened by our vague, perhaps retroactive, sense that she has foetalized the victim in her remarks immediately before about the "fatal entrance of Duncan / Under [her] battlement." But the failure of distinction between willful blindness and the unseen act is most evident at the rhetorical level, in the various suggestions of a severing of her "fell purpose" from itself even as Lady Macbeth articulates her desire to "unsex" herself thus. "Thick Night" covers itself and the "keen knife see[s] not the wound it makes," as if the inanimate forms had lives of their own, and the "sightless substances" of the mediating spirits suggest there may in fact be no distinguishing between the blind seer and the invisible forms she apostrophizes.

The quality of rhetorical drift, so vital to the calculated *frisson* of the passage, is equally evident when we turn to the other side of the sexual equation and consider Macbeth's conjuring of the "sightless substance" of the bloody dagger as he moves "with Tarquin's ravishing strides" toward *his* "fell purpose." The ghostly form of that phallic apparition can be taken as the sign of an enabling disavowal. "Is this a dagger, which I see before me, / The handle toward my hand?" says he, as if such murderous solicitations were not his own (II. i. 33–4). But if anything, Macbeth seems anxious to insist that such bloody impulses are his own: "Thou marshal'st me the way that I was going, / And such an instrument I was to use" (42–3).

As the passage continues, however, this motivational riddle gives way to a sense of a more drastic severing of purpose from effect. It is not just the phallic dagger that takes on the form of a ghost:

> Wither'd Murther,
> Alarum'd by his sentinel, the wolf,
> Whose howl's his watch, thus with his stealthy pace,
> With Tarquin's ravishing strides, towards his design
> Moves like a ghost.—Thou sure and firm set earth,
> Hear not my steps, which way they walk, for fear
> Thy very stones prate of my where-about,
> And take the present horror from the time,
> Which now suits with it.
>
> (52–6)

We can recognize repudiation in Macbeth's likening himself to a ghost, or rather in his disappearing into the abstract personification, "wither'd Murther," and giving *it* the form of an apparition. But it is more difficult to see purposiveness in the sort of disappearances brought about by the apostrophe that follows. The difficulty consists in knowing just how much of the passage *is* apostrophe. The odd impersonality of the phrase "for fear" causes a hesitation between direct address—"Earth, hear not my steps"—and description—"the earth hears not my steps for fear ..." The effect is heightened with the phrase, "take the present horror from the time." The line seems to continue the account of what is to be feared—that the stones "prate" and so "take the present horror from the time / Which now suits with it." But the disquieting way the fear of being betrayed thus slides into a mere aesthetic concern—a worry that such prating would *reduce* the appropriate horror of the moment—pressures description back toward apostrophe: "Hear not my steps ... *take* the present horror from the time." "Horror," in this case, would consist in the prating of the stones, not their silence: "Stones have been known to move and trees to speak," Macbeth fearfully announces after the deed. The division in Macbeth's articulated desires—does he fear or enjoin present horror?—reflects a more fundamental equivocation in the rhetoric of the tyrant. The vague impression that the passage describes a form of "prating" which somehow steals away the horror it echoes and evokes coincides with a wavering between apostrophe and description, between enunciation and enunciated, which produces the effect of a ghostly eclipsing and absorption of the speaker himself.

For the phallic ravisher as much as for the castrating virago desire seems to take the form of a ghostly "unsexing" realized in the process of its articulation. The logic of that tendency toward enactment becomes apparent in the one account we receive of the fatal wound itself:

> Here lay Duncan,
> His silver skin lac'd with his golden blood,
> And his gash'd stabs look'd like a breach in nature
> For ruin's wasteful entrance: there, the murtherers,
> Steep'd in the colours of their trade, their daggers
> Unmannerly breech'd with gore. Who could refrain,
> That had a heart to love, and in that heart
> Courage to make's love known?
>
> (II. iii. 109–16)

Macbeth's punning is tendentious. He is describing the scene in order to justify his "rash" killing of the king's attendants, and so binds the "breech'd" swords to the "breach" they have committed. But here too the speaker's fell purpose eludes itself. For the pun raises the possibility that there is no difference between the one form of breaching and the other—between opening and closing over—or between the wound and the dagger that produces it, as if to be "unmannerly breech'd" were at the same time to be unmanned and breached. The pun crystallizes the redounding logic of an act in which wounding amounts to scaling up, and sealing up merely reproduces the wound it would conceal. Again, the reversionary effect is played out at the level of the discourse itself. Just as tell-tale blood assumes the form of an artificed mask in Macbeth's gorily ornamental account, so in the rhetoric of the passage generally the very absoluteness of the force of gilding denial brings the account close to guilty confession.

If *Macbeth* dramatizes a sexual anxiety, then, it is not at the prospect of sexual inversion but at the possibility of a fundamental relationship between "unsexing" and desire itself—the possibility, for instance, that the phallus might only appear in the form of a ghost.[16] At the same time, the paradox of belated beginnings implied by that understanding of sexuality suggests difficulties for approaching the play's sexual politics in terms of any firm distinction between Oedipal and pre-Oedipal conditions. Janet Adelman argues that the play is organized around a sustained fantasy of escape from "the maternal matrix." The fiend's riddling prophecy that "none of woman born / Shall harm Macbeth" becomes a talisman for Macbeth assuring escape from "the universal condition" of maternal origination. Even as it repudiates that fantasy, Macduff's pronouncement that he "was from his mother's womb / Untimely ripp'd" (v. viii. 15–16) sustains the dream of exemption. "The prophecy itself both denies and affirms the fantasy of exemption from women: in affirming that Macduff has indeed had a mother, it denies the fantasy of male self-generation; but in attributing his power to his having been untimely ripped from that mother, it sustains the sense that violent separation from the mother is the mark of the successful male."[17] Given the play's explicit preoccupation with irreducible forms of equivocation, we might suspect that Macduff's words represent, in particularly grim and misogynistic terms, neither the unavoidable "fact that all men are, after all, born of women"[18] nor the fantasy of self-generation, but a condition of original "untimeliness" that troubles the distinction between the two.

Certainly *Macbeth's* blazoning of the ambiguities of castration and phallic desire might suggest that the real source of anxiety in the play is the "breachless" and undifferentiated condition of pre-Oedipal existence. That state is repeatedly evoked in the play, generally in a mode of queasy, unsteady idealization:

> I have given suck, and know
> How tender 'tis to love the babe that milks me:
> I would, while it was smiling in my face,
> Have pluck'd my nipple from his boneless gums,
> And dash'd the brains out, had I so sworn
> As you have done to this.
>
> (I. vii. 54–9)

In Lady Macbeth's famous account of the (imaginary) babe at the breast, the idealized reciprocity of the mirroring mother and child tilts uneasily into a momentary suggestion of avariciousness just where such a threat is most directly excluded, in the unsettling description of the infant's "boneless gums." Instead of representing a "horror of the maternal function itself," however, that accident of proleptic evocation—a conjuring of what you want to deny—signals the intrusion of the phallic signifier, and the contingencies of the symbolic order, even here at the breast; with the phrase "his boneless gums," "it" becomes momentarily gendered.

As the passage suggests, rather than escaping the symbolic domain, the maternal seems to function as something of a symbolic lure in the play. Take Lady Macbeth's invocation of her "unsexing" spirits:

> Come to my woman's breast,
> And take my milk for gall, you murth'ring ministers,
> Wherever in your sightless substances
> You wait on Nature's mischief!
>
> (I. v. 47–50)

Adelman writes: "Most modern editors follow Johnson in glossing 'take my milk for gall' as 'take my milk in exchange for gall,' imagining in effect that the spirits empty out the natural maternal fluid and replace it with the unnatural and poisonous one. But perhaps Lady Macbeth is asking the spirits to take her milk *as* gall, to nurse from her breast and find in her milk their sustaining poison. Here the milk itself is the gall; no transformation is necessary."[19] But in thus opening up one equivocation in the phrase, Adelman arrests another one—the equivocation bearing on the very matter of how one takes the phrase. For the question of where the poison originates remains, depending as it does on whether we take the apostrophaic "take" as an injunction to literal action—take it for the gall it is—or interpretive action—take it figuratively as if it were gall. Rather than uncovering a maternal ground and origin, the phrase merely draws us into an irresolvable wavering; if Lady Macbeth enacts the unsexing she calls for in her own unmoored apostrophe, it is because however far back it is pursued—even to the breast—that poisoning loss of proper and literal ground has already transpired. What is significant about this equivocal injunction to "take" the breast, however, is the determinate way it captures us. To cut off—or "stop up"—such equivocations at the source may be the condition for generating a steady voice and meaning out of the ungrounded apostrophe, but it is also to renew the unsexing wound blindly. The more anxiously we limit the unstable address, then, the more completely we inscribe ourselves within it in the position of the "murth'ring ministers" the virago invokes.

The captivating effects of the address—its effectiveness as a lure to take all takers—seem to arise from the way it conjoins an ambiguous rhetorical moment with the intense identificatory investments mobilized by the maternal. That conjunction can reach spectacular intensity in *Macbeth*, as with the appearance of the "bloody child" (IV. i). That apparition, which speaks the fatally ambiguous prophecy that "none of woman born shall harm Macbeth," looks forward to Macduff's revelation that he had been "untimely ripp'd" from the womb, but also back to Lady Macbeth's infanticidal fantasy.[20] The specter presents interpretive uncertainty in a fabulously loaded form; we can resolve the figure either in the direction of infanticide or matricide. Given the nature of that choice, the apparition could indeed be seen to play upon parturition anxiety: separate, whatever the consequence, just so long as you separate.

But the very extravagance of these bloody options suggests they may give resolute form to a more slippery equivocation. The bloody child might be taken as figure for the more thoroughgoing and inescapable indeterminacies of its own "breach" birth. Representing the cauling, "breeching," blood that marks its advent and the blood of its "breached" and fatally abortive demise as one and the same, the babe figures the unresolvable ambiguities of its own apparitional condition; to "cut-off" the figure is to conjure it anew in all its spectral luridness. However terrible it is, the overcharged option between the blood of the mother and the blood of the child may simply ground the more troubling, because more inescapable, ambiguity of the hallucinatory figure itself. Still, one cannot escape a suspicion that, at moments such as this in the play, equivocation itself is being a bit too decisively offered for our taking.

Why is *Macbeth* so unequivocally equivocal? However extravagant they may seem, moments of interpretive irresolution have the resolute form of a trap in *Macbeth*. Rather than undoing it, the play's reflexive turns reinscribe the traitor's redounding "faith-breach," making it the grounds for a remarkably self-enforcing form of theatrical reception. *Macbeth* is able to sustain that regulatory effect because it casts interpretive and sexual uncertainty in a distinctive form—as a matter of vision.[21] Rhetorically, the threat of drift tends to crystallize in the "sightless couriers" and "sightless substances" which pass through the discourse of the play as if with a life of their own. More dramatically, interpretative uncertainty coalesces in the form of hallucinatory reveries and terrors—of rapture.

V

In their very exorbitancy, *Macbeth's* spectacular transports would have been familiar stuff to a Renaissance audience. Although we associate melancholy with Hamlet's antic sorrows, the disease was understood to be the fated condition of political tyrants, as well as musing scholars, and would have been recognized in Macbeth's more violent "fit[s]." The most theatrical of psychic conditions, melancholy is the disease that prompts the brain "without externall occasion, to forge monstrous fictions, and terrible to the conceit."[22] Reading contemporary accounts of melancholy, however, one is struck less by the monstrousness of its groundless fictions than by the relatively unanxious way in which they are evoked. With melancholy, radical equivocation assumes a coded and workable form.

Where do melancholy fictions come from? Renaissance commentators are careful to distinguish melancholic delusion from madness. Melancholy does not touch the soul or mind itself, Timothy Bright insists. Instead, the disease results entirely from the perturbations brought about by the subtle, but nevertheless organic, "spirits," or "copulas" which mediate between body and soul. Melancholia amounts to a failure of representation: "onely therein lieth the abuse and defect, that the organicall parts which are ordained embassadours, and notaries unto the mind in these cases, falsifie the report, and deliver corrupt recorder" (112). Melancholy fear arises, not from the humors themselves, but from this action of "eclipsing" (151)—a form of severing comparable to that performed by Lady Macbeth's "ministers": "The body thus possessed with unchearefull, and discomfortable darkness of mencholie, obscurity the Sonne and Moone, and all the comfortable planets of our natures, in such sort, that if they appeare, they appeare all darke, and more than halfe eclipsed of this mist of blackeness" (106). The effects thus produced "are not in the nature of the humor, but as it disturbeth the active instrumentes, no more than darkness causeth some to stumble, other some to go out of their way and wander ... al[l] as they be disposed and occupied which take them to their business in the dark, and not through any such effectuall operation of darkness, which is naught else but meere absence of light" (108).

If it is not darkness as such, but the act of eclipsing the spiritual light that elicits fear, then at some level melancholics would never truly lose touch with their own clear natures. To get at the full terrors of melancholy, Bright must, like any good melancholic, be at odds with himself. He distinguishes the melancholic's inward eclipse from the fear prompted by outward darkness: "Now the internall darkness affecting more nigh by our nature, then the outward, is cause of greater fears, and more molesteth us with terror, then that which taketh from us the sight of sensible things: especially arising not of absence of light only, but by a presence of a substantiall obscurity, which is possessed with an actual power of operation: this taking hold of the brayne by process of time giveth it an habite of depraved conceite, whereby it fancieth not according to truth" (103). The paradox of this double eclipse—a division within which also amounts to an ineluctable sealing-off—lies at the heart of melancholic uncertainty, and can be summarized in a single, punning term: "You mean by your wordes," Guazzo says in Pettie's translation of *The Civile Conversation*, "to include mee in the number of the melancholike, which have their wit so *breeched*, that they cannot discerne sweet from sowre. But if I flatter not myselfe, I have a whole minde within my crasie body. "[23]

There is nothing concealed about this equivocation. The phantasmatic uncertainties about the source of the "breeched" mind's fears define the disease in its essence; melancholy "causeth the senses both outward and inward preposterously to conceive" (108). In melancholy, the inward-turning gaze of sadness explicitly mingles with a terrible paranoiac apprehension. Melancholy is able to sustain that contradictory structure because it remains a thoroughly speculative phenomenon—even at its most exorbitant, a matter of the eye filled with sorrow. In his account of the radically immanent, anti-Aristotelian nature of Baroque *Trauerspiel*, Walter Benjamin draws attention to this captivating, specular characteristic of the melancholic condition:

> Mourning is the state of mind in which feeling revives the empty world in the form of a mask, and derives an enigmatic satisfaction in contemplating it. Every feeling is bound to an *a priori* object, and the representation of this object is its phenomenology. Accordingly, the theory of mourning, which emerged unmistakably as a *pendant* to the theory of tragedy, can only be developed in the description of that world which is revealed under the gaze of the melancholy man.

With mourning, contemplation assumes a "drastic externality," discerning itself in the hollow mask of the "empty world." Yet, out of that very alienation, under the mourner's gaze, the empty object recovers an enigmatic reserve: "the most simple object appears to be a symbol of sonic enigmatic wisdom because it lacks any natural, creative relationship to us."[24] Benjamin's account of the relation between mourning and externality—the "ostentation" of grief—recalls Queen Isabel, and lets us recognize melancholy's combination of inwardness and dread in her specular sorrow. But "mysterious externality," Benjamin's wonderful phrase for the world sustained beneath melancholy's eye, might equally describe the evocative opacity, the exorbitancy, but also the reserve, all desire seems to take on in *Macbeth*.

Recent psychoanalytic reflections on mourning bear out the relationship between melancholy and speculation. In his analysis of Hamlet,

Lacan associates melancholy with the significant moment when the decline of the Oedipal complex is accomplished through the expedient of symbolic castration. For Lacan, mourning is first and foremost mourning for the phallus. At the same time, mourning confirms Freud's intuition that the relation between the subject and the phallus is narcissistic. The necessity of mourning prompts a vigorous and originary narcissistic coalescence amounting to, in Lacan's terms, "the composition of the imaginary register." For the subject in mourning, the phallus—primordial signifier of difference—is doubly spectral, Lacan implies. It appears as a revenant forever lost, but also as a specular, narcissistically invested form. It appears, that is, as a hallucinatory apparition.[25]

For Lacan, mourning is a reflective phenomenon, bearing less on the origin of desire than on how the subject "himself must situate himself in desire."[26] But Lacan's account of this significant juncture between symbolic and imaginary orders is suggestively ambiguous. The disappearance of the phallic signifier, he says, demands mourning and the compensatory aggrandizements of narcissism. But could not Lacan's account not equally suggest that, at least from the perspective of the subject, it is mourning and the narcissistic investments it prompts that first invest the phallic signifier with meaning? Julia Kristeva's interest in melancholy arises from this possibility of a primordial mourning, with its important implication about the contingent, narcissistically bolstered, nature of the symbolic order as a whole.[27]

For Kristeva, melancholy narcissism is inseparable from a primitive experience at the limits of symbolization which she terms "abjection," a mixture of dejection and dread which would have been familiar to Renaissance theorists of irreducible sorrow. Melancholy abjection arises, Kristeva argues, from a significant "interspace" after a (more or less conjectural) state of original narcissism has begun to dissolve but before an opposition between subject and object has been securely established under the aegis of paternal prohibition and the Oedipus complex. In that moment of dissolving boundaries, which is also an advent of sorts for the subject, the subject will experience phobia, but a phobia which, in lieu of an object, seizes on "*the symbolic activity itself.*" That momentary investment of the ungrounded sign—"the degree zero of signification"—takes the peculiar form of an intense visual cathexis with no object—in Kristeva's terms, "the hallucination of nothing":

> To speak of hallucination in connection with such an "object" suggests at once that there is a visual cathexis in the phobic mirage—and at least a speculative cathexis in the abject. Elusive, fleeting, and baffling as it is, that non-object can be grasped only

as a sign. It is through the Intermediary of a *representation*, hence a *seeing*, that it holds together. ... For the absent object, there is a sign. For the desire of that want, there is a visual hallucination.[28]

Much as it would seem to represent a breakdown of the paternal function, abjection is actually "eminently productive of culture," Kristeva argues, for its speculative mirage secures the sign, and the symbolic order itself, against greater dissolutions.[29]

Kristeva's description recalls the fleeting, and critical, intersection of sight and sign which constitutes the traitor's groundless shame in *Henry V*. But "the hallucination of nothing" also brings to mind the peculiar character of the rapture experienced by a more fully realized traitor. I want to make my way back to *Macbeth* by way of a passage from another play describing another moment of transport. In *Hamlet*, the first player recites a narrative of the bloody actions of a vastly overdetermined tyrant, "horridly trick'd / With blood of fathers, mothers, daughters, sons," in whom Hamlet sees his own destiny densely figured: Pyrrhus' encounter with the aged Priam represents the tyranny the Prince must overcome, the decisive action he must imitate, but also the paralysis that arrests him. "O'er-sized with coagulate gore," masked by the blood that reveals him, the tyrant might also be seen to densely figure the impenetrable wound at the center of *Macbeth*. But it is the related issue of the tyrant's tendency toward rapture that most provokes speculation. "Hellish Pyrrhus" comes upon the ancient King:

> Anon he finds him
> Striking too short at Creeks. His antique sword,
> Rebellious to his arm, lies where it falls,
> Repugnant to command. Unequal match'd,
> Pyrrhus at Priam drives, in rage strikes wide,
> But with the whiff and wind of his fell sword
> Th' unnerved father falls. Then senseless Ilium,
> Seeming to feel this blow, with flaming top
> Stoops to his base, and with a hideous crash
> Takes prisoner Pyrrhus' ear; for to his sword,
> Which was declining on the milky head
> Of reverent Priam, seem'd i' th' air to stick.
> So as a painted tyrant Pyrrhus stood
> And, like a neutral to his will and matter,
> Did nothing.
> (*Hamlet*, II. ii. 468–82)

The passage spells out the Oedipal context of the redounding "breach" which structures the ethics of power in *Macbeth*. In his overmastering power, the tyrant swings wide, and misses altogether, the "unnerved father" who is already, who in Oedipal terms has always been, little more than a ghost. As the passage continues, the reversionary violence of the tyrant's stroke is recast in the form of an "unnerving"—a castrating—split between "will and matter," or between "fell purpose" and "effect," which leaves the tyrant oddly suspended at the moment of his fatal act.

The tyrant's Pyrrhic violence is appropriate to a drama in which the conflation of paternal and usurping roles in the figure of the adversary compels the revenger to confront, with paralysing effect, the fatal redundancy of Oedipal desire itself. For our purposes, however, what is most interesting is the form that suspension of will takes. Pyrrhus is captivated through the ear, just as we are by the player's rhetoric. And, with that captivation, he becomes a tableau—for a moment, nothing more than a "painted tyrant." "Between the acting of a dreadful thing / And the first motion, all the interim is / Like a phantasma, or hideous dream" (*Julius Caesar*, II. i. 63–5). Judging from the "painted tyrant," what is most phantasmic about this interim of rapture is its capacity to absorb the conceiver within its overmastering, and visibly theatrical, effects.

Why this "unnerving" movement into spectacular rapture? In the first player's speech, Pyrrhus' transformation seems to lead beyond the Oedipal drama altogether. During the interval when all becomes suspended, the source of captivating power shifts beyond the agonistic confrontation to the fall of "senseless Ilium"; as in the accounts of the king's theatricalizing presence, individual agency seems momentarily lost to the larger entity of the political state. At the same time, for the audience, the particulars of the drama momentarily fall away before the still tableau of the theatrical tyrant. Nevertheless, our consideration of melancholy suggests that this eviscerating passage into specular reverie represents the last recourse, not the undoing, of symbolic and patriarchal power.

We can see that by considering *Macbeth*'s passage from agonistic drama to the fixed spectacle of a painted tyrant. Such a movement is apparent in the play's increasingly mask-like and reflexively theatrical qualities. But it also occurs more specifically. Toward the close, after Macbeth vows he will not fight Macduff, his adversary replies:

> Then yield thee, coward,
> And live to be the show and gaze o' th' time:
> We'll have thee, as our rarer monsters are,

Painted upon a hole, and underwrit,
"Here may you see the tyrant."

(V. viii. 23–7)

The traitor's threatened end coincides with the most reduced form of theater
itself: on the one hand, a painted visage, on the other, the sparest deictic
inscription: "Here may you see the tyrant." Macbeth both refuses that fate—
he chooses to fight—and accedes to it—he will return to the stage as a
theatrical prop. The arresting effect of that return can be seen as a
consequence of the simple reconvergence of those two theatrical elements
Macduff's threat had so minimally distinguished—a potent crossing of sight
and inscription.

[Re-Enter Macduff, with Macbeth's head]

MACDUFF: Hail, King! for so thou art. Behold, where stands
   Th' usurper's cursed head: the time is free.
   I see thee compass'd with thy kingdom's pearl,
   That speak my salutation in their minds;
   Whose voices I desire aloud with mine,—
   Hail, King of Scotland!
ALL: Hail, King of Scotland! [*Flourish*]

(V. ix. 19–26)

Macduff's deference to the unspoken thoughts of the onlookers is politically
expedient. At moments of transition—and in particular, ambiguous
transitions involving usurpers usurped—it is best that the precise source of
the legitimizing impulse remain forever uncertain. But this is also a critical
moment in the emergence of sovereign power as such—the fleeting interval
between the cease of one king and the affirmation of the next when
sovereignty appears in its truest, most phantasmal form. Indeed, we may not
be perfectly certain whom we should be "all hail[ing]" during this
momentary interim. After Banquo's ghost and Lady Macbeth's somnambulist
wanderings, the reappearance of the tyrant, with his eyes wide and empty of
speculation, amounts to a revival of the haunting Gorgon, "compass'd" now
on the stage by the "kingdom's pearl."

When the new king goes on to speak of those who have "fled the snares
of watchful tyranny," he only heightens our suspicion that death has affirmed
the tyrant's watchful potency. At the close, political and theatrical power
settle into the form of a specular trap—a tyrannical "snare" for the watchful.
The more we reduce the tyrant to a "show and gaze o' th' time," the more
we will conjure that empty speculator as the condition and origin of our own

"all-seeing" powers. The more we gaze, the more we feel ourselves subject to an alien and phantasmal gaze. *Macbeth* concludes under the sway of the "all-seeing" and "penetrant" eye that James invokes at the opening of *Basilikon Doron*, and that oversees our reading of *Leviathan*.[30]

However depletionary it may seem, *Macbeth*'s movement into the form of an empty mask serves a critical organizing function. More than simply extending the redounding effects of a "faith-breach" beyond theater's margins, rapture galvanizes symbolic exorbitancy into a regulated play of affirmation and denial, faith and transgression, through its limitless specular returns. A complex set of pressures is necessary to sustain this sovereign "interim" when all—spectator and spectacle alike—become "a phantasma." There is a threat to the watcher involving the inordinate powers of the symbolic domain, but also a narcissistic coalescence, an "enigmatic satisfaction," and even a contentment of sorts. According to the pamphlet on the Royal Entertainment of the French Prince Francis at Antwerp, spectacles of state, particularly martial ones, have the power to "drive the beholder into an astonishment, setting him after a sort besides himselfe; and yet nevertheless filling him with joy and contention surmounting all others."[31] It is not accidental, or simply ironic, that the kingdom consolidates beneath this ambiguous gaze.

For the Renaissance spectator the mingled experience of loss and indentificatory consolidation may have been evident in the very notion of rapture. The most explicit contemporary account of the political function of theater hinges, I think, on a single double-edged term:

> What English blood seeing the person of any bold English presented and doth not hug his fame and hunny at his valour, pursuing him in his enterprise with his best wishes and as being wrapt in contemplation, offers him in his heart all prosperous performance, as if the performer were the man personated? so bewitching a thing is lively and well spirited action, that it hath power to new mould the hearts of the spectators.[32]

To be "rapt"—carried out of one's thoughts by a "bewitching" power—was at the same time to be "wrapt"—sealed and protected within a greater absorbing contemplation; the terms were considered to be synonymous. Theatrical rapture was a matter of being breached and of being breached.

We can gather that power of "new moulding" back to the figure of the king by comparing Macbeth's painted tyrant with a more magisterial image of sovereignty—Holbein's portrait of Henry VIII at Whitehall. Across their heightened oppositions, certain elements of the death's head and the king converge. Both are glaringly phallic: Henry with his looming codpiece, Macbeth elevated on a pole around which all within the wooden O and beyond now gather—we are reminded of the captivating "blind-boy" at the close of *Henry V*. Both are snares for the watchful; amid the averted gazes of the family members gathered around Henry, only the painted eye of the king engages the eye of the spectator directly. But what joins the figures most is the response they solicit. A sixteenth-century visitor to Whitehall said he felt "abashed, annihilated" in the presence of the painted king.[33] The phrase represents a particularly condensed expression of the groundless shame, the oddly bracing intersection of emptiness and exposure, which comes from speculating on sovereignty. It might also be taken as a condensed expression of the "new moulding" produced by the combination of exorbitancy and mimetic familiarity which defined Renaissance theater as a whole.

This may align Renaissance drama too sweepingly with the theater of rapture. There are other possibilities for viewing theater, of course. Indeed, there may be other possibilities for rapture. We should consider a further ambiguity at the close of *Macbeth*. The uncertainty about who is being hailed during the interim of power at the end would have been heightened by the real or implied presence of James in the audience, "compassed" by his "kingdom's pearl." What if we imagine the king, too, contemplating the source of his "all-seeing" power in the painted tyrant? Jonathan Goldberg has suggested the subversive potential in the play's parade of mirrored kings; even as it realized the attendant king's fantasy of a self-generated and endless lineage, the witches' show would have shown regal authority to be subject to the "uncontrolled duplications" and "menacing heterogeneity" of representation.[34] Such subversiveness might come to a head, so to speak, at the close of the play in the form of an exorbitant regal rapture which shows the king "nothing afeared" of the "strange images of death" he himself makes. Then again, James more than anyone knew how to derive "enigmatic satisfaction," and considerable power, from contemplating phantasms.

NOTES

1. Howard Felperin compares *Macbeth* to Medieval morality plays, arguing that the form reflects the character's own efforts at depersonalization as well as Shakespeare's commentary on social ritualism ("A Painted Devil: *Macbeth*," in Harold Bloom (ed.), *Modern Critical Interpretations: Macbeth* (New York: Chelsea House, 1987), 91–111). Richard Ide speaks of Macbeth's transformation into a "stereotypical villain," associating the change with the play's movement toward a "God-like" perspective ("The Theatre of the Mind: An Essay on Macbeth," *English Literary History* 42 (1975), 353).

2. A form evident in Ide's title, "The Theatre of the Mind: An Essay on Macbeth."

3. David Wilbern, "Phantasmagoric Macbeth," *English Literary Review* 16 (1986), 520–7.

4. Harry Berger, Jr, "The Early Scenes of *Macbeth*: Preface to a New Interpretation,"

English Literary History, 47 (1980), 5.

    5. ibid., 7–14.

    6. Note to II. ii. 55–6 in *Macbeth*, ed. Kenneth Muir, the Arden Shakespeare (London and New York: Methuen, 1951).

    7. Paul, *Royal Play*, 44–60.

    8. William O. Scott discusses the contradictory and self-divisive nature of Macbeth's logic in his soliloquies in terms of the "liar's paradox" ("Macbeth's—And Our—Self-Equivocations," 165–74).

    9. Richard Ide associates the moment with Macbeth assuming the role of playwright in relation to his own drama ("Theatre of the Mind," 342).

    10. Marjorie Garber considers the play in terms of its pervasive and uncanny boundary-crossing effects in *"Macbeth*: The Male Medusa" (*Shakespeare's Ghost Writers* (New York and London: Methuen, 1987), 87–118).

    11. Stephen Gosson, *Plays Confuted in Five Actions* (1582), in *Markets of Bawdrie: The Dramatic Criticism of Stephen Gosson*, ed. Arthur F. Kinney (Salzburg: Institut für Englische Sprache und Literatur, 1974), 192–3.

    12. Anthony Munday, *A Second and Third Blast of Retrait from Plaies and Theaters* (London, 1590), 95–6. For Anti-theatricality, see Introduction, n. 10.

    13. See Alexander Leggat, "Macbeth and the Last Plays" in J.C. Gray (ed.), *Mirror Up To Shakespeare: Essays in Honour of G.R. Hibbard* (Toronto: University of Toronto Press, 1984), 189–207. Muriel Bradbrook sees in *Macbeth* the influence of King James's spectacular entry into London as well as of court theater (*The Living Monument: Shakespeare and the Theatre of His Time* (London: Cambridge University Press, 1976), 127, 134, and Jonathan Goldberg reads the play in relation to the demonic and empowering anti-masque in Jonson's *Masque of Queens* ("Speculations: *Macbeth* and Source," in Richard Machin and Christopher Norris (eds), *Post-Structuralist Readings of English Poetry* (Cambridge, London, New York: Cambridge University Press, 1987), 47–54).

    14. *James I*, 61–2. On the indeterminate—at once receptive and creative—version of "fantasy" animating the royal masque, see Roy Strong and Stephen Orgel, *Inigo Jones: The Theater of the Stuart Court* (London: Sotheby Parke Bernet and Berkeley: University of California Press, 1973) 2 vols, i. 5.

    15. See Peter Stallybrass, "*Macbeth* and Witchcraft," in *Focus on Macbeth* 196–206; on the threat of sexual inversion in the play, see Coppélia Kahn, *Man's Estate: Masculine Identity in Shakespeare* (Berkeley, Los Angeles, and London: University of California Press, 1981), 172–92: Madelon Gohlke, "'I wooed thee with my sword': Shakespeare's Tragic Paradigms," in Murray Schwartz and Coppélia Kahn (eds), *Representing Shakespeare: New Psychoanalytic Essays* (Baltimore: The Johns Hopkins University Press, 1980), 175–7; Harry Berger, Jr., "Text against Performance in Shakespeare: The Example of *Macbeth*," *Genre*, 15 (1982), 49–80. Marjorie Garber focuses on the Medusa's head in the play as a representation of "gender undecidability as such": "*That* is what is truly uncanny about it, and it is that uncanniness that is registered in the gender uncertainties in *Macbeth*" (*Shakespeare's Ghost Writers*, 110). On the relation between the Medusa's head and castration in the context of political anxieties, see Neil Hertz, "Medusa's Head. Male Hysteria under Political Pressure," in *The End of the Line: Essays on Psychoanalysis and the Sublime* (New York: Columbia University Press, 1985) 161–93.

    16. I take up the issue of the "phallic ghost" below, p. 166.

    17. J. Adelman "'Born of Woman': Fantasies of Maternal Power in *Macbeth*," in *Cannibals, Witches, and Divorce: Estranging the Renaissance* (Selected Papers from the English Institute, 1985; Baltimore: The Johns Hopkins University Press, 1987), 105, 108.

18. ibid., 90.

19. Adelman, "Born of Woman," 98.

20. ibid., 104.

21. On the visual emphasis in the play see D.J. Palmer, "'A New Gorgon': Visual Effects in *Macbeth*," in *Focus on Macbeth*, 54–72, Lucy Gent, "The Self-Cozening Eye," *Review of English Studies*, 34 (1983), 419–28, and H. Diehl, "Horrid Image, Sorry Sight, Fatal Vision: The Visual Rhetoric of *Macbeth*," *Shakespeare Studies* 16, (1983), 191–203.

22. Timothy Bright, *A Treatise of Melancholy* (London, 1586; New York: The Facsimile Press Society & Columbia University Press, 1940), 102; cited parenthetically hereafter.

23. *"The Civile Conversation" of M. Stephan Guazzo ... the First Three [Books] Translated out of French by G. Pettie [the Fourth out of the Italian by Bartholomew Young]* (London: Thomas East, 1586), fo. 4^r; cited by L.M. Harris, "*Macbeth*'s 'unmannerly breech'd with gore,'" *Modern Language Notes*, 21 (1906), 11–12. Pettie is translating the French, "le cerueau *obfusque*."

24. *The Origin of German Tragic Drama*, trans. John Osborne (London: New Left Books, 1977), 139, 140.

25. "Desire and the Interpretation of Desire in *Hamlet*," in Shoshana Felman (ed.), *Literature and Psychoanalysis: The Question of Reading: Otherwise* (Baltimore and London: The Johns Hopkins University Press, 1977), 46, 47–8, 52.

26. ibid., 49.

27. "On the Melancholic Imaginary," in Shlomith Rimmon-Kenan (ed.), *Discourse in Psychoanalysis and Literature* (London and New York: Methuen, 1987), 107–10.

28. *Powers of Horror: An Essay on Abjection*, trans. Leon S. Roudiez (New York: Columbia University Press, 1982), 44, 42, 46. My understanding of the significance of Kristeva's analysis is indebted to Neil Hertz, *The End of the Line*, 231–3, and Cynthia Chase, "'Transference' as Trope and Persuasion," in *Discourse in Psychoanalysis and Literature*, 223–9.

29. Kristeva, *Powers of Horror*, 45. See also Timothy Murray's account of the fleeting prospect in Abbé du Bos's work of a form of theatrical energy associated with "the flip-side of the ideological institution of objectivity, the Other of the symbolic institution of arbitrary signification" (*Theatrical Legitimation: Allegories of Genius in Seventeenth-Century England and France* (New York and Oxford: Oxford University Press, 1987), 210.

30. Stephen Mullaney argues that the entrance of Macbeth's lifeless head stabilizes and "reforms" the drama; after merging "for a brief time" with the unmasterable ambiguities associated with the figure of the traitor, Shakespeare's dramaturgy reasserts its divergence from the spectacle on the scaffold (*Place of the Stage*, 128–9). I am suggesting that the death's head solicits just such a desire to stabilize its uncertainties. Recalling Freud's account of the apotropaic properties of the Medusa's head, Marjorie Garber speaks of the way the Gorgon's head is "transformed from an emblem of evil to a token of good" at the close (*Shakespeare's Ghost Writers*, 115).

31. "The Roiall Intertainement of the French Prince at Antwerpe" (1581), in Raphael Holinshed, *Chronicles of England, Scotland, and Ireland*, 6 vols (London, J. Johnson, 1807–8), iii. 466.

32. Thomas Heywood, *An Apology for Actors* (1612), ed. Richard H. Perkinson (New York: Scholars' Facsimiles and Reprints, 1941), G/1–2.

33. C. van Mander, *Livre des Peintres* (1604) trans. Henri Hymans (Paris: J. Rouan, 1884), 2 vols, i. 218. See Roy Strong, *Holbein and Henry VIII* (London: Routledge & Kegan Paul, 1967), 39.

34. "Speculations: *Macbeth* and Source," 53–4.

H.W. FAWKNER

Deconstructing Macbeth

As I now approach the dramatic crisis of murder itself, my criticism will situate itself inside what is loosely known as the "Noble-murderer interpretation." This is the reading favored by actors like Garrick and Olivier and discussed by quite a number of significant critics. The basic idea, here, is that Shakespeare's genius does not bother to stage the banal notion of a bad man entering evil but of a very good man entering evil. However, and this is a crucial dimension of the current enterprise, I do not myself read this transition (in the noble-murderer reading) from good to evil as a "fall" from good, as a common type of tragic "tainting." I do not think that Macbeth at any point "becomes evil" in order to become a murderer (although murder in itself obviously is evil). I think, with John Bayley, that it "is essential to the hypnotic tension of the play that Macbeth should not seem in any ordinary way 'responsible' for his actions."[1] (The stress here is on "ordinary"; one is not freeing Macbeth from responsibility.) In short, my position is this: anyone arguing that Macbeth "turns evil" and that this inner darkening is the crucial trigger device for the murder and the tragic action is not only misconceiving Shakespeare's dramatic design but also disfiguring the imaginative and aesthetic potentials of the play.

In fact, that type of secondary-school reading also disfigures most of the enormous psychological potentials of Macbeth. Several critics are generously willing to acknowledge the greatness of the play, while at the

From *Deconstructing Macbeth*. ©1990 Associated University Presses, Inc.

same time voicing the curious prejudice that Shakespeare is a poor psychologist who sacrifices psychological truth for the sake of dramatic effect. One is willing to recognize the feeling of tragicgreatness, but finding that this greatness does not fit any logocentric model of psychological causation, one decides that the play is successful in spite of its psychology. I hold precisely the opposite view. I think there is a very special psychology in this play, and I think that critics replacing this psychology (which is beyond their ken) with their own "temptation-and-fall" theories (taken from popular logic) are simply transforming the play into something that is more immediately manageable for them than it really is. E.E. Stoll has argued that the tragic thrill comes from seeing the good man falling into horror, but that Macbeth's deeds would be more in keeping with psychological realism had the hero had some real cause to dislike Duncan.[2] This, to me, is the silliest possible notion. If Macbeth really has had a grievance, then the whole play called *Macbeth*, far from being one of the most brilliant dramas ever devised, would sink into mediocrity and indifference. In this same vein and fashion, Gustav Rümelin tells us that Shakespeare "exaggerates" at the expense of real "psychological truth" but still somehow creates a play that is his most powerful and mighty tragedy.[3] In his review of these two positions, J.I.M. Stewart limply follows suit (with respect to this particular issue) by stating that Shakespeare was always prepared to use a "non-realistic" move[4] and that tragic fall might be related to the fad that "everybody" is subject to weak moments of exposure in which some "lurking" evil runs through us.[5]

The idea that Macbeth is "treacherous" (in the ordinary sense) is no doubt promoted by his tendency, shown from the outset, to speak in asides. The "Cumberland" aside (1.4.48–53) is a case in point here: "Stars, hide your fires! / Let not light see my black and deep desires." But two things need to be said about the incriminating asides. First, the "Cumberland" aside, as the only really "evil" one, is almost certainly an interpolation—as Granville-Barker, Fleay, and others have observed (KM, 25).[6] I suspect that this interpolation was introduced by someone with precisely the kind of attitude exemplified by Stoll and Rümelin above: that Shakespearean psychology had to be "improved" (indeed introduced!) so that tragic intentionality could be "made clear." Second, the hero's tendency to speak in asides is not necessarily a social event, denoting undercover action and withdrawal, but a technical necessity: Shakespeare wants to display a transition toward introversion, and the only way of giving the audience access to this introversion is to use asides and soliloquies.

My own view is this: that Macbeth never has had the intention to murder Duncan, and that *throughout the play he never has any such intention*. His intention is not only absent, it is structurally absent.

Absence, generally, is structural in Macbeth; and absent intentionality is the specific form that tragic crisis gives to this general absence. I cannot really see how the play as a whole can function in its specifically Shakespearean form of suggestion without there being a (conscious or unconscious) recognition of this peculiar organization.

In a sense—and this is what is truly terrifying in Macbeth—there is simply nothing of the murderer in the hero. Partly, this murderous emptiness inside the murderer can be explained in terms of constitutional weakness; one can posit a failure of nerve, of proper disposition, or even (as we have seen in Bayley's criticism) of dramatic suitability: the hero's mind is "unfitted for the role that tragedy requires of it."[7] But things can be taken much further—in a sense logically have to be taken much further. The murderous emptiness is not only the function of "weakness" but a function of strength—of an intensity of mind that is unprecedented. Tragic paralysis, in *Macbeth*, is not a merely passive event; on the contrary, it is highly active. Tragic action, while being interiorized so as to mostly take place inside the mind, does not dissipate its energies there, become mere misty sluggishness. Macbeth wrestles with a spell, and in a sense with a paralyzing one: but the paralysis affects his bodily actions and military readiness, not his mind. The spell, far from being something that drugs his intellect, is something that keenly awakens it to unprecedented acuteness and sensitivity. What this extra-lucid intellection now comes to engage with (as I shall argue in a moment) is the activity of an unthinkable watchfulness: Macbeth begins the weird process of watching the absence of his own intention (to murder).

Because of this Shakespearean move, the scene presenting the hallucinated dagger cannot (as Olivier and others recognized) be turned into a conventional horror scene, full of mere knee-knocking and guilt. In Olivier's performance, there was no melodramatic recoiling from the air-drawn dagger, and the soliloquy was spoken as if in dreaming. Delivering his speech as drugged whisper, Olivier managed to create a sense of total unreality. Although Macbeth appeared as a man of immense sensibility, this sensibility did not sensitize him to the murder itself but made him rather indifferent to it (indifferent to its presence). Sensibility was now directed toward something else. His comments after returning from the king's clamber were delivered in a strangely flat tone, signifying a lack of real self-involvement.[8] It might be argued here that Macbeth is not actually interested in murder but in the aura of absences around it, that he is not hypnotized by murder as action but by the ever-receding (non)supports in which it is embedded. Macbeth's intellect is from this viewpoint a deepening of a process identified by Margaret Ferguson in Hamlet: the hero's tendency to be attentive to the passive rather than the active: "Hamlet does not inquire very deeply ... into the meaning of his action [when killing Rosencrantz and

Guildenstern, etc.]. This seems odd, since he has shown himself so
remarkably capable of interrogating the meaning of his inaction."[9] In spite
of the larger inclination toward action of Macbeth, the remark remains
relevant for him too—for as I will be continuing to argue, action for him
tends to presence itself in terms of inaction. This fact applies to all the
temporal phases: past action, present action, and future action. Thus the
"dialectic" between action and inaction as it surfaces in Hamlet is here taken
down into a deeper state of reciprocation, for here one side of the dialectic is
often sensed to actually amount to its polar opposite.

The idea of Macbeth as one immersed in "ambition" seems to me to be
a red herring in this general context. We are told that he is exceedingly
ambitious—so ambitious, in fact, that he is prepared to commit a terrible
crime against a sovereign who is politically innocent and not even an
ordinary "political enemy." But while Lady Macbeth is the ambitious one,
and the one trying to persuade her husband that he is her equal in this
respect, Macbeth hardly ever displays political behavior that betokens
ambitious thoughts. The end of the "If it were done" soliloquy is interesting
from this viewpoint:

> I have no spur
> To prick the sides of my intent, but only
> Vaulting ambition, which o'erleaps itself
> And falls on th'other—
>
> (1.7.25–29)

From the orthodox perspective the meaning is that ambition is pure cause, the
only cause. There is a circle of ambition, so that ambition itself causes
ambition. But if ambition is circular and solipsistic in this sense, the circularity
("Vaulting") surely refers to effect rather than cause. Ambition is circular as
effect. In Macbeth there are in a sense only effects (as I shall presently argue).
The ambition is "vaulting" and circular because it has no punctual source or
origin; it does not originate from any empirical fact, whether of treacherous
mind or political actuality. The "ambition" is ultimately empty of substance,
of empirical content; and for this very reason it is nonambition. Macbeth does
not say that he has "only ambition"—or only an ambition that, sadly, happens
to be vaulting. He says that he only has vaulting ambition. It does not overleap
its target (since it has none), it "o'erleaps itself." It traces only the formal
presence of its formal possibility. It "falls on th'other— ... what? Side? In any
case it falls on something else, on something beyond itself, on something that
has nothing to do with ambition.

I would now like to forward the first of the three main critical notions in this subsection. This is the notion that the idea of the murder is stronger for Macbeth than the murder, and that he therefore in a strange way has to perform the murder in order to murder the idea of it.

This line of reasoning presupposes certain assumptions similar to those made by John Bayley. "Macbeth may seem simple enough, but it is also in fact the play with the clearest and most terrifying discrepancy between inner consciousness and action."[10] This fracturing of the spirit, leading to extreme inwardization, is what I have been identifying as "metaphysical servitude". In fact Bayley at one point happens to use this very word ("servitude") in a similar fashion: Shakespeare shows us social chaos but he also shows us chaos in the mind, "its nightmare servitude to an irrevocable act."[11] My commentary would only add this single qualification: that it is not to the act that Macbeth ultimately is the slave, but to the idea of it. This difference may seem slender, "academic." But in fact the whole drama pivots on it—and it is by ignoring this very difference that criticisms tend to prematurely wreck their logic. It is clear that if the "servitude" of the tragic hero is a servitude to the idea rather than to the actual act as such, the servitude can precede the act and thus in a sense come to be viewed as causal.

There are two main ways of explaining the crucial difference between a murder/idea nexus where murder is dominant and a murder/idea nexus where idea is dominant, and I begin with a procedure that discusses this particular notion in relation to the cardinal concept of the entire play: Truth.

Those favoring the theory of ambition will no doubt point to units such as: "Glamis, and Thane of Cawdor: / The greatest is behind" (1.3.116–17) and "Two truths are told, / As happy prologues to the swelling act / Of the imperial theme" (1.3.127–29). The first of these units appears to indicate that Macbeth is now ambitiously looking forward to the remaining third of his monarchial career; but while I can agree with the fact that he certainly is looking forward, I cannot agree with the idea that he is looking forward mainly in terms of ambition. The forward-looking is engineered logically, not emotionally. If a gypsy looks in a crystal ball and tells me I win eight hundred dollars next Wednesday at seven o'clock, and that I win eight million dollars the following Wednesday at seven o'clock, then it is not particularly surprising that I will be looking forward with a thumping heart to that second Wednesday evening if the first Wednesday evening to my surprise brings me in exactly eight hundred dollars and exactly at seven o'clock. But what does this new thrill depend on? It depends exclusively on my quite normal ability to perform cognitive acts of simple induction. This is precisely the mechanism that Shakespeare is working with in Macbeth: and the brilliant point about it all is that subjectivity as causal agent in an important way can be bracketed. My hopes, just like those of Macbeth for the crown, are in a sense *not* monitored by a subjective act of will. Although we have come to desire the promised thing, the "approach" of that thing, its coming into the horizon of our ownmost view, its closeness, is not a function of desire. Instead a rather abstract and lofty mechanism of logic out there in the world has presented these bewildering hopes; they are, as such, beyond my control and influence. Indeed, there can only come into action the sense of a really self-determined subjective mastery through a negation of the hopes: only by resisting them can I gain back the initiative that right now has slipped away into chance, weird predestination, or whatever you want to call it. "Glamis, and Thane of Cawdor: / The greatest is behind." If the lines are spoken with the gluttony of poorly concealed expectation, then Macbeth, I admit, is already implicitly a murderer and a villain, a new *Richard III*. But I do not think the lines should be spoken with the dark glow of intense ambition radiating from the eyes, and I do not think that Macbeth in any significant way recapitulates *Richard III*. The words might better be spoken in stunned, mechanical, incredulous reverie.

The idea of the "happy prologues" does not really endanger this reading, for "happy" does not necessarily at all refer to an emotion (a growing happiness inside the cogito "Macbeth") but, indeed, to "prologues." It is not happiness (as a subjective state of mind) that is at stake; here, but the idea of happiness; and this idea is an ideal: happiness as the completion of the perfectly drawn metaphysical circle Glamis–Cawdor–King. The happiness lies most of all in the completion of the circle, in the happy presence to itself of the circle's possible realization. The "prologues" are happy because their identities as prologues are quickly being enhanced by the general turn of events.

The second way of discussing the ascendancy of "idea of murder" over "murder" is to call attention to certain psychological states involving delinealized temporality and reversed causation. Macbeth, we know, suffers right from the first encounter with the sisters from a "fit"—call it a "murder fit." But this fit is not an emotion or passion in which he suddenly, like Mr. Hyde, realizes that he wants to murder; instead the fit is a state where he realizes that his identity-as-murderer is already formed "out there" in logical space. The entity Macbeth-as-murderer "exists," immediately, as a ready-made thing out there. It is premature and trivial to call this thing an "idea" or a "thought"—because Shakespeare is perhaps in the final analysts shaking our confidence in being able to state what an idea or a thought is. What is a thought? What is an idea? These questions do not simply follow the Macbeth-problematic as "interesting points" to be made about a finished dramatic experience; rather, these questions are internal to the dramatic experience as such—not as questions, but as movements charged with questioning possibility.

The "fit" that seizes Macbeth can be compared with the one that seizes many people who come to a precipice. What is interesting here is the mechanism of "original reaction" or "originary fear." It is related to what I discussed a while ago as "originary healing." The psychological mechanism only appears in humans, though certain higher apes have similar tendencies. In this type of experience, there is not first a perception of the abyss, then a fear of it, and then a readiness to jump off—in order, as it were, to cancel the horrible swelling of the fear. Instead there is from the outset a sense of vertigo: the very first perception of the abyss is the perception of one's horrible fate at its bottom. That, precisely, is what the abyss is all about: that all along it has been waiting for you there; or, to make things more gruesome and Shakespearean: that all along you have been waiting down there. "You." A corpse. The fallen you waits for you, just as in our play the fallen Macbeth (who already has murdered Duncan) "waits" for the not-fallen Macbeth. In a sense greets him, quite solemnly. "Hail Macbeth!" The existence of specters in such a world does not at all surprise one from this viewpoint: corpses, rising from the abyss; an absolute beyond speaking from inside the bosom of one's tightest self-presence.

This mechanism can be theorized in minute detail with reference to the hero's system of reflexes. Macbeth does not first feel that he might eventually want to murder Duncan and then see the bloody scenario in front of him and then finally find himself in full flight from the feeling/thought/image. This reassuring sequentiality is what afflicts Mr. Smith in the common horror story; but Macbeth is not Mr. Smith and Shakespeare is not "into" horror stories. What happens to Macbeth, instead, is that he begins with the horror/flight. He begins not with the flight from something, but just with "from": the flight-from. He does not begin with the horror of something, but just with "of": horror-of. Gradually he has to "fill in" the missing object, make it present and self-present.

> My thought, whose murder yet is but fantastical,
> Shakes so my single state of man,
> That function is smother'd in surmise,
> And nothing is, but what is not.
>
> (1.3.139–43)

Here, it is not only that the consequences of murder have not yet been fully grasped; murder is not "fantastical" merely because it is unreal and unfamiliar as a fully developed notion. The unit "fantastical" instead indicates that murder at this point refuses to be, precisely, "a fully developed notion." Thought, still, has not formed the idea "murder," and conversely "murder" is not yet part of thought but part of what is "fantastical." "Murder," from this viewpoint is weird ("fantastical"), and the important word sequence "thought, whose murther" (which hits the spectator as word sequence, not idea) indicates that thought itself is drawn into the dangers, risks, and unrealities of "murder," that "thought" and "murder" are coimplicative—but in a way that cannot yet (or perhaps ever) be understood.

The idea I am trying to promote, here, is that repulsion in a difficult sense is primal and originary in Macbeth; repulsion is "causal" as it is in cases of deathward anguish near the precipice. Because one is so frightfully repelled by the horrible abyss, one is sucked down into it. Analogously: because noble Macbeth is so frightfully repelled by the idea of murder, he is drawn relentlessly into it.

The important soliloquies of the opening act are all structured by this primacy of repulsion. Thus Shakespeare does not make us feel that Macbeth is a pulsional man, full of the blood-hot passion of murderous desire, and that metaphysical deliberation is some kind of hesitant latecomer, some mere process of deferral. Instead Shakespeare makes us feel that repulsion "organizes" pulsion, that the repulsive reflex is so dominant and intense that whatever eventually gets done in the name of its opposite (in the name of murder) really in a fundamental way is structured, determined, and limited by that original and irremovable repulsionism.

This queer organization can be felt in the important "If it were done" soliloquy. Here, already, and under the influence of Lady Macbeth's manipulations, the hero is beginning to try to think out his revulsion in terms of its opposite: "real" desire to murder. But precisely because revulsion still plays the leading part—the part it remains playing for the duration of the tragedy—the soliloquy does not take Macbeth where "he"/murder would have liked it to go.

Soliloquy

If it were done, when 'tis done, then 'twere well
It were done quickly: if th'assassination
Could trammel up the consequence ...

(1.7.1–3)

There is pragmatic calculation here, a man prepared to overlook transcendental issues ("jump the life to come," 1.7.7) in order to carefully consider the worldly consequences of a mean deed. So goes the common reading. And it will be supported by critics like Bertrand Evans, theorists who argue that Macbeth has no moral awareness at all, and that this soliloquy reveals the shallowness of his moral capacities.[12] We are told that Macbeth in no true way is raising moral objections to murder in this soliloquy, that his moral logic is lame and insufficient.[13] I agree entirely. But for the opposite reasons. Why is this pro-and-con soliloquy empty of moral substance? Evans says it is because Macbeth lacks moral sensibility; I say that it is because Macbeth has moral sensibility. The moral debate is superfluous (and thus structurally empty for Macbeth as "dialectic" or inner tug-of-war) precisely because he has absolute insight into the immorality of the deed. If Evans's notion of Macbeth as a moral idiot were true, we would have no tragedy at all. In Shakespeare's complex organization of the tragic mechanism, the very murder requires an absolute recoil as a first trigger for its later effectuation. For Evans the hero's rhetoric only indicates that the murder is assessed as being "particularly risky,"[14] and the unit "We'd jump the life to come" is identified as a "casual" pronouncement.[15] Macbeth's feeling that the murder will be blown in every eye is said to refer to the villain's fear of punishment as a consequence of universal protest.[16]

> If it were done, when 'tis done, then 'twere well
> It were done quickly: if th'assassination
> Could trammel up the consequence, and catch
> With his surcease success; that but this blow
> Might be the be-all and the end-all—here,
> But here, upon this bank and shoal of time,
> We'd jump the life to come.—But in these cases,
> We still have judgment here; that we but teach
> Bloody instructions, which, being taught, return
> To plague th'inventor: this even-handed Justice
> Commends th'ingredience of our poison'd chalice
> To our own lips.
>
> (1.7.1–12)

The trouble with distortions and simplifications of Macbeth's tragic mind is not only that the hero's subtle character gets ruined but also that we end up with a falsification and sentimentalization of the relationship between Macbeth and Lady Macbeth. Because Bertrand Evans thinks that Macbeth is a moral idiot, he also thinks that Lady Macbeth knows Macbeth in a very deep manner. Indeed, in their conjoint "understanding" of Macbeth as a moral idiot (and therefore also a pathetic coward) Evans and Lady Macbeth form a perfect pair. Their readings of the man Macbeth and of the particular nature of his inner predicament are equally acute. This "superlative wife," we are informed, reads Macbeth like a "primer."[17] His expressed reluctance to proceed with the evil plan is the function of "lame" rationalization, a pathetically "whining" set of excuses.[18] She only has to tell him the "plain truth"[19] and show him how to avoid getting caught in order to demolish his dams of resistance.[20]

Shakespeare, of course, is really doing something utterly different in this soliloquy. Murder is a completely monstrous thing for Macbeth, and the soliloquy ends up in the constatation that murder is out of the question. It may seem that this decision is a function of the foregrounding of all the nasty "consequences" of murder; yet as the end of the speech indicates, the final sensation has nothing to do with "consequences" but with the apprehension of a vast visionary nothingness in which the nullity of motivation and the nullity of desire are beginning to be indistinguishable.

> his virtues
> Will plead like angels, trumpet-tongu'd, against
> The deep damnation of his taking-off;
> And Pity, like a naked new-born babe,
> Striding the blast, or heaven's Cherubins, hors'd
> Upon the sightless couriers of the air,
> Shall blow the horrid deed in every eye,
> That tears shall drown the wind.—I have no spur
> To prick the sides of my intent, but only
> Vaulting ambition, which o'erleaps itself
> And falls on th'other—
>
> (1.7.18–28)

Although murder (and not merely its "consequences") is prominently horrible for Macbeth in the soliloquy, he permits some distant part of his mind to mechanically go through what amounts to an elaborate *hypothesis of murder*: quite simply to clarify the absurdity of the deed's possibility. The academic silliness of taking various linguistic units at their surface value quickly emerges from a consideration of "We'd jump the life to come" as it appears at the beginning of the speech (1.7.7). Far from indicating a callous readiness to obliterate the transcendental horizon, this unit merely indicates the highly provisional suppression of that idealist notion. It is obvious that instead of being a worldly pragmatist caring only for mundane consequences the hero is in deep levels of his being profoundly conscious of the transcendental dilemma. Macbeth remains a transcendentally oriented figure throughout the play. And, what is more, all his moments of crisis are in the final analysis monitored and organized by his intense transcendentalism—the very transcendentalism that Shakespeare troubled to clarify in his opening scenes. Indeed, none of the hero's moments of tragic crisis are adequately grasped if they are not viewed in relation to the hero's sustained idealism. Although he starts, in this soliloquy, with a lower-than-divine sphere of reference ("here, / But here"), it is eminently clear that the latter parts of the speech reveal a very strong sense of divine infringement: "The *deep damnation* of his taking-off" (1.7.20). In his misreading, Evans fails to see that rhetoric overpowers "meaning." if you look at the end of the soliloquy, with all its images of "heaven's Cherubins" and nakedly new-born Pity, it is easy to see that the generally moral and religious frame of reference is precisely what is most vivid and important in Macbeth's state of mind. Who, in this speech, is not in "deep damnation" if not Macbeth?

But if part of the soliloquy can be viewed as a function of the very moral inclination in Macbeth that certain critics refuse to acknowledge, another part is a function of a vaster mechanism that is still not fully developed but which can nevertheless be intuited at this early stage. This mechanism is perhaps best described as a form of staging. Macbeth begins a highly imaginative process of self-projection where the extravagance of image and sentiment at once flattens and deepens the sense of personal involvement. This involvement, now at one and the same time growing more shallow and more troubled, is an engagement with a "new" Macbeth, or a Macbeth on the "other side"—a person somehow possible at the farther side of "murder," behind and beyond its reality. In this staging—theatrical in an almost melodramatic manner that will not fade in subsequent scenes—it is not merely the question of nonmurderous Macbeth learning how to project himself into the cold-bloodedness of murder; rather, it is the question of quite stable Macbeth learning how to become the absence-from-Macbeth that he already to some extent is on account of prophecy and on account of the weird "original guilt" promoted in the what-is-not soliloquy.[21] The more absent Macbeth learns to become, the more does he become present to the self-absence that already is his odd destiny and tragedy. This process of increasingly melodramatic and forced staging can be related to Bayley's notion (discussed recently) that the hero is unfit to play his part in tragedy. Michael Goldman thinks along similar lines when he speaks of Macbeth "learning to perform" the murder, "as an actor might."[22] In psychoanalytic terms: the more one "plays" being "the murderer" (whether positively or negatively, whether "sincerely" or hypothetically), the less does one have to answer for murder personally. But the play's mechanism does not exactly parallel the Freudian notion that revulsion from murder secretly indicates murderous desire; here, rather, it is the other way around: desire, curiously enough, betokens revulsion, betokens what I have referred to as "originary revulsion" or "originary repulsion."

Two main "levels" can thus be identified in the "if it were done" soliloquy—and both of them unbalance the "stage-villain" reading forwarding this great speech as a discourse on worldly obstacles. First there is the clear view of Macbeth as a morally conscious man—a view deliberately and elaborately staged by Shakespeare. Macbeth, searching his heart, finds that murder is not tolerable as a political deed or human act. But precisely because Macbeth is so obviously moral, precisely because he himself is so profoundly conscious of his own ingrained idealism, the "moral dimension" of his thought is almost automatized: he does not have to carefully think out the reasons for not murdering Duncan but instead merely has to call them into view. Indeed, we feel that part of his mind is absent from this cataloguing of moral considerations. As we have seen, there are critics who prematurely rationalize this slight absence in Macbeth from the moral issues as a "moral lack." But the lack is not a moral lack but a lack. Just that, a vacuity and minus. Macbeth listens to himself go through a routine act of logical argumentation, but what interests him is the astonishing fact that he can at all deliberate such matters in a reasoning manner. As the sense of dreamy unreality intensifies, he can fuel the absence-oriented process by permitting his sense of slipping foothold to merge with the "deep damnation" in Duncan's "taking-off." Macbeth actually himself takes off, joining those equally unreal creatures in the aerial corridors of sightless couriers and heavenly cherubim.

It is clear by now that the "If it were done" soliloquy simultaneously forwards the sense of two opposite movements—and that discourse, deconstructing the oppositionality of this (dialectical) opposition, unifies *and* separates the "two" motions in one and the "same" operation. On the one hand the act in which Macbeth makes "murder" more present as an imaginatively developed structure of mind is indistinguishable from his desire to explode that structure and ride recklessly away on the fantastical improbability of its reality. On the other hand, and conversely, the very negation of murder has a striking suggestion of being an imaginative effort to dig into its possible reality, to discover its possibility *as* real. The real equivocation, in summary, is not produced by the pros and cons of murder, by advantages and disadvantages, but by the fact that the collapse of dialectical oppositionality opens a "unified" sphere of precarious suggestion in which the *entire* corpus of the soliloquy can work at once for aim against murder. Macbeth desires the absence of his presence to murder, but he also desires the presence of his absence from murder. From the deconstructionist viewpoint these "two" movements are (1) the same thing, and (2) not the same thing. The space "between" these two last alternatives is unthinkable, or is to be thought only in terms of unthinkability. The space "between" these two last alternatives is not a space. It cannot be intellectually "visualized"—but exists "in" (or through) discourse as a non-spatio-logical "instance."

"Present fears / Are less than horrible imaginings" (1.3.137–38). Yes. But the presence of the horrible imaginings themselves is at once a move in the reassuring direction of "present fears" and a move away from what can be present. It is this "double" (and yet not double) movement that I shall consistently track throughout *Macbeth*: that Macbeth in servile fashion frantically presses all entities into their reassuring presence; but that this presenting in a sense is a mock-presenting of mock-presences, since "what" is made present is somehow always already intuited as empty of (full) presence. Thus Macbeth in a sense walks into a trap (the trap of "presence"); but since he has darkly foreseen the abyssal absence in the bosom of all presence, we may be entitled to feel that his self-entrapment is partly self-organized. Macbeth rids himself of "Macbeth," paradoxically, by setting out to find him: he vaguely realizes that the prey, once caught, will vanish and thus cease to bother him.

NOTES

1. *Shakespeare and Tragedy*, p. 191.

2. Quoted by J.I.M. Stewart in "Sleep Tragic Contrast: *Macbeth*," in *Shakespeare: The Tragedies*, ed. Clifford Leech (Chicago and London: University of Chicago Press, 1965), p. 106.

3. Ibid., p. 108.

4. Ibid., p. 119.

5. Ibid., p. 114.

6. Muir argues that the eye-versus-hand imagery "is Shakespearian" (KM, 25); but it could be argued that the too-obvious Shakespearean stress here is exactly what looks suspicious. The passage contains the Shakespearean building blocks, but does it contain the Shakespearean way of assembling these blocks?

7. *Shakespeare and Tragedy*, p. 69.

8. See Bartholomeusz, *Macbeth and the Players*, p. 259.

9. "Hamlet: Letters and Spirits," p. 299.

10. *Shakespeare and Tragedy*, p. 69.

11. Ibid.

12. *Shakespeare's Tragic Practice* (Oxford: Clarendon Press, 1979), pp. 200–201.

13. Ibid., p. 201.

14. Ibid., p. 202.

15. Ibid., p. 201.

16. Ibid., p. 202. I should perhaps emphasize, here, that I am in favor of retaining the Folio punctuation. This is not the place to undertake a critique of the "emendation" currently institutionalized; all I can say at this moment, by way of a general remark, is that

the grammatically "correct" punctuation that we now have is an ontologizing construct that spoils a number of crucial spacings in the text. The cryptoromantic and ultra-ontologizing "bank and shoal of time" instead of "bank and school of time" is another interesting "improvement"—especially from the viewpoint of a critique of metaphysical presence.

17. Ibid.

18. Ibid.

19. Ibid.

20. Ibid., p. 203.

21. It may be objected that in discussing a process of "absencing" in Macbeth, I am contradicting my main thesis: that the hero gradually shifts over into a quest for metaphysical presence. But matters cannot be oversimplified. It all very much depends on what we mean by "Macbeth." There certainly is a Macbeth who in the most alarming and conspicuous manner falls into a quest for presence. But the name "Macbeth" is never reducible to a presence: "other" Macbeths are operative "offstage." In addition, as I argue all along, the structural impossibility of (metaphysical) presence, of presence as absolute self-presence, ensures the production of an absent Macbeth by the production of a present one.

22. "Language and Action in *Macbeth*," p. 146.

REBECCA W. BUSHNELL

Thriftless Ambition:
The Tyrants of Shakespeare and Jonson

Shakespeare and Jonson portray tyranny by showing how sexual and political desire both shapes an ambitious tyrant's image and undoes it. More specifically, Richard III and Sejanus (and in a different way, Macbeth) combine ambition with the tyrant's traditional attribute of lust when they rely on seduction in grasping for the crown. In doing so, however, they trap themselves in a web of dependency, for in the end they need to be desired themselves as much as they want the crown. In this confusion, where the seducer abases himself to achieve power, the traditional opposition between the masculine king and effeminate tyrant is both set up and deconstructed. By the time they achieve their purpose, these tyrants find that the power and self they built up through the process of gaining the crown are highly unstable.[1]

In developing this link between ambition and sexual desire, Shakespeare's and Jonson's tyrant plays thus demonstrate an acute self-consciousness of how the traditional rhetoric of statecraft worked in forming the sovereign's as well as the tyrant's image. In these plays, both tyrants and kings manipulate the traditional images of tyrannical lust and effeminacy in seeking to consolidate their own power; in doing so, however, they expose the conventional nature of that imagery. Even as these plays support the earlier characterization of the tyrant as fragmented by desire and subjected

Excerpted from "Thriftless Ambition: The Tyrants of Shakespeare and Jonson," *Tragedies of Tyrants: Political Thought and Theater in the English Renaissance*. ©1990 Cornell University Press.

to women, by focusing on how power is acquired and legitimized through use of that characterization, they reveal its ideological basis. The morality plays dismantle the prince's character when he gives into temptation and desire; Shakespeare's and Jonson's plays, however, more in the fashion of Buchanan's *Baptistes*, demonstrate how to create a political image in a tradition of rhetoric that defines authority by moral character and gender identity. This exposure of the political process extends beyond the uses of sexuality and gender to strip bare the complex strategies of using antithesis to paint a political character. (…)

Macbeth also explores the roles of desire and gender identity in the shaping of the tyrant's image. Like Richard, Macbeth confesses only to "vaulting ambition," not lust. Yet each is compromised by sexual desire in his drive to the throne: Richard by his investment in seduction, and Macbeth by his uxoriousness, which impels him to kill Duncan but deserts him when he is king. Many readers have seen Macbeth's dependence on his wife and the Witches as a sign that legitimacy is associated with patriarchy. The restoration of the proper king and virgin Malcolm by Macduff, not of woman born, is taken to signify the victory of what is masculine and proper over what is feminine and unruly.[2] Yet, while the play thus evokes tyranny's traditional link with effeminacy, apparently opposing Malcolm's and Macduff's masculinity to Macbeth's submission to his wife, Macbeth is uxorious mostly when he is ambitious to be king. When he actually holds the throne, Macbeth becomes increasingly estranged from his wife, in contradiction to the usual pattern, which shows the reigning tyrant dominated and eventually undone by his passion for a woman.

When Malcolm gives Macbeth the full complement of labels traditionally associated with tyranny, he accuses him of being "luxurious"; yet in the play we see no direct evidence of Macbeth's supposed luxuriousness or lustfulness. He can be seen as luxurious only insofar as he is uxorious, that is, insofar as subjection to his wife marks his being mastered by lust for her.[3] The "black and deepe desires" that Macbeth confesses to having are called ambition, but he himself never seems to want the crown as much as his wife wants it for him.[4] Once he admits that he has "no spur / To prick the sides of my intent, but only / Vaulting ambition" (1.7.25–27), his lady enters to prick him with her spurs. Unlike Richard III, Macbeth does not present his lust for the crown as a substitute for the desire for women; for Macbeth, they are intermingled.

At the same time that the tyrant's uxoriousness is thus introduced, it is complicated by the play's confusion of masculinity and femininity, which allows gender to be manipulated in political rhetoric.[5] Lady Macbeth's plea to the spirits to unsex her and fill her full of direst cruelty is usually interpreted as her rejecting her femininity in favor of a Masculine code of blood and ambition. Yet, while Lady Macbeth asks the spirits to unsex her, she also asks them to convert her female sexuality into a form of cruelty (milk to gall), adapting "feminine" weakness to feminine power, and thus fulfilling John Knox's fear that while women are naturally weak, in "experience" they are "variable and cruel."[6] More than simply "manly," her actions are shrewish, when she commands her husband to "hie thee hither, / That I may pour my spirits in thine ear, / And chastise with the valor of my tongue / All that impedes thee from the golden round" (1.5.25–28). Not entirely "unfeminine," her behavior fulfills men's fears of what happens when women get power.[7]

The lady's following scene with Macbeth emphasizes Macbeth's own effeminacy, at the same time that she fashions a model of "manly" action for him to follow. Any movement that Macbeth makes away from killing Duncan his lady calls unmanly, although it is implicitly unmanly that he should submit to her plans in the first place. When he first begins to resist going ahead with the murder, she challenges him with being effeminate (so green and pale)[8] and with failing in his love for her—a love that defines his uxoriousness (1.7.38–39). Macbeth clearly perceives this speech as a threat to his manliness. Indeed, it is threatening that she says it at all: "Prithee, peace!" he begs, "I dare do all that may become a man; / Who dares [do] more is none" (1.7.45–47). He thus defends his masculinity against her shrewishness as much as he rejects the murder plan. Lady Macbeth, in turn, diverts his attention by interpreting his "man" in terms of the opposition of man and beast, rather than man and woman. Thus he can feel that instead of obeying her, he simply embraces a more inclusive concept of manliness. In the end, Macbeth appears sufficiently convinced that he has not really given in to her. He does not praise her as a man but rather as a woman who is capable of creating men: "Bring men-children only! / For thy undaunted mettle should compose / Nothing but males" (1.7.73–75).

The audience thus sees Macbeth giving in to his wife and her "sexual blackmail,"[9] but his lady has prevented him from realizing he is doing so by persuading him that it is manly to do what she proposes. While Macbeth's decision to proceed clearly echoes earlier images of the tyrant's uxoriousness, it is also different because in following his wife, Macbeth supposedly upholds masculine values. Insofar as Cambyses' love for his Lady is expressed in threats and cruelty, this conjunction of tyrannical "masculinity" and effeminacy is implied; in *Macbeth*, however, the relationship is expressed explicitly in the lady's description of his tyrannical usurpation (in fulfillment of *her* desires) as a "manly" and not an effeminate act.

In Cambyses' case, the tyrant's infatuation represents or at least parallels the climax of his bloody and vicious career; in *Macbeth*, however, Macbeth's submission accompanies his rise to the throne. *After* Duncan's murder, the "manly" Macbeth drifts apart from Lady Macbeth.[10] In his terror after committing the deed, he barely seems to hear her when she admonishes him to "consider it not so deeply" (2.2.27). When she commands him to take the daggers back to where Duncan lies, Macbeth refuses to do so. The moment following the murder scene thus signals his drawing away from her influence, insofar as he disregards and disobeys her. The next time we see them together in private, Lady Macbeth complains that Macbeth keeps apart (3.2.8). Before the banquet scene he still addresses her with endearments, but he does not tell her his secrets (3.2.45–46). In the banquet scene itself, when Macbeth is crazed by Banquo's ghost, Lady Macbeth again accuses him of unmanliness: "Are you a man?" she asks (3.4.57); is he "quite unmann'd, in folly?" (3.4.72). She sees his actions as feminine "flaws and starts" that "would well become / A woman's story at a winter's fire / Authoriz'd by her grandam" (3.4.62–65). While Macbeth attempts to confront the specter "like a man," this time he cannot give in to her vision of himself and of events as he did before the murder. Even as he appears most "unmanly" in the grip of fear and illusion, he is detaching himself from her influence and so is no longer uxorious.

After the banquet scene in act 3, we do not see the husband and wife together again, and Macbeth reacts to the news of his lady's death without emotion. When he hears the cry of women, he says, "I have almost forgot the taste of fears" (5.5.9). Although fear above all dominated his first actions as a tyrant, now even fear seems to have left him. The only identifiable emotion he retains is a warrior's anger, a sanctioned "manly" emotion in this play.[11] Macbeth's development as a tyrant, in contrast to Cambyses', thus ends with his loss of passion and feeling, the hallmarks of the feminine and of the traditional tyrant.

Linda Bamber argues that in Shakespeare's plays "the tragic process," or tragic experience of the male self, parallels a process of separation from the feminine, the consequent abuse of women, and a moving beyond anger and loss to a new vision of the self. But, as she notes, that pattern does not occur in *Macbeth*.[12] For Bamber, it is absent because the play lacks a dialectic between the feminine and masculine, when Lady Macbeth values "the world of men above everything else."[13] Yet the feminine is not, as she claims, "irrelevant to the dialectic of the tragedy":[14] it is located in Macbeth's uxoriousness, which he sheds in the play's course. Macbeth's tyranny is accentuated by his gradual separation from his wife, and his lack of desire serves as the ultimate proof of his tyranny.

In suggesting that Macbeth pays both too much and not enough attention to his wife, *Macbeth* thus evokes and challenges the conventional function of gender in political imagery. While in *Cambyses* the tyrant translates uxoriousness into cruelty, in *Macbeth* uxoriousness and tyranny are ultimately divided, because even though Macbeth is "effeminate" in becoming a tyrant, he then *abandons* the emotions that are traditionally feminine. The doubleness of the feminine, in which passion is both strength and weakness, surfaces in Lady Macbeth, whose excessive "femininity" becomes shrewishness. Yet it also is reflected in her husband, who is most "manly"—and most depleted—in his full tyranny. Even if Macduff is not of woman born and Malcolm is a virgin, by the play's end Macbeth's condition establishes that separation from women is not an absolute virtue: Malcolm and Macduff must share that state with the tyrant Macbeth.

In focusing on Richard's and Macbeth's becoming tyrants, as well as on their actions once they have seized the throne, *Richard III* and *Macbeth* thus dislocate the conventional relationships between tyranny and desire, and tyranny and gender, developed in both the morality plays and the statecraft tradition. While Shakespeare's plays adapt many of the traditional conventions concerning tyranny's association with effeminacy and lust, they also demonstrate how those conventions are used to shape an image of a sovereign self. Richard III distances himself from sexual desire and effeminacy to define Edward as a tyrant yet uses these attributes to construct his own image as the legitimate king. Such a construction undermines him once he comes to rule, when his "effeminacy" becomes weakness and his roles as lover and beloved falter. In *Macbeth*, too, the attribute of uxoriousness is essential to the shaping of Macbeth's image as tyrant-usurper: once *he* comes to rule, however, his "effeminacy" is shed, converted into a more terrifying "masculinity." The play thus offers a devastating reply to Tyndale's insistence that a cruel tyrant is a better ruler than an effeminate king.

NOTES

1. See Robert N. Watson, *Shakespeare and the Hazards of Ambition* (Cambridge, Mass.: Harvard University Press, 1984), for an account of this process. One clear exception to this description of tyranny is the portrait of Claudius in *Hamlet*; since that play is concerned more with tyrannicide than with the tyrant, however, I have chosen not to consider it here. On the treatment of tyrants and tyrannicide in *Hamlet*, see Roland Mushat Frye, *The Renaissance Hamlet: Issues and Responses in 1600* (Princeton, N.J.: Princeton University Press, 1984), chap. 2.

2. See Leonard Tennenhouse, *Power on Display: The Politics of Shakespeare's Genres* (London and New York: Methuen, 1986), pp. 127–32; Peter Stallybrass, "Macbeth and Witchcraft," in *Focus on Macbeth*, ed. John Russell Brown (London: Routledge and Kegan

Paul, 1982); and Janet Adelman, "'Born of Woman': Fantasies of Maternal Power in *Macbeth*," in *Cannibals, Witches and Divorce: Estranging the Renaissance: Selected Papers from The English Institute, 1985*, n.s., no. 11, ed. Marjorie Garber (Baltimore, Md.: Johns Hopkins University Press, 1987).

3. David Norbrook notes that "Macbeth appears as a ravisher only in the symbolic sense, in comparing himself to Tarquin" ("*Macbeth* and the Politics of Historiography," in *The Politics of Discourse: The Literature and History of Seventeenth Century England*, ed. Kevin Sharpe and Steven N. Zwicker [Berkeley: University of California Press, 1987], p. 103). In "History, Politics and *Macbeth*," Michael Hawkins notes that uxoriousness is an essential part of Macbeth's image as a tyrant (in *Focus on Macbeth*, ed. John Russell Brown [London: Routledge and Kegan Paul, 1982], pp. 164–65). For a psychoanalytic interpretation of Macbeth's surrender to feminine "spirits," also see Coppélia Kahn, *Man's Estate: Masculine Identity in Shakespeare* (Berkeley: University of California Press, 1981), p. 178.

4. Robert Ornstein, in *The Moral Vision of Jacobean Tragedy* (Madison: University of Wisconsin Press, 1960) concludes that "Macbeth no more murders for ambition than Raskolnikov murders for money. Like Raskolnikov, he kills for himself, for 'peace'—the end of the restless torment of his imagination. He must prove to himself under the goading of his wife that he is a man" (p. 231).

5. Robert Kimbrough, "Macbeth: The Prisoner of Gender," *Shakespeare Studies* 16 (1983): 175–90, sees *Macbeth* as demonstrating the "personal and social destructiveness of polarized masculinity and femininity" (p. 177); for him Shakespeare's "works move toward liberating humanity from the prisons created by inclusive and exclusive gender labeling" (p. 175). I would suggest rather that Shakespeare uses gender to criticize conventions of political discourse.

6. See chap. 2, p. 65, of this volume. Adelman argues that here Lady Macbeth "localizes the image of maternal danger" (p. 98).

7. See Harry Berger, Jr., "Text against Performance: The Example of *Macbeth*," in *The Power of Forms in the English Renaissance*, ed. Stephen Greenblatt (Norman, Okla.: Pilgrim Books, 1982), p. 73, on the witches' and Lady Macbeth's violent femininity. Dennis Biggins, "Sexuality, Witchcraft and Violence in *Macbeth*," *Shakespeare Studies* 8 (1975): 255–77, also suggests that "witchcraft is associated with sexual domination and unnatural sexual infatuation" (p. 263). Cf. Stallybrass on the witches' association with "female rule and the overthrowing of patriarchal authority, which in turn leads to the 'womanish' (both cowardly and instigated by women) killing of Duncan, the 'holy' father who establishes both family and state" (p. 201).

8. See Adelman, p. 101, on this metaphor.

9. D.F. Rauber, "Macbeth, Macbeth, Macbeth," *Criticism* 11 (1969): 61.

10. Kahn, however, suggests that during this time "Macbeth moves to passive identification with the mysterious, evil feminine powers" (p. 185), while Wilson sees that "as her husband yields to the id, Lady Macbeth gradually becomes superfluous, much in the way Lear's Fool becomes superfluous: when the protagonist internalizes the companion's voice, the companion can disappear from the stage" (p. 119).

11. On the "newly Homeric valorization of anger" in the Renaissance, see Gordon Braden, *Renaissance Tragedy and the Senecan Tradition: Anger's Privilege* (New Haven, Conn.: Yale University Press, 1985), p. 75.

12. Linda Bamber, *Comic Women, Tragic Men: A Study of Gender and Genre in Shakespeare* (Stanford, Calif.: Stanford University Press, 1982), p. 105.

13. Bamber, p. 91.

14. Bamber, p. 107.

ROBERT LANIER REID

Macbeth's Three Murders

Macbeth is a milestone in man's exploration of ... this "depth of things"
which our age calls the unconscious.
—Harold Goddard, *The Meaning of Shakespeare*

Shakespeare inherited a five-act dramaturgical pattern that he refined into
a symmetrical 2–1–2 series of cycles, focusing each cycle on a central
"epiphanal encounter," a moment of intense recognition. In the mature
tragedies, *Macbeth* and *King Lear*, those three cycles (and epiphanal
moments) form stages of psychological development: a comprehensive inner
plot. What transpires in the protagonist's soul during each of the three
phases, and how does each prepare for the next? What holistic psychological
development occurs in the course of each play?

Interpreters of *Macbeth* have focused almost exclusively on the first
murder, the killing of a king in acts 1–2, as the basis for understanding the
play—its social, psychological, and metaphysical meanings. Macbeth's
subsequent two assassinations, of Banquo in act 3, and of Macduff's wife and
children in acts 4–5, either are ignored, or are treated simply as efforts to
secure the usurped crown, or perhaps as a kind of Freudian "repetition
compulsion"—the blooded man's first heinous kill engendering serial
slayings.[1] Neither of the subsequent murders has been accorded its own

---

From *Shakespeare's Tragic Form*. ©2000 Associated University Presses, Inc.

distinctive meaning and psychological motivation; they are seen as mere shadowy reenactments of the Oedipal complex which is presumed to underlie the one essential crime, the slaying of the patriarchal king.[2]

As R.A. Foakes pus it, "the murder of Duncan was the equivalent in mountaineering terms of scaling Everest, and after this [Macbeth] has no trouble with lower hills."[3] This exclusive highlighting of the regicide (as the "be-all and end-all" of the play) entails, however, that the final three acts must dwindle from real theatrical power to melodramatic spectacle[4]—a result of the victims' shrinking symbolic import and, correspondingly, the shrinking spiritual grandeur of the protagonists, who deliver fewer and fewer eloquent soliloquies, consign their villainies to hired thugs, and finally are swept aside by the nobler (but less charismatic) avengers, Macduff and Malcolm. Many astute critics of the play—including Bradley, Rossiter, Heilman, Sanders, Jorgensen, Mack, Kirsch, and Muir—have struggled with this central conundrum: can the playwright sustain great tragedy if the only true kingly spirit is dispatched at the outset?[5]

Like most of these critics, I believe that Macbeth's capacious mind, despite its moral degeneration, remains at center-stage, showing the horrific consequences of a truly heroic spirit embracing evil. But instead of conceiving the tragedy as one great cosmos-shaking act of regicide followed by two subordinate aftershocks, I would characterize the Macbeths' journey into darkness as three equally significant stages of spiritual catastrophe, three distinctive and theatrically potent dimensions of evil as it evolves and festers in the human psyche. Macbeth murders first a politically authoritative *parental ruler*, then a *brotherly friend* (his "chiefest friend" according to Holinshed), and finally a *mother and her children*.[6] His victims thus represent the three fundamental human bonds, together comprising (in reverse order) the three basic stages of human maturation, or the three essential cathexes of the human psyche. Thus, in the course of the three murders Macbeth deconstructs the entire psychological infrastructure of human identity. Shakespeare's awareness of this pattern is underscored by its earlier prototypical appearance in *Richard III*, where that villain-hero similarly kills a king (Henry VI), then a brother (Clarence), then children (the Princes).[7] In *Macbeth*, however, the playwright is far more apprised of the scheme's psychological implications, which he methodically exploits.

The dramaturgical design of *Macbeth* precisely emphasizes this three-phase pattern: acts 1 and 2 present, in a continuous sequence, the regicide and its immediate consequences; act 3 shows the murder of Banquo and then its impact on Macbeth at the banquet; acts 4 and 5, another continuous cycle of action, presents the slaughter of Macduff's family, then its social and psychological consequences.[8] This 2–1–2 structure, the dramaturgic pattern of all of Shakespeare's mature tragedies, perfectly accommodates his treatment of Macbeth's three murders.

To attain this neatly coherent pattern of psychological devolution, Shakespeare has drastically altered Holinshed's *Chronicles*[9]—first, by condensing all the major crises of Duncan's six-year reign and of Macbeth's seventeen-year reign into the two-hour traffic of the stage. The entire battery of wars and assassinations seems to transpire in a matter of days, rather than a quarter of a century, making the three murders (as well as the broader framework of political violence in acts 1 and 5) seem closely and causally connected.

Equally striking is Shakespeare's moral reshaping of the victims, casting them as iconically benevolent members of the human family, in order to accommodate his three-phase tragic pattern. Instead of the chronicles' portrait of a weak, cowardly, and greedy king about the same age as his cousin Macbeth, Shakespeare portrays Duncan as aged, humble, and generous—an ideal, almost saintly monarch. Though some recent critics, in the radically revisionist spin of New Historicism, interpret Duncan's "womanliness" as Shakespeare's indication of his unkingly impotence, I believe Wilbur Sanders's view is correct: Duncan's nurturing, fertile, self-mortifying traits contribute positively to Shakespeare's portrait of "a most sainted king" (4.3.109). Duncan begins where Lear and Cymbeline end, as a king who can "see feelingly."[10]

Similarly Banquo, in the chronicles a co-conspirator in regicide, is recast as a devoted friend in life's warfare, modestly resisting each temptation to which his colleague falls prey. Many critics have questioned the probity of Banquo even more than Duncan. Berger's and Calderwood's subtle criticism of Duncan's "aggressive giving" would also pertain to Banquo's lavish praise of his warrior-colleague (1.4.54–58).[11] Yet that Duncan's and Banquo's compliments are essentially benevolent is underscored not only by their repeated association with "royalty" and "grace," but also by the contrast with Macbeth's deceitful, murderous mode of "aggressive giving"—especially his forceful invitation of Banquo to the feast (3.1.11–39) and flattery of the missing guest (3.2.30–31, 4.41–44, 91-92). Though Shakespeare implies political shortcomings in Duncan's aged weakness and in Banquo's Hamletlike inertia after the regicide (thus qualifying the playwright's compliment to James I), nevertheless in reviving the chronicles Shakespeare has taken pains to idealize the moral character of both victims; their frailties, like Hamlet's, derive more from warring evils of the world than from their own innate urges.

Likewise Macduff, who in the chronicles enters the story belatedly, mainly seeking personal revenge, is transmuted by Shakespeare into an ever-present touchstone of charitable social compassion. He is the Man of Feeling, who enacts what his wife and babes, those "strong knots of love," have engendered: the most primitive human bond. Adelman and Hunter devalue Macduff's moral character by taking seriously Lady Macduff's anxious but wittily exaggerated accusations of her husband (4.2.6–14, 14–45);[12] yet even the child appreciates the irony of her remarks. In spite of the pointed criticisms leveled at Macduff by his wife, by Malcolm (4.3.26–28), and, most emphatically, by himself (4.3.224–27), it is clear that he is moved by generous compassion for Scotland as a whole, and that his compassion grows out of the intense family feeling manifested by his wife and child. It is Macduff's horrified response to Duncan's murder that initiates the knocking of conscience in the Macbeths; and it is his patriotic opposition to the usurper that galvanizes Scotland and England into a retributive force.

Shakespeare's radical reconstruction of the chronicles, especially his amelioration of the victims' moral character, thus emphasizes the destruction of three primordial human bonds. This three-phase sequence of psychological disintegration (and implicit affirmation of the values destroyed) provides a paradigm of Shakespeare's mature tragic form.

Killing Duncan: Usurping and Dismantling Superego

In presenting an initial assault on regal or parental authority in acts 1–2, *Macbeth* is comparable to all the tragedies from *Hamlet* to *Coriolanus*. The murder of a parentlike king, reflecting the Macbeths' aspiration to Godlike greatness and power, is an Oedipal repudiation of superego (as commentators since Freud and Jekels have acknowledged). Yet the gender implications of Duncan's rule have been too reductively construed by Oedipal-oriented psychoanalysts. For centuries it has been assumed that Duncan's *fatherliness* forms the basis of his comprehensive social identity (Scotland) and of his Christlike spiritual identity ("The Lord's anointed temple," 2.3.70)—that as *patriarch* he, like Lear and Cymbeline, represents the acme of psychological development, the mature conscience of the race, or, in Freudian terms, "superego."[13] Critics persistently construe the regicidal motive as all Oedipal antagonism, citing Lady Macbeth's distress at Duncan's fatherly appearance during the assault (2.2.12–13), to which one might add Macbeth's condemnation of the murder as a "parricide," projecting his own Oedipal urges onto Malcolm and Donalbain (3.1.31).

Yet the Macbeths envision Duncan not just as a *father*, who "hath been / So clear in his great office" (1.7.17–18), but also as a *mother*, who vies with

Lady Macbeth in expressing love for her husband and for the other thanes, and who is cast as Lucrece to Macbeth's "ravishing Tarquin" with his phallic dagger (2.1.33–55). In addition, both Macbeths at critical moments in their soliloquies envision the monarch as a vulnerable and soul-like *child*, the heavenly infant that Lady Macbeth would deny the chance to "peep through the blanket of the dark, / To cry, 'Hold, hold!'" (1.5.53–54), and which Macbeth projects apocalyptically as a "naked new-born babe" of Pity (1.7.21). Thus, in psychoanalytic (or "object-relational") terms Duncan is not just the father, but all aspects of the human family—perhaps most poignantly, mother and child. By their own gender obsessions, the Macbeths have promoted the erroneous and reductive conception of sovereignty as a pure patriarchy. As recent critics have noted, the Macbeths' urge for sovereign greatness is expressed as a fantasy of becoming exclusively "manly" by taking up phallic weaponry to eliminate womanly and childlike characteristics.[14]

Similarly, in acts 1–2 of each mature tragedy Shakespeare portrays an assault on conscience or synteresis (or Freudian superego), not merely as a fatherly or kingly power, but increasingly as a consolidating, androgynous figure of authority: Othello and Desdemona defend themselves conjointly before the Venetian council; Lear's initial attempt to arrogate and then to suppress female nurture confirms the flaw in his sovereignty; Duncan is androgynous; Antony and Cleopatra struggle toward that communion; in contrast, Coriolanus, like Macbeth, seeks a constrictive autonomy and absoluteness through eliminating "female" relationality and compassion. As Stephen Orgel and Lotus Montrose have observed, both Elizabeth I and James I promoted the idea of their monarchy as an androgynous consolidation of paternal authority and female nurture.[15]

The Macbeths' notable series of monologues in acts 1–2, fueled by willful hyperbole, confirms their aspiration to a male-oriented version of "greatness" (a word whose variants appear seventeen times in act 1, more than in the other four acts combined). To the extent that we as audience identify with the Macbeths' grand speechmaking, hypnotic role-playing, and cosmic aspiration for greatness in these acts, we must also experience the ironies that emerge in the actual performance of the murder: pettiness, furtiveness, cowardice, and utter deceit.

As the hyperbolic fantasy of these early soliloquies reveals, the ego function informing this regicidal-parenticidal stage of Macbeth's career in villainy is *sublimation* but in its most perverted form. Anna Freud describes sublimation as the highest phase of psychic functioning in the construction of selfhood, the ultimate means of enriching the ego.[16] Ideally, sublimation resolves the Oedipal struggle (a struggle for the final, genital stage of sexual maturation), not by evading bodily consummation of sexual energies, nor by suppressing their female component, but, as Loewald and Kohut have shown, by promoting comprehensive and free interplay between gender-components of the self. Thus the Macbeths' brutish rape of kingly greatness works exactly contrary to authentic sublimation. By furtively killing the king they not only destroy the bond with this androgynous parent, they also violate the illuminating and consolidating powers of their own superego, or conscience, inducing a sleeper regression into self-divisive and annihilative ego defenses.

KILLING BANQUO: ENVYING THE EGO IDEAL

The murder of Macbeth's "chiefest friend" in act 3 is motivated not by further aspiration to greatness, but by rivalrous envy of a brotherly alter-ego. In acts 1–2 Macbeth's basic motivation was not envy of Duncan, Banquo, or Malcolm (though the basis for later envy is established): in spite of anxiety over Duncan's appointing his son Prince of Cumberland, Macbeth never considers killing Malcolm along with Duncan (leaving the unappointed Donalbain to shoulder the guilt). In his initial embracing of evil Macbeth is preoccupied with the sublime fantasy of regicide as the "be-all and end-all," conferring inviolable supremacy; only on discovering its failure to provide such aggrandizement does he turn to bitter envy of others, now conceived as rivals. According to Aquinas, "After the sin of pride [whereby Lucifer aspired to be a deity] there followed the evil of envy ... whereby he grieved over man's good."[17] Macbeth's fury toward Banquo is thus a second stage of evil, resulting from the failure to satisfy the hunger for greatness, just as Cain's envious fratricide stemmed from his parents' frustrated desire to emulate God.[18] Envy, and the rivalrous doubling and splitting that necessitates confronting distasteful mirror-images of the self at the center of each of the tragedies, is secondary to that earlier violent effort to displace divine-regal-parental authority. The regicide-parenticide thus leads to fratricide-amiticide, a chronologically secondary but equally universal phenomenon, which carries its own momentous psychological implications.

This assault on a warrior-friend who is virtually the mirror-image or double of Macbeth ("all hail, Macbeth and Banquo! / Banquo and Macbeth, all hail!" 1.3.68–69) is a direct violation of ego, involving a psychological "splitting" into self and shadow-self, as Macbeth perversely identifies with the darker, more illusory component. Though he rationalizes the murder of Banquo in only one soliloquy, far less grandiose than the monologues of acts 1–2, Macbeth throughout act 3 continues the fiery expression of his inner powers by a number of intense dialogues in which he no longer effectively communicates his deeper meaning either to his auditors or to himself. They can only guess at the dark nuances in his spate of bestial images: serpents and scorpions (3.2.13–15, 36; 3.4.28–30); bat, "shard-bound beetle," and crow (3.2.40–42, 50–53); "greyhounds, mongrels, spaniels, curs" (3.1.92–94); "Russian bear, arm'd rhinoceros, or th'Hyrcan tiger" (3.4.99–100); "magot-pies, and choughs, and rooks" (3.4.121–24). Jorgensen calls these speeches (like the similar ravings of Lear in act 3) "soliloquies made public."[19] Equally important, they are soliloquys made obscure through intense repression, so that neither Macbeth and Lear nor their auditors can easily fathom the profound self-divulgence in their speeches. If acts 1–2 show a perverse mode of hyperbolic aspiration (appropriating sublimation as a means of overthrowing the superego or conscience), this furtive imagery of act 3 shows Macbeth's regression to the prior psychic function of *projection*, the defensive externalization of his depraved and problematic qualities onto others, which enforces a general process of "decomposition" and "splitting" of the ego.[20] At its best, projection (an expulsive psychic function deriving from the anal stage of infancy) plays a key role in the development of selfhood, enabling one to influence others by projecting onto them one's own ego ideals and inadequacies, and also enabling one thereby to experiment with and test those values and identities. But at its worst, as in malicious rituals of murder and scapegoating, projection revises reality so drastically that "nothing is, / But what is not," and the murderer's own selfhood, his "single state of man," is increasingly shaken and disjoined (1.3.134–42).

Envy, and the resultant splitting of selfhood, dictates the entire sequence of act 3: Macbeth's spiteful soliloquy in which he feels "rebuked" by Banquo's "royalty of nature"; his strange ranking of dogs in the abusive hiring of the assassins, humiliating them, even as he claims to raise and "make love" to them; his furtive insecurity even with his wife (rehearsing her part while concealing his full intent); and his "half-participation" in the murder itself, perhaps as the third murderer. In spite of Macbeth's show of surprise at Fleance's survival (3.4.20–24), it is tempting to believe that Macbeth is the mysterious third assassin[21]—so that he only half-participates in the second murder. That Macbeth can hardly admit (even to himself) his involvement suggests the extent of his splitting psyche: for if he *is* the third murderer, it reveals both a deepening insecurity and a growing obsession with rational control (utter self-repression, and anal attentiveness to detail, and a host of other defensive mechanisms aimed at sustaining to others and to himself the illusion of kingship, including the pretense of shock on learning of Fleance's escape—which resembles his extravagant show of dismay on learning of Duncan's death). Macbeth's furtive pretense of uninvolvement even for his own cutthroats would thus demonstrate his increasing cowardice, alienation, and lack of a stable central self. Hence, for the second murder Macbeth both is and is not an active participant, owing to his descent into psychic bifurcation.

George Williams notes that performing the play with Macbeth as the third murderer "necessitates a staging that twice violates the 'Law of Reentry.'"[22] Though the assignment of a third murderer may indicate Macbeth's growing anxiety and may vicariously show his grasping for control (attending more closely than the other assassins to the usurper's crucial purposes), stage convention would thus seem to argue against Macbeth's schizoid reappearance as monarch-cutthroat-monarch in such rapid sequence. Yet if we consider the extraordinary liberties and experimentation in the staging of other Shakespearean plays of this period (e.g., the Dover cliff scene in *King Lear*), one wonders at the theatrical ingenuity of having Macbeth immediately reenter, perhaps with a dark cape only thinly disguising his kingly garments, so that the audience would actually be *aware* of his devious schizophrenic "doubling." If so, it is the most stunningly purposeful violation of the Law of Reentry in the Shakespearean canon.

Macbeth's self-division builds to a climax during the banquet when his vacillation between noblemen and assassins, between true and feigned selves, gives way to a sleeper vacillation between conscious and unconscious realities. His obscene praise of the missing guest ("And to our dear friend Banquo, whom we miss") serves the psychic function of invoking his double's macabre presence, filling the central seat to which Macbeth himself is inexorably drawn. In "*Macbeth*: King James's Play" George Williams notes that the ghost of Banquo rather than of Duncan holds sway in the drama's central scene, thus inflating the compliment to King James I though it subverts decorum. Williams also explains the symbolic seating that underlies the doppelgänger effect at the banquet: "Macbeth does not sit in his throne (the "state" where Lady Macbeth remains)—to which he has no spiritual right; he does expect to sit at the table—a level to which he does have a right." The "place reserved" for Banquo, to which Macbeth is drawn as to his own natural place, is centrally located: "Both sides are even: here I'll sit i' th' midst" (3.4.11).[23] Almost exactly the same event occurs in Dostoyevsky's *The Double*, and similar psychic displacements occur in James's *The Turn of the Screw* and Conrad's "The Secret Sharer"; but only Macbeth confronts a double who represents not his sinister shadow, but the ruination of his better self.[24]

Throughout act 3 Macbeth's insecurity focuses no longer on the proud aspiration for kingly greatness, but on envious rivalry with his antithetical friend Banquo, who is to him what Edgar is to Edmund, Hal to Hotspur, Orlando to Oliver: the child favored with a loving heart, who calls into question the unloving self's entire "being" and must be utterly eliminated:

> every minute of his being thrusts
> Against my near'st of life: and though I could
> With bare-faced power sweep him from my sight,
> And bid my will avouch it, yet I must not,
> For certain friends that are both his and mine,
> Whose loves I may not drop.
>
> (3.1.116–21)

Instinctively Macbeth envisions the bond with his "chiefest friend" in the context of a universal siblinghood, making the murder of Banquo as broadly symbolic as that of Duncan: first he eliminates the universal parent or greater self, then the archetypal sibling or mirror-self. In each of the mature Shakespearean tragedies this shattering confrontation with an antithetical self-image occurs at the play's center, the middle of act 3: Othello's temptation by Iago (3.3), Lear's discovery of "Poor Tom" (3.4), Macbeth's spectral encounter with Banquo (3.4), Antony's battle with Octavius and (more important) the interplay with his alter-ego, Cleopatra (3.7–13). This positing of an "indissoluble tie" (*Macbeth* 3.1.15–18) between self and shadow-self (or alter-ego) occurs at the exact center of *Othello* and *Macbeth* (and, with more benevolent implications, at the center of *King Lear*). At this moment each protagonist confronts the darkest possibilities of selfhood: the imputed treachery of Desdemona, the feigned sins of Poor Tom, the butchery inflicted by Macbeth himself. As in Lear's meeting with the mad beggar, Macbeth's rencontre with his mutilated alter-ego engages him in full awareness of fraternal Otherness; but while this stunning encounter leads the kingly Lear instinctively to affirm the oneness of human souls, it provokes the usurper Macbeth to repudiate "that great bond" (3.2.49). In discarding Banquo, Macbeth thus divests himself of brother-love, the homoerotic bond, the second crucial cathexis forming the normative identity of the human psyche.

KILLING LADY MACDUFF AND HER CHILDREN: ANNIHILATING THE ID, AND ALL OTHERNESS

In acts 4 and 5, focusing on the slaughter of a mother and children (and the immediate social and psychological consequences of that deed), Macbeth eliminates the third and most fundamental human bond as he violates the primitive core of selfhood, what Freud called the id. Most critics treat this third assault as mere "fourth-act pathos," as a dim echo of the previous kills, or as a hasty and illogical afterthought testifying to a kind of madness in the tyrant, since these victims offer neither militant opposition nor patrilineal threat to Macbeth's royal claim.[25]

But Macbeth's essential motive for the third murder is not a reenactment of the Oedipal struggle (casting Macduff as the new parent-power to be deposed); nor is it another envious rivalry with a mirroring sibling (seeing Macduff's goodness, like Banquo's, as a galling comparison to his own evil). Rather, building upon and blossoming out of those two previous modes of aggression, Macbeth's "black and deep desires" now enter a third and culminating phase: scornful annihilative hatred of the simple passional core, the mother-and-child matrix of selfhood—the healthy "oral-narcissist" bonding which contrasts the perverse narcissism now unfolding in Macbeth.[26] Macbeth's contemptuous repudiation and perversion of the affective-cognitive human core (the "id") informs this final sequence of psychic degradation in acts 4 and 5. The ego-function which dominates this earliest phase of psychic development (and which most pertinently informs the final two acts of Shakespeare's mature tragedies) is *introjection*, the ego's incorporation of desired aspects of the nurturant other in order to construct its own identity.[27] Introjection of the beloved, for the purpose of achieving (or re-achieving) total selfhood, is the psychological principle that is either violated or embraced in the final phase of each of Shakespeare's major tragedies. Acts 4 and 5 invariably draw their cathartic and transforming energy not from the killing of a king, but from the heroic male's reaction to the destruction of a *beloved maiden* (Ophelia, Desdemona, Cordelia) or, in the final tragedies, a *mother with children* (Lady Macduff and Lady Macbeth, Cleopatra, Virgilia and Volumnia).[28]

A wholesome mode of introjective bonding informs the poignant scene of Lady Macduff and her son (4.2), where in the father's absence she frets over the child's continued sustenance. But the boy's affirmation that Providential if not parental care will feed him, echoing Matthew 6.26, suggests the dignity of what he has thus far introjected from his parents. This humane and spiritual nurture contrasts the strikingly perverse mode of introjection in the preceding scene: the witches' materialistic, cannibalistic ritual. Into their womblike cauldron's mouth (the *vagina dentata*)[29] they fling fragments of poisonous and ravenous beasts (toad, snake, dragon, wolf, shark, tiger) and parts representing the erotic and sensory powers of non-Christians (Jew's liver, Turk's nose, Tartar's lips)—including those lower senses of smell and taste involved in feeding. This travesty of Otherness (like Othello's suicidal reminiscence of killing a Turk in the service of Christianity) is a too-appropriate symbolism for what the witches and Macbeth himself have come to represent.

The final and focal object in the witches' catalogue of dismembered parts is "Finger of birth-strangled babe / Ditch-deliver'd by a drab" (4.1.26–31). Thus, from the "pilot's thumb" of the witches' early scene

(1.3.28), symbolizing the perversion of parental guidance or superego, Macbeth regresses inexorably to the aborted potency of the child (or id), as symbolized by the foetal "finger" or phallus, "strangled"—castrated—devoured by the cauldron-womb-mouth of the Voracious Mother, the "drab" or prostitute. Introjection (an incorporative mode of identification deriving from the experience of sucking and swallowing during the oral stage of infancy) is thus materialized and brutalized by the witches to secure worldly power.

From the vicious opening ritual of act 4 (which provokes the entire cycle of action in acts 1–5), Macbeth embraces the witches' omnivorous perversion of the primal introjective principle. Each of his three murders has been associated with imagery of feasting, but it is particularly in his impulsive butchering of mother and babes that Macbeth has willingly and unhesitatingly "supp'd full with horrors" (5.5.13). Thus the third murderous assault, a Herodlike massacre of innocents from which Macbeth completely distances himself, but which Shakespeare exposes to the audience with the most excruciating intimacy, brings us to the peak of horror, the breaking of the deepest taboo, which violates the very rudiment of selfhood and of social bonding.

Far more than King Duncan and Banquo, whose entrammelment in political motivations partly cloaks their essential being, the intimacy of mother and child brings us closest to the core of human nature. In each of Shakespeare's mature tragedies, the final cathartic sequence of acts 4–5 jeopardizes the primal psychic ground of being, the inception of love: the drawing of woman, "fool," or child into the web of deceit and violence promotes in the male authority-figures not merely revulsion against evil, but clear and intense awareness of the rich essence of life which has been lost. Macbeth himself, in his finest show of inner light, envisioned the soul's greatest power as its early innocence and in its affective mode of "pity": "like a new-born babe / Striding the blast" (1.7.19–20). As he loses touch with that childlike and woman-nurtured essence in himself, Macbeth also loses his capacity for true sovereignty.

NOTES

1. Freud's argument for the second instinctual drive, the aggressive death-wish, grew out of his reflections on the "repetition compulsion"—obsessive reenacting of a pleasurable sensation, or of a painful and self-destructive behavior. The motive, he felt, was not simply to sustain pleasure or pain, but subconsciously to use it as a means of recovering primal experience, especially in the case of the aggressive and destructive obsession, which he attributed to a desire to return to peaceful nothingness. See Bibliography, 5H, "Repetition Compulsion."

2. See Bibliography, 5F, "Oedipal Conflict (*Macbeth*)." For revisionary studies of gender-psychology, shifting attention from embattled father to devouring mother, or reformulating gender roles, see Bibliography, 5F, "Preoedipal Conflict (*Macbeth*)," and 5B, "Gender Stereotyping, Reversal, and Transference."

3. Foakes, "Images of Death: Ambition in *Macbeth*," *Focus on Macbeth*, ed. John Russell Brown (London: Routledge and Kegan Paul, 1982), 18.

4. Julian Markels, "The Spectacle of Deterioration: Macbeth and the 'Manner' of Tragic Deterioration," *SQ* 12 (1961): 293–303.

5. Heilman, Muir, and Sanders insist on Macbeth's greatness of spirit but also on the sordid depths of his degradation (Robert B. Heilman, "The Criminal as Tragic Hero: Dramatic Methods," *ShS* 19 [1966]: 12–24; Kenneth Muir, introduction, *Macbeth*, New Arden Ed. [London: Methuen, 1987], xliii–liii, lxv; Wilbur Sanders, *The Dramatist and the Received Idea* [Cambridge: Cambridge University Press, 1968], 253–316). Cf. A.C. Bradley, *Shakespearean Tragedies*, 2nd ed. (1905; reprint, New York: Macmillan, 1949), 349–65; A.P. Rossiter, *Angel with Horns*, ed. Graham Storey (New York: Theatre Arts, 1961), 209–34; Paul A. Jorgensen, *Our Naked Frailties: Sensational Art and Meaning in Macbeth* (Berkeley: University of California Press, 1971), 185–216; Maynard Mack, Jr., *Killing the King* (New Haven: Yale University Press, 1973), 138–85; Arthur Kitsch, "Macbeth's Suicide," *ELH* 51 (1984): 269–96.

6. This "object relations" pattern was (in slightly different form) first noted by L. Veszy-Wagner, "*Macbeth*: 'Fair is Foul and Foul is Fair,'" *AI* 25 (1968): 242–57. Though she subordinates each victim to a patriarchal version of the Oedipal struggle, she acutely observes that Macbeth's "main problem is ... uncertain identity" with regard to gender.

7. See Jones, *Scenic Form in Shakespeare*, 195–224.

8. For detailed treatment of this three-part structure of *Macbeth*, see *ibid.* For discussion of three stages of self-discovery in Shakespeare's tragic form, see Maynard Mack, "The Jacobean Shakespeare," 11–42.

9. See Muir's Introduction to *Macbeth*," xxxvi–xliii; Muriel C. Bradbrook, "The Sources of *Macbeth*," *ShS* 4 (1951): 35–48; David Norbrook, "*Macbeth* and the Politics of Historiography," in *Politics of Discourse: The Literature and History of 17th-Century England*, ed. Kevin Sharpe and Steven N. Zwicker (Berkeley and Los Angeles: University of California Press, 1987), 78–116.

10. Sanders, *The Dramatist and the Received Idea*, 253–316. Cf. Harry Berger, Jr., "The Early Scenes of *Macbeth*. Preface to a New Interpretation," *ELH* 47 (1980): 1–31; James L. Calderwood, *If It Were Done: Macbeth and Tragic Action* (Amherst: University of Massachusetts Press, 1986), 119–21; Graham Bradshaw, *Shakespeare's Skepticism* (New York: St. Martin's Press, 1987), 244–50; Adelman, "'Born of Woman,'" 93–94.

11. Berger, "The Early Scenes of *Macbeth*," Calderwood, *If It Were Done*. Other sharp questioners of Banquo include Bradley, *Shakespearean Tragedies*, 379–87; Roy Walker, *The Time Is Free* (London: Andrew Dakers, 1949), 89–92; Richard J. Jaarsma, "The Tragedy of Banquo," *L&P* 17 (1967): 87–94.

12. Adelman, "'Born of Woman'"; Hunter, "Doubling, Mythic Difference."

13. See Bibliography, 5J, "Superego-formation."

14. See D.W. Harding, Robert Kimbrough, Marilyn French, Coppélia Kahn, Janet Adelman, and Dianne Hunter in Bibliography, 5B, "Gender Stereotyping, Reversal, and Transference," and 5F, "Preoedipal Conflict."

15. See Stephen Orgel and Louis A. Montrose in *Rewriting the Renaissance: The Discourses of Sexual Difference in Early Modern Europe*, ed. Margaret W. Ferguson, Maureen Quilligan, and Nancy J. Vickers (Chicago: University of Chicago Press, 1986), 58–59,

65–87. For the Renaissance view of conscience or synteresis as a means of consolidating mental powers and gender-components of human nature, see Pierre de la Primaudaye, *The French Academie*, 2:364–511, esp. on restoring the Edenic communion between heart (437–511) and head (364–136).

16. See Bibliography, 5I, "Sublimation." In *The Ego and the Mechanisms of Defense* Anna Freud described ego-functions as not only defensive but constructive. Hartmann and other ego psychologists, by replacing "sublimation" with "neutralization" and "desexualization," tended to vilify the libido and to ignore the constructive activity of sublimation. It plays a vital role in the struggle for what Kohut calls "grandiose selfhood," the process so travestied by the Macbeths. For discussion of the closely-related processes of sublimation, superego formation, and therapeutic transference, see Loewald, *Sublimation*, chaps. 1–2; and Kohut, *The Analysis of the Self*, 309–24.

17. Aquinas, *Summa Theologica*, 2 vols. (Chicago: Encyclopedia Britannica, 1952), 1.63.2.

18. For a different view of the analogy between Cain and Macbeth, see Jorgensen, *Our Naked Frailties*, 47–51, 190–95, 200, 213.

19. Ibid., 194. Robert Weimann similarly explains Lear's drifts from dialogue to monologue during his madness (*Shakespeare and the Popular Tradition in the Theater*, 217–21). Cf. Barry Weller, "Identity and Representation in Shakespeare," *ELH* 49 (1982): 356–58.

20. On the key role of projection in psychological development, see Bibliography, 5G, "Projection and Projective Identification." Melanie Klein, in "Notes on Some Schizoid Mechanisms" and in *The Psychoanalysis of Children* (142–48, 178), established a pattern in childhood development of *introjection-projection-reintrojection*. But the reintrojection-phase occurs on a higher level, as in sublimation, and this higher level is made possible by the stimulating effect of projection. Thus reintrojection, like Wordsworth's "recollection in tranquillity", is a culminating mode of psychic internalization and identity-construction occurring on a more comprehensive, controlled, and "sublime" level. Cf. Knight, "Introjection, Projection, and Identification"; and Anna Freud, *The Ego and the Mechanisms of Defense*, 50–53.

21. This theory, first advanced by Allan Park Paton, *N&Q* (1869), was lucidly reformulated by Harold Goddard in Vol. 2 of *The Meaning of Shakespeare*, 122–26.

22. George W. Williams, "The Third Murderer in *Macbeth*," *SQ* 23 (1972): 261.

23. George W. Williams, "*Macbeth*: King James's Play," *SoAR* 47 (1982): 12–21.

24. See Bibliography, 5A, "Dissociation, Doubling, Multiple Personality, and Splitting." No critic has fully considered Banquo as Macbeth's "double." Robert N. Watson briefly mentions Banquo as "doppelgänger" ("'Thriftless Ambition,' Foolish Wishes, and the Tragedy of *Macbeth*," in *William Shakespeare's Macbeth*, ed. Harold Bloom [New York: Chelsea House, 1987], 142–47); James Kirsch describes the "participation mystique" of the two men, Macbeth being more attuned to the unconscious, but the weaker ego (*Shakespeare's Royal Self* [New York: G. P. Putnam, 1965], 331–39); Matthew N. Proser describes Banquo's ghost "as a kind of analogy for Macbeth's mutilated soul" (*The Heroic Image in Five Shakespearean Tragedies* [Princeton: Princeton University Press, 1965], 76–78). In *A Psychoanalytic Study of the Double in Literature*, Robert Rogers builds on Freud's reading of *Macbeth* when he identifies Macbeth and Lady Macbeth as doubles; Rogers does not distinguish between the customary homoerotic phenomenon of mirror-transference (between close friends, sibling rivals, or hero and alter-ego) and the more complex psychic transference between heterosexual partners in marriage.

25. Hogan, "*Macbeth*: Authority and Progenitorship," sees the slaughter as repeating

the Oedipal struggle, an indirect blow at Macduff as threatening authority and as fertile progenitor.

26. See Bibliography, 5D, "Narcissism and Self-love." One must distinguish Macbeth's tyrannous infantilism (culminating in narcissistic rage) from the healthy oral-narcissistic bond, involving mutual respect between parent and child during the sucking stage. For negative aspects of narcissism, see S. Freud, "On Narcissism: An Introduction"; Kernberg, *Borderline Conditions and Pathological Narcissism*; and the important Shakespearean studies by Kirsch, "Macbeth's Suicide"; and Adelman, "'Born of Woman'" and "'Anger's My Meat.'" For positive modes of narcissism, see Kohut, "Forms and Transformations of Narcissism"; and Benjamin, *The Bonds of Love*. Shakespeare seems particularly attuned to this primitive cathexis which forms the core of human identity, emphasizing not just negative but positive aspects of mother–child bonding in the cathartic sequence of each mature tragedy, most strikingly in Cleopatra's death-scene ("Dost thou not see the baby at my breast / That sucks the nurse asleep?").

27. See Bibliography, W, "Introjection, Internalization, Identification."

28. Though the cathartic valuation of womanly/matronly nurture in acts 4–5 holds true for all of Shakespeare's major tragedies, *Hamlet* requires qualification. Never fully reunited with Ophelia or Gertrude, Hamlet only incipiently comprehends the meaning of a grave holding his "fool" and his beloved (a synthesis so richly explored in *King Lear*). *Hamlet's* final focus on the killing of a false parent-king, of an inadequate sibling-double (Laertes), and of a disloyal nurturing mother suggests unresolved Oedipal (and pre-Oedipal) anxieties and an incomplete quest for identity.

29. See Bibliography, 5K, "Vagina Dentata and Penis Dentata," especially Roy Schafer, *Language and Insight*, who provides a broad gender analysis (153–60). The demoniac symbolism in *Macbeth* combines male and female perversions. In tempting Macbeth to annihilate children, the demon masters' "armed head" (*penis dentata*) joins the witches' devouring cauldron (*vagina dentata*) (4.1.69–86). This satanic collusion of perverted gender components, a marital travesty which promotes mutual deception and annihilation rather than mutual support and procreation, evolves throughout the play.

Character Profile

G. Wilson Knight described *Macbeth* as Shakespeare's "most profound and mature vision of evil," even as four centuries of critics have probed the nature of good and evil in Shakespeare's representation of the Scottish king and his queen. Macbeth's evil, often interpreted as a conscious and painful capitulation of the good that strains for spousal affirmation before it is ultimately denied, is rarely understood as an innate or inevitable nature in the man. He is the play's villain, but one that takes up his dark cloak only gradually, as fear and guilt feed treachery upon treachery to culminate in a bloody tyranny that becomes his epithet. At the play's end, Macbeth seems unrecognizable from the man he was at its opening. As general in the King's army and Thane of Glamis, Macbeth is hailed as a returning hero and heaped with praise from all quarters. Even before he returns to Court, news of his success is relayed to Macbeth. The nobleman Rosse congratulates him: "As thick as hail,/Came post with post; and every one did bear/ Thy praises in his kingdom's great defence, And pour'd them down before him" (I.iii.96–99). Indeed, in the preceding scene, a captain severely wounded in battle nonetheless troubles to speak three speeches to paint Macbeth's valor while his gashes stream blood on Duncan's court. The official introduction of Macbeth to the audience, therefore, is no foreboding of doom. According to the captain, he is "brave Macbeth (well he deserves that name)," whose sword on the battlefield flashed with the justice of an avenging angel, not to rest until he had executed, against the odds of Fortune itself, the royal mission to slay the traitor to the king (I.ii.16–23). The captain's endorsement is immediately justified by Duncan, who agrees: "O valiant cousin! worthy gentleman!" (I.ii.24)

Although he gives no explicit physical description of the man, Shakespeare insists on Macbeth's physical prowess, on the battlefield as well as in his domestic sphere. Duncan arrives at the Macbeths and banters at the Lady:

> Where's the Thane of Cawdor?
> We cours'd him at the heels, and had a purpose
> To be his purveyor: but he rides well;
> And his great love, sharp as his spur, hath holp him
> To his home before us.
>
> (I.vi.20–20–24)

Here, the king compliments his general's riding skill, playing a pun as well on Macbeth's "sharp" love for his wife, which has sped him home ahead of the rest of the party. The audience knows what Duncan does not—that the husband hurries to catch his wife alone from a darker motivation than spousal (or sexual) haste after his absence from home. But the king's jest may not be wasted; for all we come to know of Macbeth as a man who lives in the depth of his imagination, his eye turned inward to the conflicts of his secret ambitions and insecurities, the general is perceived as a physical man by his king—whose impression of Macbeth in this case is all too narrow.

If Duncan is mistaken in his estimation of Macbeth, Lady Macbeth makes no such error. Her knowledge of her husband's character is terrifyingly precise as she sums up his weaknesses not in his predilection to evil, but to good. After receiving his written recount of the witches' prophecy, she permits herself only a line and a half to gloat at his success before she turns to worrying that he does not possess the ruthlessness she feels is necessary to fulfill his destiny:

> Yet do I fear thy nature:
> It is too full o'th'milk of human kindness,
> To catch the nearest way. Thou wouldst be great;
> Art not without ambition, but without
> The illness should attend it.
>
> (I.v.16–20)

Lady Macbeth's observation of her husband is unforgiving of the good that threatens to reveal itself. She sees that he is too timid, even childish, in his intolerance of his own duplicity, and she scolds him to set a braver face in front of his guests, whom they mean to destroy: "Your face, my Thane, is as a book, where men/ May read strange matters" (I.v.62–63).

Still, Macbeth is not so transparent as his wife would have him believe. After his murders of the king and his two grooms, who are framed for the regicide and immediately eliminated for their treachery (or, innocence, rather), Macbeth is asked how he came to kill these men, the responsibility for whose slaughter—unlike that of the king—he does not evade. He answers: "Who can be wise, amaz'd, temperate and furious,/ Loyal and neutral, in a moment? No man:/ Th'expedition of my violent love/ Outrun the pauser, reason" (II.iii.106–109). That he was overcome by emotion so fierce that he could not control his rage against the murderers of the king is Macbeth's explanation for his crime. His rationale, however, is doubly ironic, as is recognized or suspected by his interrogators and the audience alike. By now, the audience is well aware of the weakness of his noble emotions against those ignoble in him. Despite his protest to the contrary here, Macbeth's acts of violence throughout the play fulfill his ultimately *rational* machinations for power. Although he is by no means in emotional control here or in any of his increasingly brutal acts of violence, his emotions—noble or otherwise—are always submerged beneath his conscious desire to take and keep the crown of Scotland. Here, even his plea of emotional derangement following the allegedly retributive murders of the royal guards manifests his rational qualifications, just as the actual events of murder of the king and his groomsmen demonstrate Macbeth's emotional incompetence in the face of his own uncertain evil.

His paranoia reaches a climax when he sees the ghost of the recently murdered Banquo at his table. Unable to ignore this apparition, Macbeth exposes his sickly conscience to those present at his feast. Addressing the ghost, he raves:

> What man dare, I dare:
> Approach thou like the rugged Russian bear,
> The arm'd rhinoceros, or th'Hyrcan tiger;
> Take any shape but that, and my firm nerves
> Shall never tremble: or, be alive again,
> And dare me to the desert with thy sword;
> If trembling I inhabit then, protest me
> The baby of a girl.
>
> (III.iv.98–105)

This is no bravado. Instead, it is the lament of a warrior whose strengths of battle are physical, and who therefore finds himself overmatched in his ineffectual struggle with the supernatural. Macbeth, the general-turned-king, knows himself to be no coward before any mortal enemy, man or beast, but his courage fails him against this ghostly shape whom he recognizes as his former colleague and confidante. In Macbeth, Shakespeare portrays a man who is enormously vulnerable to his imagination, to the extent that though he may command his body to superlative effect, he cannot master the complexities of the mind, by which he is ultimately frustrated and enslaved.

As destiny hovers over the king whose royalty was prophesied to end with his person, Shakespeare gives an extended account of Macbeth's growing notoriety among his subjects in the conversation between Macduff and Malcolm, Duncan's prince. Macduff, who holds the extreme opinion of Macbeth's nature, says of the new king: "Not in the legions/ Of horrid Hell can come a devil more damn'd/ In evils, to top Macbeth" (IV.iii.55–57). Yet Malcolm, uncertain of his own fate in Macbeth's murderous state and less forgetful of better times, reminds the nobleman: "This tyrant, whose sole name blisters our tongues,/ Was once thought honest: you have lov'd him well" (IV.iii.12–13). Malcolm agrees that Macbeth is treacherous and a tyrant, adding to these grievances more: "I grant him bloody,/ Luxurious, avaricious, false, deceitful,/ Sudden, malicious, smacking of every sin/ That has a name" (IV.iii.57–60). But Malcolm, if not forgiving, mitigates the nature of Macbeth's downfall, as he speaks of the more general treachery of the man's political position: "A good and virtuous nature may recoil/ In an imperial charge" (IV.iii.19–20). For Macbeth, whom the same Malcolm eulogizes as "this dead butcher" in the last speech of the play, the earlier mitigation proves the most generous of his life's account.

In the last moments of his life, Macbeth finally abandons the power of the prophecy that has both crowned him king and defeated his mind. As the fate foretold by the witches comes to its end at last, Macbeth takes up his sword in an uncharacteristic refusal of the destiny that he has heretofore followed as an actor merely playing out his script:

> I will not yield,
> To kiss the ground before young Malcolm's feet,
> And to be baited with the rabble's curse.
> Though Birnam wood be come to Dunsinane,
> And thou oppos'd, being of no woman born,
> Yet I will try the last: before my body
> I throw my warlike shield: lay on, Macduff;
> And damn'd be him that first cries, 'Hold, enough!'
>   (V.ix.27–34)

Although there is none on this stage to speak well of the fame of Macbeth, Shakespeare gives the villain a hero's death. The villain, who is arguably more sensitive to his own evil than even his most accurate critics on the stage, remains protective of his person to the last. Shakespeare's Macbeth insists that he die like a man if not a hero.

Contributors

HAROLD BLOOM is Sterling Professor of the Humanities at Yale University. He is the author of over 20 books, including *Shelley's Mythmaking* (1959), *The Visionary Company* (1961), *Blake's Apocalypse* (1963), *Yeats* (1970), *A Map of Misreading* (1975), *Kabbalah and Criticism* (1975), *Agon: Toward a Theory of Revisionism* (1982), *The American Religion* (1992), *The Western Canon* (1994), and *Omens of Millennium: The Gnosis of Angels, Dreams, and Resurrection* (1996). *The Anxiety of Influence* (1973) sets forth Professor Bloom's provocative theory of the literary relationships between the great writers and their predecessors. His most recent books include *Shakespeare: The Invention of the Human* (1998), a 1998 National Book Award finalist, *How to Read and Why* (2000), *Genius: A Mosaic of One Hundred Exemplary Creative Minds* (2002), and *Hamlet: Poem Unlimited* (2003). In 1999, Professor Bloom received the prestigious American Academy of Arts and Letters Gold Medal for Criticism, and in 2002 he received the Catalonia International Prize.

G. WILSON KNIGHT's works include *Imperial Theme, Shakespearian Production, The Crown of Life, The Mutual Flame, The Sovereign Flower, Byron and Shakespeare, Shakespeare and Religion, Poets of Action,* and *The Starlit Dome.*

BERNARD McELROY was Professor of English at Loyola University. He is the author of *Shakespeare's Mature Tragedies* (1971) and *Fictions of the Modern Grotesque* (1989).

HOWARD FELPERIN is Professor of English at Macquarie University, Sydney. He is author of *Shakespearean Representation: Mimesis and Modernity in Elizabethan Tragedy*, *The Uses of the Canon: Elizabethan Literature and Contemporary Theory*, *Beyond Deconstruction: The Uses and Abuses of Literary Theory*, *Shakespearean Romance*, and *Dramatic Romance: Plays, Theory, and Criticism*.

ROBERT N. WATSON is Professor of English at UCLA. He is author of *The Rest is Silence: Death as Annihilation in the English Renaissance*, *Ben Jonson's Parodic Strategy: Literary Imperialism in the Comedies*, *Shakespeare and the Hazards of Ambition*, and editor of *Critical Essays on Ben Jonson (Critical Essays on British Literature)*.

KAY STOCKHOLDER was Professor Emerita of English at University of British Columbia and former president of the B.C. Civil Liberties Association. She was the author of *Dream Works: Lovers and Families in Shakespeare's Plays*.

CHRISTOPHER PYE is Professor and Chair of the English Department at Williams College. He is author of *The Vanishing: Shakespeare, the Subject, and Early-Modern Culture (2000)* and *The Regal Phantasm: Shakespeare and the Politics of Spectacle (1990)*.

H.W. FAWKNER is an Anglo-Scandinavian critic who has lectured in various universities. His studies of John Fowles and John Cowper Powys were published in 1984 and 1986, respectively.

REBECCA W. BUSHNELL teaches in the English Department at the University of Pennsylvania. She is the author of *Prophesying Tragedy: Sign and Voice in Sophocles' Theban Plays*.

ROBERT LANIER REID is Henry Carter Stuart Professor of English and chair of the English Department at Emory & Henry College. He has published articles on Shakespeare, Spenser, and Renaissance psychology and is currently writing a book on the contrary psychologies of Spenser and Shakespeare.

Bibliography

Adam, R. J. "The Real Macbeth: King of Scots, 1040–1054." *History Today* 7 (1957): 381–87.

Adelman, Janet. "'Born of Woman': Fantasies of Maternal Power in *Macbeth*." In *Cannibals, Witches, and Divorce: Estranging the Renaissance*, edited by Marjorie Garber. Baltimore: Johns Hopkins University Press, 1987, pp. 90–121.

Amneus, Daniel. "Macbeth's 'Greater Honor.'" *Shakespeare Studies* 6 (1972): 223–30.

Anderson, Ruth L. "The Pattern of Behavior Culminating in *Macbeth*." *ELH* 14 (1947): 114–26.

Baird, David. *The Thane of Cawdor: A detective Study of* Macbeth. London: Oxford University Press, 1937.

Bamber, Linda. "*Macbeth* and *Coriolanus*." In *Comic Women, Tragic Men: A Study of Gender and Genre in Shakespeare*. Stanford: Stanford University Press, 1982, pp.91–107.

Barroll, J. Leeds. *Artificial Persons: The Formation of Character in the Tragedies of Shakespeare*. Columbia: University of South Carolina Press, 1974.

Bartholomeusz, Dennis. *Macbeth and the Players*. Cambridge: Cambridge University Press, 1969.

Baxter, John. "*Macbeth: Style and Form*." In *Shakespeare's Poetic Styles: Verse into Drama*. London: Routledge & Kegan Paul, 1980, pp. 196–220.

Berger, Harry, Jr. "The Early Scenes of *Macbeth*: Preface to a New Interpretation." *ELH* 47 (1980): 1–31.

Bernad, Miguel A. "The Five Tragedies in *Macbeth*." *Shakespeare Quarterly* 13 (1962): 49–61.

Berryman, John. "Notes on *Macbeth*." In *The Freedom of the Poet*. New York: Farrar, Straus & Giroux, 1976, pp. 56–71.

Birenbaum, Harvey. "Consciousness and Responsibility in *Macbeth*." *Mosaic* 15, No. 2(June 1982): 17–32.

Bradshaw, Graham. "Imaginative Openness and the *Macbeth*—Terror." In *Shakespeare's Scepticism*. New York: St. Martin's Press, 1987, pp. 219–56.

Bryant, Joseph A., Jr. "*Macbeth* and the Meaning of Tragedy." *Kentucky Review* 8, No. 2 (Summer 1988): 3–17.

Burton, Philip. "Macbeth." In *The Sole Voice: Character Portraits from Shakespeare*. New York: Dial Press, 1970, pp. 356–79.

Calderwood, James L. *If It Were Done:* Macbeth *and Tragic Action*. Amherst: University of Massachusetts Press, 1986.

Cartelli, Thomas. "Banquo's Ghost: The Shared Vision." *Theatre Journal* 35 (1983): 389–405.

Curry, Walter Clyde. "The Demonic Metaphysics of *Macbeth*." *Studies in Philology* 30 (1933): 395–426.

Daalder, Joost. "Shakespeare's Attitude to Gender in *Macbeth*." *AUMLA* No. 70 (November 1988): 366085.

Elliott, G.R. *Dramatic Providence in* Macbeth. 2nd ed. Princeton: Princeton University Press, 1960.

Empson, William. "*Macbeth*." In *Essays on Shakespeare*. Edited by David B. Pirie. Cambridge: Cambridge University Press, 1986, pp. 137–57.

Farnham, Willard. "*Macbeth*." In *Shakespeare's Tragic Frontier: The World of His Final Tragedies*. Berkeley: University of Berkeley Press, 1950, pp. 79–137.

Fergusson, Francis. " 'Killing the Bond of Love': Ugolino and Macbeth." In *Trope and Allegory: Themes Common to Dante and Shakespeare*. Athens: University of Georgia Press, 1977, pp. 23–48.

Ferrucci, Franco. "*Macbeth* and the Imitation of Evil." In *The Poetics of Disguise: The Autobiography of the Work in Homer, Dante, and Shakespeare*. Translated by Ann Dunnigan. Ithaca: Cornell University Press, 1980, pp. 125–58.

Foster, Donald W. "*Macbeth*'s War on Time." *English Literary Renaissance*16 (1986): 319–42.

French, Marilyn. "*Macbeth*." In *Shakespeare's Division of Experience*. New York: Summit Books, 1981, pp. 241–51.

Greene, James J. "Macbeth: Masculinity as Murder." *American Imago* 41 (1984): 155–80.

Grenander, M.E. "*Macbeth* as Diaphthorody: Notes toward the Definition of Form." *Yearbook of Comparative Criticism*10 (1983): 224–48.

Hartwig, Joan. "Parodic Scenes in *Macbeth*: The Porter, the Murderers, and Malcolm." In *Shakespeare's Analogical Scene*. Lincoln: University of Nebraska Press, 1983, pp. 43–65.

Hopkins, Lisa. *The Shakespearean Marriage: Merry Wives and Heavy Husbands*. Palgrave Macmillan, 1997.

Horwich, Richard. "Integrity in *Macbeth*: The Search for the 'Single State of Man.'" *Shakespeare Quarterly*29 (1978): 365–73.

Jekels, Ludwig. "The Riddle of Shakespeare's Macbeth." *Psychoanalytic Review*30 (1943): 361–85.

Jorgensen, Paul A. *Our Naked Frailties: Sensational Art and Meaning in Macbeth*. Berkeley: University of California Press, 1971.

Kimbrough, Robert. "Macbeth: The Prisoner of Gender." *Shakespeare Studies* 16 (1983): 175–90.

Kirsch, Arthur. "Macbeth's Suicide." *ELH* 51 (1984): 269–96.

Kirsch, James. "Macbeth's Descent into Hell and Damnation." In *Shakespeare's Royal Self*. New York: Putnam's, 1966, pp. 321–422.

Knight, G. Wilson. "The Milk of Concord: An Essay on Life-Themes in *Macbeth*." In *The Imperial Theme*. 3rd edition. London: Methuen, 1951, pp. 125–53.

———. *Shakespeare's Dramatic Challenge: On the Rise of Shakespeare's Tragic Heroes*. London: Croom Helm; New York: Barnes & Noble, 1977.

Lyman, Stanford M., and Marvin B. Scott. "*Macbeth*." In *The Drama of Social Reality*. New York: Oxford University Press, 1975, pp. 7–20.

Mathur, K.C. "Macbeth and the Will to Power." *Indian Journal of English Studies* 15 (1974): 13–26.

McAlindon, Thomas. *Shakespeare's Tragic Cosmos*. New York: Cambridge University Press, 1991.

Nevo, Ruth. "*Macbeth*." In *Tragic Form in Shakespeare*. Princeton: Princeton University Press, 1972, pp. 214–57.

Pack, Robert. "Macbeth: The Anatomy of Loss." In *Affirming Limits: Essays on Mortality, Choice and Poetic Form*. Amherst: University of Massachusetts Press, 1985, pp. 67–83.

Paris, Bernard J. "Bargains with Fate: The Case of *Macbeth*." *American Journal of Psychoanalysis* 42 (1982): 7–20.

Rosenberg, Marvin. *The Masks of Macbeth*. Berkeley: University of California Press, 1978.

Sinfield, Alan. "*Macbeth*: History, Ideology and Intellectuals." *Critical Quarterly* 28 (1986): 63–77.

Slights, Camille Wells. "Equivocation and Conscience in *Macbeth*." In *Casuistical Tradition in Shakespeare, Donne, Herbert, and Milton.* Princeton: Princeton University Press, 1981, pp. 106–32.

Smidt, Kristian. "Double, Double, Toil and Trouble." In *Unconformities in Shakespeare's Tragedies.* New York: St. Martin's Press, 1990, pp. 150–62.

Sypher, Wylie. "Duration: *Macbeth*." In *The Ethic of Time: Structures of Experience in Shakespeare.* New York: Seabury Press, 1976, pp. 90–108.

Van den Berg, Kent T. "From Community to Society: Cultural Transformation in *Macbeth*." In *Playhouse and Cosmos: Shakespearean Theater as Metaphor.* Newark: University of Delaware Press, 1985, pp. 126–47.

Acknowledgements

"Brutus and Macbeth" by G. Wilson Knight. From *The Wheel of Fire*. ©1998 by Routledge. Reprinted by permission.

"*Macbeth*: The Torture of the Mind" by Bernard McElroy. From *Shakespeare's Mature Tragedies*. ©1973 Princeton University Press, 2001 renewed PUP. Reprinted by permission of Princeton University Press.

"A Painted Devil: *Macbeth*" by Howard Felperin. From *Shakespearean Representation*. ©1977 Princeton University Press, 2005 renewed PUP. Reprinted by permission of Princeton University Press.

"'Thriftless Ambition,' Foolish Wishes and the Tragedy of *Macbeth*" by Robert N. Watson. From *Shakespeare and the Hazards of Ambition*. ©1984 by the President and Fellows of Harvard College. Reprinted by permission of Harvard University Press.

"'Blanket of the Dark': Stealthy Lovers in *Macbeth*" by Kay Stockholder. From *Dream Works: Lovers and Families in Shakespeare's Plays*. ©1987 by University of Toronto Press. Reprinted by permission of the estate of Kay Stockholder.

"*Macbeth* and the Politics of Rapture" by Christopher Pye. From *The Regal Phantasm*. ©1990 Christopher Pye. Reprinted by permission.

"Deconstructing *Macbeth*" by H.W. Fawkner. From *Deconstructing* Macbeth. ©1990 by Associated University Presses, Inc. Reprinted by permission.

"Tragedies of Tyrants" by Rebecca W. Bushnell. From *Tragedies of Tyrants: Political Thought and Theater in the English Renaissance*. ©1990 Cornell University. Used by permission of the publisher, Cornell University Press.

"Macbeth's Three Murders" by Robert Lanier Reid. From *Shakespeare's Tragic Form*. ©2000 by Associated University Presses, Inc. Reprinted by permission.

Index